THE PRECIOUS BLOOD

THE
PRECIOUS BLOOD

OR

THE PRICE OF OUR SALVATION

BY

FREDERICK WILLIAM FABER, D. D.

Author of

"All for Jesus," "Spiritual Conferences," "Bethlehem,"
"The Foot of the Cross," "The Blessed Sacrament," etc., etc.

"Habet magnam vocem Christi Sanguis in terra, cum eo accepto ab omnibus gentibus respondetur Amen. Hæc est clara vox Sanguinus, quam Sanguis ipse exprimit, ex ore fidelium eodem Sanguine redemptorum."

— S. AUGUSTIN. *contra* Faustum l. xii. c. 10.

NEW EDITION

TAN BOOKS AND PUBLISHERS, INC.
Rockford, Illinois 61105

Nihil Obstat

JOSEPH A. M. QUIGLEY

Censor Librorum

Imprimatur

✠ J. CARD. O'HARA, C.S.C.
Archiepiscopus Philadelphiensis

Feast of the Assumption of the Blessed Virgin Mary, 1959

Originally published by the John Murphy Co., Baltimore Maryland. This edition originally published in 1959 by The Peter Reilly Co., Philadelphia.

Library of Congress Catalog Card Number: 78-66300

ISBN: 0-89555-075-X

Printed and bound in the United States of America

TAN BOOKS AND PUBLISHERS, INC.
P. O. Box 424
Rockford, Illinois 61105

1978

CONTENTS

TO THE MEMBERS OF THE CONFRATERNITY
OF THE MOST PRECIOUS BLOOD
IN THE CHURCH OF THE LONDON ORATORY.

MY DEAR FRIENDS:

I have written this little book for you, and now dedicate it to you with feelings of the warmest affection. It is ten years next August since the Holy Father set up our Confraternity. Since then we have enrolled upwards of thirty-eight thousand members, and a hundred and four Religious Communities. Besides this, several other Confraternities of the Precious Blood have been set up and affiliated with ours; and their members are also very numerous. Some others have been erected in imitation of ours, and independently of it, and are successfully propagating our favorite devotion.

The meetings at the Oratory on Sunday nights testify to the abundant blessing which our Lord has given to this apostolate of prayer. Letters are arriving daily, and from the remotest quarters of the world, either asking our prayers, or returning thanks for unexpected answers to prayer, or recounting signal conversions, obtained through the intercession of the Confraternity. Of late these divine favors have greatly increased; and, while this is a fresh motive for the love of God and for confidence in prayer, it also deepens our feeling of our own unworthiness, and greatly humbles us. The Confraternity is now so extended that the correspondence includes letters from Ireland and Scotland, from France and Germany, from Canada and Newfoundland, from the

United States and Central America, from California and Brazil, from Australia and New Zealand, from the East Indies and the Chinese Missions, from the Cape of Good Hope and other British Dependencies. When we think of all this, we must prize more and more the privileges of this grand union of intercessory prayer. The success of the Confraternity is naturally an object of lively interest both to you and me. To you, because it is connected now with so many secret joys and sorrows of your lives, and so many hidden mercies and sweet answers to prayer, which are known only to yourselves: to me, because it is the realizing of my hopes beyond what I ever could have dreamed: and to both of us, because it is an humble increase of the glory of our dearest Lord.

I have watched the growth of the Confraternity with a pleased surprise; and the tokens of God's blessing upon it have over-whelmed me with gratitude and confusion: and I have thought what I could do. Though many of you are present at the London Oratory every Sunday evening by your letters, comparatively few of you can be there in person. Yet I have felt that we belong to each other, and that I should satisfy my own feelings, while I should be gratifying yours, if I could make some affectionate offering to the whole of my dear Confraternity.

Therefore I have written this little book. I have tried to tell you all I know about the Precious Blood, all that many years of hard study and much thought have enabled me to learn; and I have tried to tell it you as easily and as simply as I could. I thought I could not please you better than by this. I thought I could not show my gratitude to our Blessed Redeemer better than by striv-ing to increase a devotion which he himself, by his blessing on the Confraternity, has shown to be so pleasing to him. I believed we could not repay the paternal kindness of the Sovereign Pontiff, our Father and Founder, who has enriched us with Indulgences, in a manner more welcome to himself than by an effort to propa-gate the devotion to the Precious Blood, in whose honor he has established a new feast in the Church of God. I know that I could not please myself better, than by magnifying the Precious Blood, which of all the glorious objects of Catholic devotion has been for years the dearest to my heart.

Accept, then, this little but loving gift. Let it stand as a memorial of my love of you, of your love of Jesus, of the filial devotion of both of us to the Holy Father, and of our united thanksgiving to our Blessed Savior for his goodness to our Confraternity, and for our salvation through his Blood.

Your affectionate Servant and Father,

FREDERICK WILLIAM FABER,
Priest of the Oratory.

The London Oratory.
Feast of the Conversion of St. Paul,
1860.

CHAPTER I

THE MYSTERY OF THE PRECIOUS BLOOD

CHAPTER I

THE MYSTERY OF THE PRECIOUS BLOOD

SALVATION! What music is there in that word — music that never tires but is always new, that always rouses yet always rests us! It holds in itself all that our hearts would say. It is sweet vigor to us in the morning, and in the evening it is contented peace. It is a song that is always singing itself deep down in the delighted soul. Angelic ears are ravished by it up in heaven; and our Eternal Father himself listens to it with adorable complacency. It is sweet even to him out of whose mind is the music of a thousand worlds. To be saved! What is it to be saved? Who can tell? Eye has not seen, nor ear heard. It is a rescue, and from such a shipwreck. It is a rest, and in such an unimaginable home. It is to lie down forever in the bosom of God in an endless rapture of insatiable contentment.

"Thou shalt call his name Jesus; for he shall save his people from their sins." Who else but Jesus can do this, and what else even from him do we require but this? for in this lie all things which we can desire. Of all miseries the bondage of sin is the most miserable. It is worse than sorrow, worse than pain. It is such a ruin that no other ruin is like unto it. It troubles all the peace of life. It turns sunshine into darkness. It embitters all pleasant fountains, and poisons the very blessings of God which should have been for our healing. It doubles the burdens of life, which are heavy enough already. It makes death a terror and a torture, and the eternity beyond the grave an infinite and intolerable blackness. Alas! we have felt the weightiness of sin, and know that there is nothing like it. Life has brought many sorrows to us, and many fears. Our hearts have ached a thousand times. Tears have flowed. Sleep has fled. Food has been nauseous to us, even when our weakness craved for it. But never have we felt any thing like the dead weight of a mortal sin. What then must a life of such sins be? What must be a death in sin? What the irrevocable eternity of unretracted sin?

From all this horror whither shall we look for deliverance? Not to ourselves; for we know the practical infinity of our weakness, and the incorrigible vitality of our corruption. Not to any earthly power; for it has no jurisdiction here. Not to philosophy, literature, or science; for in this case they are but sorry and unhelpful matters. Not to any saint, however holy, nor to any angel, however mighty; for the least sin is a bigger mountain than they have faculties to move. Not to the crowned queen of God's creation, the glorious and the sinless Mary; for even her holiness cannot satisfy for sin, nor the whiteness of her purity take out its deadly stain. Neither may we look for deliverance direct from the patience and compassion of God himself; for in the abysses of his wisdom it has been decreed, that without shedding of blood there shall be no remission of sin. It is from the Precious Blood of Jesus Christ alone that our salvation comes. Out of the immensity of its merits, out of the inexhaustible treasures of its satisfactions, because of the resistless power of its beauty over the justice and the wrath of God, because of that dear combination of its priceless worth and its benignant prodigality, we miserable sinners are raised out of the depths of our wretchedness, and restored to the peace and favor of our Heavenly Father.

Is hope sweet where despair had almost begun to reign? Is it a joy to be emancipated from a shameful slavery, or set free from a noxious dungeon? Is it gladness to be raised as if by miracle from a bed of feebleness and suffering, to sudden health and instantaneous vigor? Then what a gladness must salvation be! For, as there is no earthly misery like sin, so is there no deliverance like that with which Jesus makes us free. Words will not tell it. Thought only can think it, and it must be thought out of an enlightened mind and a burning heart, dwelt on for a long, long while. The first moment after death is a moment which must infallibly come to every one of us. Earth lies behind us, silently wheeling its obedient way through the black-tinted space. The measureless spaces of eternity lie outstretched before us. The words of our sentence have scarcely floated away into silence. It is a sentence of salvation. The great risk has been run, and we are saved. God's power is holding our soul lest it should die of gladness. It cannot take in the whole of its eternity. The least accidental joy is a world of beatitude in itself. The blaze of the vision is overwhelming. Then the truth that eternity is eternal—this is so hard to master. Yet all this is only what we mean when we pronounce the word salvation. How hideous the difference of that first moment after death, if we had not been saved! It turns us cold to think of it. But oh, joy of joys! we have seen the face of Jesus; and the light in his eyes, and the smile upon his face, and the words upon his lips, were salvation.

But there are some who do not feel that sin is such a horror or captivity. They say it lays no weight upon their hearts. They say their lives are full of sunshine, and that time flows with them as the merry rivulet runs in summer with a soothing brawl over its colored stones, and its waters glancing in the sun. They say it is so with them; and truly they should know best. Yet I hardly believe them. If they are happy, it is only by fits and starts; and then not with a complete happiness. There is ever an upbraiding voice within. An habitual sinner always has the look of a jaded and disappointed man. There is weariness in the very light of his eyes, vexation in the very sound of his voice. Why is he so cross with others, if he is so happy with himself? Then are there not also dreadful times, private times when no one but God sees him, when he is chilled through and through with fear, when he is weary of life because he is so miserable, when the past weighs upon him like a nightmare, and the future terrifies him like a coming wild beast? When death springs upon him, how will he die? When judgment comes, what will he answer? Yet even if the sinner could go through life with the gay indifference to which he pretends, he is not to be envied. It is only a sleep, a lethargy, or a madness—one or other of these according to his natural disposition. For there must be an awakening at last; and when and where will it be? They that walk in their sleep are sometimes wakened if they put their foot into cold water. What if the sinner's awakening should be from the first touch of the fire that burns beyond the grave?

But we claim no share in any foolish happiness of sin. We are on God's side. We belong to Jesus. Sin is our great enemy, as well as our great evil. We desire to break with it altogether. We are ashamed of our past subjection to it. We are uneasy under our present imperfect separation from it. Our uppermost thought—no! not merely our uppermost thought, our only thought—is our salvation. We care for no science, but the science of redeeming grace. The cross of Christ is our single wisdom. Once we wished for many things, and aimed at many things. But we are changed now. Our lives are amazingly simplified, simplified by the fear of sin and by the love of God. Our anxiety now is, that all this may remain. We fear another change, especially a change back again. We can think calmly of no change except from little love to much love, and from much love to more love. The right of Jesus to our love, to our best love, to all our love, is becoming plainer and plainer to us. His exceeding loveliness is growing more and more attractive, because it is revealing itself to us every day like a new revelation. What depths there are in Jesus, and how wonderfully he lights them up with the splendors of his eternal love! Do we not feel every day more and more strongly, that we must be more for Jesus than we are, that of all growing things divine love is the most growing, that all idea of a limit to our love of Jesus, or of moderation in our service of him, is a folly as well as a disloyalty? He was the brightness of innumerable lives and the sweetness of innumerable sorrows, when he was but the expectation of longing Israel. What must he be now, when he has come, when he has lived, and shed his Blood, and died, and risen, and ascended, and then come back again in all the unutterable endearments of the Blessed Sacrament? Why are our hearts so cold? Why is our love so faithless, and our faith so unloving? We try, and still we do not love as we wish to love. We try again, and love more; and yet it is sadly short of the love we ought to have. We strive and strive, and still we only languish when we ought to burn. He longs for our love, sweet, covetous lover of souls as he is. He longs for our love; and we long for nothing so much as to love him. Surely there must be a time and a place, when both he and we shall be satisfied; but the place will be heaven, and the time nothing else than the great timeless eternity.

Salvation is through the Precious Blood. We will take that for our study of Jesus this time. When love is humble, it prays with David to be washed more and more from its iniquity. But there is no washing away of iniquity, except in the Precious Blood of our most dear Redeemer. When love is bold, it prays to be set on fire with the flames which Jesus came to kindle. But it is only the Precious Blood which makes our heart beat hotly with the love of him. So let us take the Precious Blood for our study now: and let us study it in a simple, loving way, not so much to become deep theologians, though deep theology is near of kin to heroic sanctity, but that our hearts may be more effectually set on fire with the love of Jesus Christ. There is so much to be said, that we cannot say it all, because we do not know it all. We must make a choice; and we will choose these six things: the Mystery of the Precious Blood, the Necessity of it, its Empire, its History, its Prodigality, and, last of all, the Devotion to it in the Church.

We must take a saint to guide us on our way. Let it be that grand lover of Jesus, the Apostle St. Paul. His conversion was one of the chief glories of the Precious Blood. Redeeming grace was his favorite theme. He was forever magnifying and praising the Blood of Jesus. His heart was filled with it, and was enlarged by grace that it might hold yet more. After the Heart of Jesus, never was there a human heart like that of Paul, in which all other human hearts might beat as if it were their own, unless it be that other universal heart, the heart of King David, which has poured itself out for all mankind, in those varying strains of every changeful feeling, by means of its sweet psalms. St. Paul's heart feels for every one, makes every one's case its own, sorrows and rejoices with those who sorrow or rejoice, and becomes all things to all men that it may save them all. Among the wonders of creation there are few to compare with that glorious apostolic heart. The vastness of its sympathies, the breadth of its charity, the unwearied hopefulness of its zeal, the delicacy of its considerateness, the irresistible attraction of its imperious love—all this was the work of the Precious Blood; and that heart is still alive even upon earth, still beating in his marvellous Epistles as part of the unquenchable life of the Church. It is impossible to help connecting these characteristics of St. Paul's heart with the manifest devotion to the Precious Blood. Let us take him then as our guide amidst the unsearchable riches of Christ and the superabounding graces of his redeeming Blood. As it was with the disciples as they walked to Emmaus with Jesus, so will it be with us as we go along with his servant Paul. Our hearts will burn within us by the way; and we ourselves shall grow hot from the heat of that magnificent heart of him who guides us.

We are then to consider, first of all, the Mystery of the Precious Blood. It was one of God's eternal thoughts. It was part of his wisdom, part of his glory, part of his own blessedness from all eternity. You know that creation, although exceedingly ancient, perhaps so ancient as to be beyond our calculations, is nevertheless not eternal. It could not be so. To be eternal is to be without beginning; and to be without beginning is to be independent of any cause or power. This is a true description of God. But creation had a time at which it began, and it was the independent act of God's most holy, most condescending will. Thus there was an eternity before creation, a vast, unimaginable, adorable life, not broken up into centuries and ages, not lapsing but always still, not passing but always stationary, a life which had no past and no future, because its whole self was always present to itself. This was the life of God before any creation, an unspeakably glorious life, which we can think of with love and adoration, but which it is quite impossible for us to understand. We shall say more of it in the third chapter. Some holy persons, like Mother

Anne Seraphine Boulier of the Visitation at Dijon, have had such an exceeding devotion to this life of God prior to creation, that they have by God's order shaped their spirituality wholly upon it. Very often, when the troubles of life vex and ruffle us, or when we are downcast and distrustful, it would do us good to think of that ancient life of God. It would fill us with quiet awe. We should feel our own littleness more sensibly, and we should care less about the judgments of the world. The thought of it would be like a bed to lie down upon, when we are weary with work or fatigued with disappointment.

Nevertheless there is a sense in which creation was eternal. It was eternally in the mind of God. It was one of his eternal ideas, always before him; so that he never existed without this idea of creation in his all-wise mind and in his all-powerful intention. Moreover, it was always part of his intention that the Creator should become as it were part of his own creation, and that an Uncreated Person should really and truly assume a created nature and be born of a created mother. This is what we call the mystery of the Incarnation. It is this which makes creation so magnificent. It was not merely a beautiful thing which God made as an artificer, and which he set outside of himself, and kept at a distance from himself to look at, to admire, to pity, and to love. He always intended to be part of it himself in a very wonderful way. So that there would have been Jesus and Mary, even if there had never been any sin: only Jesus would not have been crucified, and Mary would not have had any dolors. But the sight of sin was also with God from the beginning, that is, through all his unbeginning eternity; and thus the Precious Blood also, as the ransom for sin, was with him from the beginning. It was one of his eternal thoughts. If we may dare to say so, it was an idea which made him more glorious, a thought which rendered him more blessed. That same dear Blood, the thought of which makes us so happy now, has been part of God's happiness forever.

He created the angels and the stars. How ancient the angels are we do not know. In all ways they are wonderful to think of, because they are so strong, so wise, so various, so beautiful, so innumerable. But they do not lie in our way just now; because, although they owe all their graces to the Precious Blood, they were not redeemed by the Precious Blood. Those angels, who did not fall, did not sin, and so needed no redemption; and God would not allow those who fell to be redeemed at all. This makes us sometimes think that God was more severe with his world of angels than with his world of men. But this is not really the case. It only shows us how we owe more to Jesus than we often think of. The angels could not make any satisfaction to the justice of God for their sins. If all the angels, good and bad together, had suffered willingly the most excruciating torments for millions upon millions of ages, those willing torments could not have made up to God for the sin of the least sinful of those angels who are now devils. If our dearest Saviour had taken upon himself the nature of angels, the case would have been different. But he became man, not angel; and so his Passion, as man, satisfied for all possible sins of men. The sufferings of his Passion were greater and of more price than all the torments of countless angels. The severity of God exacted more from him upon the Cross than it ever exacted or is exacting now, from the tortured angels. Thus you see God has not been more severe with them than with us: only that Jesus made himself one of us, and took all our share of God's severity upon himself, leaving us the easy happiness of faith, and hope, and love. You see we come upon the kindness of Jesus everywhere. There is not even a difficulty in religion, but somehow the greatness of his love is at the bottom of it, and is the explanation of it. Wonderful Jesus! that was the name the prophet Isaias gave him. "He shall be called Wonderful." How sweet it is to be so hemmed in by the tokens of his love, that we cannot turn to any side without meeting them! Yet his love would be sweeter to us if we could only repay it with more love ourselves.

God made the angels and the stars. The starry world is an overwhelming thing to think of. Its distances are so vast that they frighten us. The number of its separate worlds is so enormous that it bewilders us. Imagine a ray of light, which travels one hundred and ninety-two thousand miles in a second; and yet there are stars whose light would take a million of years to reach the earth. We know of two hundred thousand stars down to the ninth magnitude. In one single cluster of stars, eighteen millions of stars have been discovered between the tenth and eleventh magnitudes. Of these clusters men have already discovered more than four thousand. Each of these stars is not a planet, like the earth; but a sun, like our sun, and perhaps with planets round it, like ourselves. Of these suns we know of some which are one hundred and forty-six times brighter than our sun. What an idea all this gives us of the grandeur and magnificence of God! Yet we know that all these stars were created for Jesus and because of Jesus. He is the head and first-born of all creation. Mary's Son is the King of the stars. His Precious Blood has something to do with all of them. Just as it merited graces for the angels, so does it merit blessings for the stars. If they have been inhabited before we were, or are inhabited now, or will at some future time begin to be inhabited, their inhabitants, whether fallen and redeemed, or unfallen and so not needing to be redeemed, will owe immense things to the Precious Blood. Yet earth, our little, humble earth, will always have the right to treat the Precious Blood with special endearments, because it is its native place. When the angels, as they range through space, see our little globe twinkling with its speck of colored light, it is to them as the little Holy House in the hollow glen of Nazareth, more sacred and more glorious than the amplest palaces in starry space.

God made the stars; and, whether the earth was made by itself from the first, or was once part of the sun, and thrown off from it like a ring, God made the earth also, and shaped it, and adorned it, and filled it with trees and animals; and then looked upon his work, and it shone forth so beautifully with the light of his own perfections, that he blessed it, and, glorying in it, declared that it was very good. We know what an intense pleasure men take in looking at beautiful scenery. When we feel this pleasure, we ought to feel that we are looking at a little revelation of God, a very true one although a little one, and we ought to think of God's complacency when he beheld the scenery of the primeval earth and rejoiced in what he saw. There was no sin then. To God's eye, earth was all the more beautiful because it was innocent, and the dwelling-place of innocence. Then sin came. Why God let it come we do not know. We shall probably know in heaven. We are certain, however, that in some way or other it was more glorious for him, and better for us, that evil should be permitted. Some people trouble themselves about this. It does not trouble me at all. Whatever God does must of course be most right. My understanding it would not make it more right; neither could I do any thing to mend matters, if I understood it ever so well. Every one should keep in his own place: it is the creature's place to believe, adore, and love.

Sin came. With sin came many fearful consequences. This beautiful earth was completely wrecked. It went on through space in the sunshine as before; but in God's sight, and in the destiny of its inhabitants, it was all changed. Jesus could no longer come in a glorious and unsuffering incarnation. Mary would have to die; and, though she was sinless, she would need to be redeemed with a single and peculiar redemption, a redemption of prevention, not of rescue. She also, the Immaculate Mother and Queen of creation, must be bought by the Precious Blood. Had it not been for Jesus, the case of earth would have been hopeless, now that sin had come. God would have let it go, as he let the angels go. It would have been all hateful and dark in his sight, as the home of the fallen spirits is. But it was not so. Earth was dimmed, but it was not darkened, disfigured, but not blackened. God saw it through the Precious Blood, as through a haze; and there it lay with a dusky glory over it, like a red sunset, up to the day of Christ. No sooner had man sinned, than the influence of the Precious Blood began to be felt. There was no adorable abruptness on the part of God, as with the angels. His very upbraiding of Adam was full of paternal gentleness. With his punishment he mingled promises. He spoke of Mary, Eve's descendant, and illumined the penance of our first parents by the prophecy of Jesus. As the poor offending earth lay then before the sight of God, so does it lie now; only that the haze is more resplendent, since the Sacrifice on Calvary was offered. The Precious Blood covers it all over, like a sea or like an atmosphere. It lies in a beautiful crimson light forever, a light softening the very shades, beautifying the very gloom. God does not see us as we see ourselves, but in a brighter, softer light. We are fairer in his sight than we are in our own, notwithstanding his exceeding sanctity, because he sees us in the Blood of his dear Son. This is a consolation, the balm of which is not easily exhausted. We learn a lesson from it also. Our view of creation should be like God's view. We should see it, with all its countless souls, through the illuminated mist of the Precious Blood. Its spiritual scenery should be before us, every thing, everywhere, goldenly red.

This is the shape, then, which our Father's love takes to us his creatures. It is an invitation of all of us to the worship and the freedom of the Precious Blood. It is through this Blood that he communicates to us his perfections. It is in this Blood that he has laid up his blessings for us, as in a storehouse. This is true, not only of spiritual blessings, but of all blessings whatsoever. That the elements still wait upon us sinners, that things around us are so bright and beautiful, that pain has so many balms, that sorrow has so many alleviations, that the common course of daily providence is so kindly and so patient, that the weight, the frequency, and the bitterness of evils are so much lightened—is all owing to the Precious Blood. It is by this Blood that he has created over again his frustrated creation. It is out of this Blood that all graces come, whether those of Mary, or those of the angels, or those of men. It is this Blood which merits all good things for every one. The unhappy would be more unhappy, were it not for this Blood. The wicked would be more wicked, were it not for this Blood. The flames of hell would burn many times more furiously, if the shedding of this Blood had not allayed their fury. There is not a corner of God's creation, which is not more or less under the benignant control of the Precious Blood.

Our Heavenly Father, then, may well call his creatures to gather round these marvellous fountains, and adore his wisdom and his love. Who could have dreamed of such an invention, an invention which grows more astonishing the more we penetrate its mystery? The angels wonder more than men, because they better understand it. Their superior intelligence ministers more abundant matter to their love. From the very first he invited the angels to adore it. He made their adoration a double exercise of humility—of humility toward himself, and of humility toward us their inferior fellow-creatures. It was the test to which he put their loyalty. He showed them his beloved Son, the Second Person of the Holy Trinity, in his Sacred Humanity, united to a lower nature than their own, and in that lower nature crowned their King and Head, to be worshipped by them with absolute and unconditional adoration. The Son of a human mother was to be their Head, and that daughter of Eve to be herself their queen. He showed them in that Blood the source of all their graces. Each angel perhaps had thousands of beautiful graces. To many of them we on earth could give no name, if we beheld them. But they were all wonderful, all instinct with supernatural holiness and spiritual magnificence. Yet there was not a single grace in any angel which was not merited for him by the Blood of Jesus, and which had not also its type and counterpart in that Precious Blood. The Precious Blood—man's Blood— was as the dew of the whole kingdom of the angels. It would have redeemed them, had they needed to be redeemed or were allowed to be redeemed. But, as it was not so, it merited for them, and was the source of, all their grace. Well then may the angels claim to sing the song of the Lamb, to whose outpoured Human Life they also owed so much, though not because it was outpoured.

Nevertheless the Precious Blood belongs in an especial manner to men. Much more, therefore, does God invite them to come to its heavenly baths, and receive therein, not only the cleansing of their souls, but the power of a new and amazing life. Every doctrine in theology is a call to the Precious Blood. Every ceremony in the Church tells of it. Every sermon that is preached is an exhortation to the use of it. Every Sacrament is a communica-

tion of it. Every supernatural act is a growth of it. Every thing
that is holy on the earth is either leaf, bud, blossom, or fruit of
the Blood of Jesus. To its fountains, God calls the sinner, that
he may be lightened of his burdens. There is no remission for
him in any thing else. Only there is his lost sonship to be found.
But the saints are no less called by God to these invigorating
streams. It is out of the Precious Blood that men draw martyrdoms, vocations, celibacies, austerities, heroic charities, and all
the magnificent graces of high sanctity. The secret nourishment of
prayer is from those fountains. They purge the eye for sublime
contemplations. They kindle the inward fires of self-sacrificing
love. They bear a man safely, and even impetuously, over the
seeming impossibilities of perseverance. It is by the Blood of
Jesus that the soul becomes ever more and more radiant. It is
the secret source of all mystical transformations of the soul into
the likeness of its Crucified Spouse. It is the wine which "inebri-
ates" the virgins of God. Out of it come raptures, and ecstasies;
and by it the strength of faith grows even to the gift of miracles.
It fills the mind with heavenly visions, and peoples the air with
divine voices. All the new nature of the man, who is "renewed in
Christ Jesus," comes from this Blood, whether it be his love of
suffering, his delight in shame, his grace of prayer, his unworldly
tastes, his strange humility, his shy concealment, his zeal for souls,
his venturous audacity, or his obstinate perseverance. Sinner,
saint, and common Christian, all in their own ways, require the
Precious Blood each moment of their lives; and, as the manna in
the mouths of the Israelites had the savor which each man wished
it to have, so is it with the sweetness, the variety, and the fitness
of the graces of the Precious Blood.

All men remember their past lives by certain dates or epochs.
Some men date by sorrows, some by joys, and some by moral
changes or intellectual revolutions. Some divide their lives according to the different localities which they have inhabited, and
some by the successive occupations in which they have been
engaged. The lives of some are mapped out by illnesses, while the
tranquillity of an equable prosperity can only distinguish itself

by the lapse of years and the eras of boyhood, youth, and age. But the real dates in a man's life are the days and hours in which it came to him to have some new idea of God. To all men perhaps, but certainly to the thoughtful and the good, all life is a continual growing revelation of God. We may know no more theology this year than we did last year, but we undoubtedly know many fresh things about God. Time itself discloses him. The operations of grace illuminate him. Old truths grow: obscure truths brighten. New truths are incessantly dawning. But a new idea of God is like a new birth. What a spiritual revolution it was in the soul of St. Peter, when the Eternal Father, intensely loving that eager, ardent follower of his Son, one day secretly revealed to him the divinity of his beloved Master! It matters not whether it were in a dream by night, or in an audible voice at prayer, or in the last noiseless step of a long-pondered train of thought. Whenever and however it came, it was a divine revelation out of which flowed that new life of his, which is the strength of the Church to this day. So in its measure and degree is every new idea of God to every one of us. The Precious Blood brings us many such ideas. One of them is the fresh picture which it presents to us of his intense yearning love of souls. If we were to form our idea of God from theology, it would be full of grandeur. We should have a perception of him as vivid as it would be sublime. But if, not hitherto having known the Bible, we were to turn to the Old Testament, and see God loving, favoring, magnifying, his own historic people, and hear him passionately pleading for their love, he would seem like a new God to us, because we should receive such a new idea of him. Indeed, it would be such an idea of him as would require both time and management before it would harmonize with the idea of him implanted in us by theology. Even our own sinfulness gives us in one sense a broader idea of God than innocence could have given. So, if we think of the almost piteous entreaties with which he invites all the wide heathen world to the Precious Blood, whether by the voice of his Church, or by the bleeding feet and wasting lives of his missionaries, or by secret pleadings down in each heathen heart, grace-solicited at every hour, we get a new idea of God, and a more complete conviction that his invitation of his creatures to the Precious Blood is indeed the genuine expression of his creative love.

There is no narrowness in divine things. There is no narrowness in the Precious Blood. It is a divine invention which partakes of the universality and immensity of God. The tribes that inhabit the different lands of the earth are distinguished by different characteristics. One nation differs so much from another, as to be often unable to judge of the moral character of the other's actions. What, for instance, would be pride in the inhabitant of one country would only be patriotism in the inhabitant of another; or what would be falsehood in one country is only the characteristic way of putting things in another. It is not that the immutable principles of morality can be changed by national character or by climate; but that outward actions signify such different inward habits in various countries, that a foreigner is no judge of them. Thus a foreign history of any people is for the most part little better than a hypothesis, and is not unfrequently a misapprehension from first to last. But the Precious Blood is meant for all nations. As all stand in equal need of it, so all find it just what they want. It is to each people the grace which shall correct that particular form of human corruption which is prominent in their natural character. The Oriental and the Western must both come to its healing streams; and in it all national distinctions are done away. In that laver of Salvation there is neither Jew nor Greek, barbarian, Scythian, bond, or free: all are one in the redeeming Blood of Jesus.

As it is with the countries of the world, so is it with the ages of the world. Each age has its own distinctive spirit. It has its own proper virtues, and its own proper vices. It has its own sciences, inventions, literature, policy, and development. Each age thinks itself peculiar, which it is; and imagines it is better than other ages, which it is not. It is probably neither better nor worse. In substantial matters the ages are pretty much on a level with each other. But each has its own way, and requires to be dealt with in that way. This is the reason why the Church seems to act differently in different ages. There is a sense in which the Church goes along with the world. It is the same sense in which the shepherd leaves the sheep which have not strayed, and goes off in search of the one that has strayed. Each age is a stray sheep from God; and the Church has to seek it and fetch it back to him, so far as it is allowed to do so. We must not make light of the differences of the ages. Each age needs persuading in a manner of its own. It finds its own difficulties in religion. It has its own peculiar temptations and follies. God's work is never done in any one age. It has to be begun again in every age. Old controversies become useless, because they cease to be convincing. Old methods are found unsuitable, because things have changed. It is on this account that theology puts on new aspects, that religious orders first succeed and then fail, that devotion has fashions and vicissitudes, that art and ritual undergo changes, that discipline is modified, and that the Church puts herself in different relations to the governments of the world. But the Precious Blood adapts itself with changeful uniformity to every age. It is always old and always new. It is the one salvation. It is coextensive with any civilization. No science innovates upon it. The world never exhausts its abundance or outgrows its necessity.

But why should we heap together these generalities? Are they any thing more than so much pious rhetoric? Let us draw nearer to the mystery and see. What strikes us at the first thought of the Precious Blood? It is that we have to worship it with the highest worship. It is not a relic at which we should look with wonder and love, and which we should kiss with reverence, as having once been a temple of the Holy Ghost, and an instrument chosen by God for the working of miracles, or as flesh and bone penetrated with that celestial virtue of the Blessed Sacrament which will raise it up at the last day in a glorious resurrection. It is something unspeakably more than this. We should have to adore it with the highest adoration. In some local heaven or other, in some part of space far off or near, God at this hour is unveiling his blissful majesty before the angels and the saints. It is in a local court of inconceivable magnificence. The Human Body and Soul of Jesus are there, and are its light and glory, the surpassing sun of that heavenly Jerusalem. Mary, his Mother, is throned there like a lovely moon in the mid-glory of the sunset, beautified rather than extinguished by the effulgence round her. Millions of lordly angels are abasing their vast grandeur before the ecstatic terror of that unclothed Vision of the Eternal. Thrills of entrancing fear run through the crowds of glorified saints who throng the spaces of that marvellous shrine. Mary herself upon her throne is shaken by an ecstasy of fear before the mightiness of God, even as a reed is shaken by the wind. The Sacred Heart of Jesus beats with rapturous awe, and is glorified by the very blessedness of its abjection, before the immensity of those Divine Fires, burning visibly in their overwhelming splendors. If we could enter there as we are now, we should surely die. We are not strengthened yet to bear the depth of that prostrate humiliation, which is needed there, and which is the inseparable joy of heaven. Our lives would be shattered by the throbs of awe which must beat like vehement pulses in our souls. But we know the limits of our nature. We know, at least in theory, the abjection which befits the creature in the immediate presence of its Creator. We can conceive the highest adoration of a sinless immortal soul as a worship which it could not pay to any creature, however exalted, however near to God. We can picture ourselves to ourselves, prostrate on the clouds of heaven, blinded with excess of light, every faculty of the mind jubilantly amazed by the immensity of the Divine Perfections, every affection of the heart drowned in some forever new abyss of the unfathomable sweetness of God. We know that we should lie in sacred fear and glad astonishment before the throne of Mary, if we saw it gleaming in its royalty. Yet we know also that this deep reverence would be something of quite a different kind from our abjection before the tremendous majesty of God. But, if we saw one drop of the Precious Blood, hanging like the least pearl of dew upon a blade of grass on Calvary, or as a dull disfigured splash in the dust of the gateway of Jerusalem, we

should have to adore it with the selfsame adoration as the uncovered splendors of the Eternal.

It is no use repeating this a thousand times; yet we should
have to repeat it a thousand thousand times, for years and years,
before we should get the vastness of this piercing truth into our
souls. We should worship one drop of the Precious Blood with
the same worship as that wherewith we worship God. Let us
kneel down, and hide our faces before God, and say nothing, but
let the immensity of this faith sink down into our souls.

If the Easter Resurrection left any red stains upon the stones,
or roots, or earth of Gethsemane, they are no longer to be found
beneath the luxuriant vegetation of the Franciscan garden there.
Neither indeed if they had been left, when Easter passed, could we
have worshipped them with divine worship; for they had already
ceased to be the Precious Blood. Whatever Jesus did not reunite
to himself in the Resurrection remained disunited from the Person of the Word forever, and therefore, however venerable, had
no claim to adoration. But, had we been in Jerusalem on the
Friday and the Saturday, we should have found objects, or rather
the multiplied presence of an object, of dreadest worship everywhere. The pavement of the streets, the accoutrements of the
Roman legionaries, the floors of their barracks, the steps of
Pilate's judgment-hall, the pillar of the scourging, the ascent of
Calvary, the wood of the Cross, many shoes and sandals of the
multitude, many garments either worn or in the clothes-presses,
ropes, tools, scourges, and many other things, were stained with
Precious Blood; and everywhere the angels were adoring it. Had
we been there, and had been wise with the holy wisdom of our
present faith, we must have adored it also. But what a picture of
the world it gives us! What an awful taking of a place in his own
creation on the part of the Incomprehensible Creator! What a
view of God it gives us! What an idea of sin! What a disclosure of
the magnificence of our salvation! The Blood of God, the human
Blood of the Uncreated, the Blood of the Unbeginning drawn
three-and-thirty years ago from the veins of a Jewish maiden, and
she, the unproclaimed queen of creation, hidden in that very city

in the depths of an immeasurable sorrow! Millions of angels intently adoring down upon the low-lying surface of the ground, as if heaven were there, below rather than above, as indeed it was, and at each spot adoring with such singular concentration, as if the Divine Life had been broken up, and there were many Gods instead of One! Meanwhile men, the very part of creation which this Precious Blood most specially concerned, were passing through the streets, and over the ruddy spots, treading on adorable things and yet never heeding, with angels beneath their sandals and yet never knowing it, compassed thickly round with mysteries the sudden revelation of which would have struck them dead, and yet with the most utter, unsuspecting ignorance. It is hard to bring such a state of things home to ourselves; and yet it is but a type to us of what we are all of us always doing with the invisible presence of God among ourselves. God is within us and without us, above, below, and around us. Wheresoever we set our feet, God is there, even if we be going to do evil. If we reach forth our hands, God is in our hand; he is in the air through which our hand passes; and where our hand touches, there is God also. He is there in three different ways, by his essence, by his presence, and by his power; and in each of those three ways his presence is more real than the hardness of the rocks, or the wetness of water, or the firmness of the earth. Yet we go our ways as we please, sinning, boasting, and committing follies, not simply in a consecrated sanctuary, but in the living God. This mystery was made manifest, by the most wonderful of revelations, in the Precious Blood, when it was scattered about Jerusalem.

But we need not go to Jerusalem, we need not have lived eighteen hundred years ago, to find the Precious Blood and worship it. Here is part of that awfulness of our holy faith, which makes us so thrill with love that it is sometimes as if we could not bear the fire which is burning in our hearts. We actually worship it every day in the chalice at Mass. When the chalice is uplifted over the altar, the Blood of Jesus is there, whole and entire, glorified and full of the pulses of his true human life. The Blood that once lay in the cave at Olivet, that curdled in the thongs and knots of the scourges, that matted his hair and soaked his garments, that stained the crown of thorns and bedewed the Cross, the Blood that he drank himself in his own communion on the Thursday night, the Blood that lay all Friday night in seemingly careless prodigality upon the pavement of the treacherous city—that same Blood is living in the chalice, united to the Person of the Eternal Word, to be worshipped with the uttermost prostration of our bodies and our souls. When the beams of the morning sun come in at the windows of the church, and fall for a moment into the uncovered chalice, and glance there as if among precious stones with a restless, timid gleaming, and the priest sees it, and the light seems to vibrate into his own heart, quickening his faith and love, it is the Blood of God which is there, the very living Blood whose first fountains were in the Immaculate Heart of Mary. When the Blessed Sacrament is laid upon your tongue—that moment and that act which the great angels of God look down upon with such surpassing awe—the Blood of Jesus is throbbing there in all its abounding life of glory. It sheathes in the sacramental mystery that exceeding radiance which is lighting all heaven at that moment with a magnificence of splendor which exceeds the glowing of a million suns. You do not feel the strong pulses of his immortal life. If you did, you could hardly live yourself. Sacred terror would undo your life. But in that adorable Host is the whole of the Precious Blood, the Blood of Gethsemane, Jerusalem, and Calvary, the Blood of the Passion, of the Resurrection, and of the Ascension, the Blood shed and reassumed. As Mary bore that Precious Blood within herself of old, so do you bear it now. It is in his Heart and veins, within the temple of his Body, as it was when he lay those nine months in her ever-blessed womb. We believe all this; nay, we so believe it that we know it rather than believe it; and yet our love is so faint and fitful. Our very fires are frost in comparison with such a faith as this.

The whole of the Precious Blood is in the Chalice and in the Host. It is not part: it is the whole. We may well tremble to think what sanctuaries we are when the Blessed Sacrament is within us.

Let us think again of the innumerable stars. Let us multiply their actual millions by millions of imaginary millions more. Let us suppose them all to be densely inhabited for countless ages by races of fallen beings. We have no figures to show the numbers of the individual souls, still less to represent the multiplied acts of sin of all those single souls or spirits. But we know this, that one drop of the thousands of drops of the Precious Blood in the glorified Body of Jesus would have been more than sufficient to cleanse all those countless fallen creations, and to absolve every separate sinner from every one of his multitudinous sins. Nay, that one drop would have given out all those worlds of redeeming grace, and yet no tittle of its treasures would be spent. The worth of one drop of the Precious Blood is simply infinite; consequently, no imaginary arithmetic of possible creations will convey any adequate idea of its overwhelming magnificence. Alas! the very copiousness of our redemption makes our view of it less clear. The very crowding of God's love causes it to have something indistinguishable about it. Who does not see that it will take us an eternity to learn Jesus, or rather that we shall never learn him, but that the endless work of learning him will be the gladness of our eternity?

But this is not all the mystery. It was no necessity which drove God to the redemption of the world by the Precious Blood. He might have redeemed it in unnumbered other ways. There is no limit to his power, no exhaustion of his wisdom. He might have reconciled the forgiveness of sin with his stainless sanctity by many inventions of which neither we nor the angels can so much as dream. There are vastnesses in him who is incomprehensible, of the existence of which we have no suspicion. He could have saved us without Jesus, according to the absoluteness of his power. All salvation must be dear: yet who can dream of a salvation which should seem at once so worthy of God and so endearing to man as our present salvation through Jesus Christ? Even then our dearest Lord need not have shed his Blood. There was no compulsion in the Blood-shedding. One tear of his, one momentary sigh, one uplifted look to his Father's throne, would have been sufficient, if the Three Divine Persons had so pleased. The shedding of his Blood was part of the freedom of his love. It was, in some mysterious reality, the way of redemption most worthy of his blessed majesty, and also the way most likely to provoke the love of men. How often has God taken the ways of our hearts as the measure of his own ways! How often does he let his glory and our love seem to be different things, and then leave himself and go after us!

The Precious Blood is invisible. Yet nothing in creation is half so potent. It is everywhere, practically everywhere, although it is not omnipresent. It becomes visible in the fruits of grace. It will become more visible in the splendors of glory. But it will itself be visible in heaven in our Lord's glorified Body as in crystalline vases of incomparable refulgence. It belongs to him, the Second Person of the Most Holy Trinity, although its work is the work of the whole Trinity. In its efficacy and operation it is the most complete and most wonderful of all revelations of the Divine Perfections. The power, the wisdom, the goodness, the justice, the sanctity, of God, are most pre-eminently illustrated by the working of this Precious Blood.

These are the first thoughts which strike us about the Precious Blood. They are the ordinary considerations which our faith has made familiar to us. We shall have to return to them again in a different connection; and upon some of them we must enlarge in another place. A minuter acquaintance with Christian doctrine teaches us much more. Some little of this much must be introduced here for the sake of clearness and in order that we may better understand what has to follow.

The Precious Blood was assumed directly to our Blessed Lord's Divine Person from his Immaculate Mother. It was not taken merely to his Body, so that his Body was directly assumed to the Person of the Word, and his Blood only indirectly or mediately as part of his Body. The Blood, which was the predetermined price of our redemption, rested directly and immediately on the Divine Person, and thus entered into the very highest and most unspeakable degree of the Hypostatic Union—if we may speak of degrees in such an adorably simple mystery. It was not merely a concomitant of the Flesh, an inseparable accident of the Body. The Blood itself, as Blood, was assumed directly by the Second Person of the Holy Trinity. It came also from Mary's blood. Mary's blood was the material out of which the Holy Ghost, the Third Person of the Most Holy Trinity, the artificer of the Sacred Humanity, fashioned the Blood of Jesus. Here we see how needful to the joy and gladness of our devotion is the doctrine of the Immaculate Conception. Who could bear to think that the matter of the Precious Blood had ever been itself corrupted with the taint of sin, that it had once been part of the devil's kingdom, that what was to supply the free price of our redemption was once enslaved to God's darkest, foulest enemy? Is it not indeed an endless daily jubilee to us, that the Church has laid upon us as an article of our faith that sweet truth which the instincts of our devotion had so long made a real part of our belief?

Moreover, there is some portion of the Precious Blood which once was Mary's own blood, and which remains still in our Blessed Lord, incredibly exalted by its union with his Divine Person, yet still the same. This portion of himself, it is piously believed, has not been allowed to undergo the usual changes of human substance. At this moment in heaven he retains something which once was his Mother's, and which is possibly visible, as such, to the saints and angels. He vouchsafed at Mass to show to St. Ignatius the very part of the Host which had once belonged to the substance of Mary. It may have a distinct and singular beauty in heaven, where by his compassion it may one day be our blessed lot to see it and adore it. But, with the exception of this portion of it, the Precious Blood was a growing thing. It increased daily, as he increased in size and age. It was nourished from his Mother's breast. It was fed from the earthly food which he condescended to take. During his three-and-thirty years it received thousands of increments and augmentations. But each one of those augmentations was assumed directly to his Divine Person. It was not merely diluted by that which had existed before. It did not share in the Hypostatic Union in any lower degree. The last

drop of Blood made in him by the laws of human life, perhaps
while he was hanging on the Cross, was equally exalted, equally
divine, equally adorable, with the first priceless drops which he
drew from his Blessed Mother.

Our dearest Lord was full and true man. He was flesh of our
flesh, and bone of our bone; and his incomparable Soul, although
it was incomparable, was simply and veritably a human soul.
Every thing in his human substance was so exalted by its union
with his Divine Person as to be adorable. Yet it was only his
Blood which was to redeem the world; and it was only his Blood
as shed which was to do so, and it was only his Blood as shed *in
death* which could be the price of our redemption. The Blood
shed at the Circumcision was adorable. The Blood shed in Gethsemane was adorable. If it be true, as some contemplatives have
seen in vision, that he sweated Blood at various times in his Infancy because of his sight of sin and of his Father's anger, that
Blood also was adorable. But it was the Blood shed upon the
Cross, or at least the Blood shed in the process of dying, which
was the ransom of our sins. Throughout the whole of the triduo
of the Passion, all his Blood, wherever it had been shed and
wherever it was sprinkled, remained assumed to his Divinity, in
union with his Divine Person, just as his soulless Body did, and
therefore was to be worshipped with divine worship, with the
same adoration as the living and eternal God. At the Resurrection, when his Precious Blood had been collected by the ministry
of the angels, and he united it once more to his Body as he rose,
some of it remained unassumed. This perhaps was for the consolation of his Mother, or for the enriching of the Church with the
most inestimable of relics. This was the case with the Blood on
the veil of Veronica, on the holy Winding-Sheet, on some portions of the Cross, and on the Thorns and Nails. But this Blood,
which was not reassumed at the Resurrection, instantly lost its
union with his Divine Person, ceased to be what is strictly called
the Precious Blood, lost its right to absolute adoration, and became only an intensely holy relic, to be venerated with a very high
worship, but not to be worshipped as divine or adored as the

Blood of God. It was no longer part of himself. But the Blood in
the chalice is the Blood of the living Jesus in heaven. It is the
Blood shed in the Passion, reassumed at the Resurrection, borne
up to heaven in the Ascension, placed at the Right Hand of the
Father there in its consummate glory and beautified immortality.
Thus it is the very Blood of God; and it is the whole of it, containing that portion which he had originally assumed from Mary.

Miraculous Blood is not the Precious Blood. Neither is it like
the unassumed Blood of the Passion. For that had once been Precious Blood, and had only ceased to be so through the special
will of our Lord, whereby he willed not to reassume it at the Resurrection. The Host has miraculously bled at Mass, to reassure
men's faith or to cause a reformation in their lives. It has bled in
the hands of Jews and heretics, as if resenting sacrilege, and striking awe into their souls, like the deep fear which fell upon Jerusalem at the Passion. Crucifixes have sweated Blood to convert
sinners, or to portend some public calamities, or to show forth
symbolically the ceaseless sympathy of our Blessed Lord with his
suffering Church. But this is not Precious Blood, nor has it ever
been Precious Blood. It has never lived in our Lord. It is greatly
to be venerated, inasmuch as it is a miraculous production of God;
and it appeals especially to the reverence of the faithful, because
of its being appointed to represent in figure the Precious Blood.
If the angel, who passed at midnight over Egypt to slay the first-
born, reverenced the blood of the Paschal lamb sprinkled on the
door-posts of the Israelites, simply because it was a type of the
Blood of Jesus, much more should we reverence the miraculous
Blood which issues from the Host or from the Crucifix, as a
higher and a holier thing than the symbolic blood of animals.
Nevertheless it is not Precious Blood, nor is it to be adored with
divine worship.

Perhaps this is enough to say of the doctrine of the Precious
Blood. There are many other interesting questions connected
with it. But they are hard to understand; and, although no minutest detail of scholastic theology is other than fresh fuel to our
love of God, yet it would not suit either the brevity or the plain-

ness of this Treatise to enter upon them here. How shall we ever raise our love up to the height of the doctrine which we have put forth already? The Precious Blood is God's daily gift, nay, rather we might call it his incessant gift to us. For, if grace is coming to us incessantly, save when we sleep, it comes to us in view of the Precious Blood, and because of it. But who can estimate the wonderfulness of such a gift? It is the Blood of God. It is not the giving to us of new hearts, or of immensely increased powers, or of the ability to work miracles and raise the dead. It is not the bestowing upon us of angelic natures. It is something of far greater price than all this would be. It is the Blood of God. It is the created life of the Uncreated. It is a human fountain opened as it were in the very centre of the Divine Nature. It is a finite thing, with a known origin and an ascertained date, of a price as infinite as the Divine Person who has assumed it. To us creatures the adorable majesty of the Undivided Trinity is an inexhaustible treasure-house of gifts. They are poured out upon us in the most lavish prodigality, and with the most affecting display of love. They are beautiful beyond compare; and they are endlessly diversified, yet endlessly adapted to the singularities of each heart and soul. Yet what gift do the Divine Persons give us, which has more of their own sweetness in it, than the Precious Blood? It has in it that yearning and tenderness which belong to the power of the Father, that magnificent prodigality which marks the wisdom of the Son, and that refreshing fire which characterizes the love of the Holy Ghost.

It is also a revelation to us of the character of God. Nothing on earth tells us so much of him, or tells it so plainly and so endearingly. How adorable must be the exactness of his justice, how unattainable the standard of his sanctity, how absorbing the blissful gulfs of his uncreated purity, if the Precious Blood is to be the sole fitting ransom for the sins of men, the one divinely-chosen satisfaction to his outraged Majesty! Yet what a strange wisdom in such an astonishing invention, what an unintelligible condescension, what a mysterious fondness of creative love! The more we meditate upon the Precious Blood, the more strange does it appear as a device of infinite love. While we are really getting to understand it more, our understanding of it appears to grow less. When we see a divine work at a distance, its dimensions do not seem so colossal as we find them to be in reality when we come nearer. The Precious Blood is such a wonderful revelation of God that it partakes in a measure of his incomprehensibility. But it is also a marvellous revelation of the enormity of sin. Next to a practical knowledge of God, there is nothing which it more concerns us to know and to realize than the exceeding sinfulness of sin. The deeper that knowledge is, the higher will be the fabric of our holiness. Hence a true understanding of the overwhelming guilt and shame of sin is one of God's greatest gifts. But in reality this revelation of the sinfulness of sin is only another kind of revelation of God. It is by the height of his perfections that we measure the depths of sin. Its opposition to his unspeakable holiness, the amount of its outrage against his glorious justice, and the intensity of his hatred of it, are manifested by the infinity of the sacrifice which he has required. If we try to picture to ourselves what we should have thought of God and sin if Jesus had not shed his Blood, we shall see what a fountain of heavenly science, what an effulgence of supernatural revelation, the Precious Blood has been to us.

No doubt it was partly this power of revelation which made our dearest Lord so impatient to shed his Blood. He longed to make his Father known, and so to increase his Father's glory. He knew that we must know God in order to love him, and then that our love of him would in its turn increase our knowledge of him. He yearned also with an unutterable love of us; and this also entered into his Heart as another reason for his affectionate impatience. At all events, he has been pleased to reveal himself to us as impatient to shed his Blood. If habits of meditation and a study of the Gospels have transferred to our souls a true portrait of Jesus as he was on earth, this impatience will seem a very striking mystery. There was ordinarily about our Blessed Lord an atmosphere of quite unearthly calmness. His human will seemed almost without human activity. It lay still in the lap of the will of God. It was revealed to Mary of Agreda that he never exercised choice, except in the choosing of suffering. This one disclosure is enough to give us a complete picture of his inward life. Yet there was an eagerness, a semblance of precipitation, a stimulating desire for the shedding of his Blood, which stand alone and apart in the narrative of his Thirty-three Years. With desire had he desired to communicate with his chosen few in the Blessed Sacrifice of the Mass, wherein his Blood is mystically shed. He shed it in that awful, miraculous reality before he shed it upon Calvary, as if he could not brook the slowness of human cruelty, which did not lay hands upon him so swiftly as his love desired. He was straitened in himself by his impatience for his baptism of Blood; and he bedewed the ground at Gethsemane with those priceless drops, as if he could not even wait one night for the violence of Calvary. It seemed as if the relief and satisfaction, which it was to him to shed his Blood, were almost an alleviation of the bitterness of his Passion. This impatience is in itself a revelation to us of the yearnings of his Sacred Heart.

The prodigality, also, with which he shed his Blood, stands alone and apart in his life. He was sparing of his words. He spake seldom, and he spake briefly. The shortness of his Ministry is almost a difficulty to our minds. It was the instinct of his holiness to hide itself. This was one of the communications of his Divine Nature to his Human. Even his miracles were comparatively few; and he said that his saints after him should work greater miracles than his. Yet in the shedding of his Blood he was spendthrift, prodigal, wasteful. As his impatience to shed it represents to us the adorable impetuosity of the Most Holy Trinity to communicate himself to his creatures, so his prodigality in shedding it shadows forth the exuberant magnificence and liberality of God. During the triduo of his Passion he shed it in all manner of places and in all manner of ways; and he continued to shed it even after he was dead, as if he could not rest until the last drop had been poured out for the creatures whom he so incomprehensibly loved. Yet, while he thus carelessly, or rather purposely, parted with it, how he must have loved his Precious Blood! What loves are there on earth to be compared with the love of his Divine Nature for his Human Nature, or the love of his ever-blessed Soul for his Body? Moreover, he must have loved his Blood with a peculiar love, because it was the specially appointed ransom of the world. His love of his dearest Mother is the only love which approaches to his love of the Precious Blood; and, rightly considered, is not one love enclosed within the other?

He has continued the same prodigality of his Blood in the Church to this day. He foresaw then that he should do so; and it was part of his love of that fountain of our redemption, that he beheld with exquisite delight its ceaseless and abundant flowing through the ages which were yet to come. There is something almost indiscriminate in the generosity of the Precious Blood. It is poured in oceans over the world, bathing more souls than it seems to have been meant for, only that in truth it was meant for all. It appears not to regard the probabilities of its being used, or appreciated, or welcomed. It goes in floods through the seven mighty channels of the Sacraments. It breaks their bounds, as if they could not contain the impetuosity of its torrents. It lies like a superincumbent ocean of sanctifying grace over the Church. It runs over in profuse excess, and irrigates even the deserts which lie outside the Church. It goes to sinners as well as saints. Nay, it even looks as if it had a propension and attraction to sinners more than to other men. It is falling forever like a copious fiery rain upon the lukewarm. It rests on the souls of hardened apostates, as if it hoped to sink in in time. Its miraculous action in the Church is literally incessant. In the Sacraments, in separate graces, in hourly conversions, in multiplied death-beds, in releases from purgatory every moment, in countless augmentations of grace in countless souls, in far-off indistinguishable preludes and drawings toward the faith, this most dear Blood of Jesus is the manifold life of the world. Every pulse which beats in it is an intense jubilee to him. It is forever setting him on fire with fresh love of us his creatures. It is forever filling him with a new and incredible gladness, which we cannot think of without amazement and adoration. Oh that he would give us one spark of that immense love of his Precious Blood which he himself is feeling so blissfully this hour in heaven!

Such is the mystery of the Precious Blood. It makes the poor fallen earth more beautiful than the Paradise of old. Its streams are winding their way everywhere all over the earth. The rivers of Eden are not to be compared to them for fruitfulness. Poets have loved the music of the mountain stream, as it tinkled down the hills amidst the stones or murmured under leafy shades. Scripture speaks of the Voice of God as the voice of many waters. So is it with the Precious Blood. It has a voice which God hears, speaking better things than the blood of Abel, more than restoring to him again the lost music of his primeval creation. In our ears also does it murmur sweetly, evermore and evermore, in sorrows, in absolutions, in communions, in sermons, and in all holy joys. It will never leave us now. For at last, when it has led us to the brink of heaven, and when, in the boundless far-flashing magnificence, the steadfast splendors and unfathomable depths of the Uncreated joy of God lie out before us, ocean-like and infinite, that Blood will still flow around us, and sing to us beyond angelic skill, with a voice like that of Jesus, which when once heard is never to be forgotten, that word of him whose Heart's Blood it is, Well done, thou good and faithful servant! enter thou into the joy of thy Lord! What is the life in heaven, but an everlasting Te Deum before the Face of God? But there also, as now in our Te Deum upon earth, we shall have a special joy, a special moving of our love, when we call ourselves "redeemed with Precious Blood"; and, as we do now in church, so there in the innermost courts of our Father's House, we shall only say the words upon our knees, with a separate gladness, and a separate depth of adoration.

CHAPTER II

THE NECESSITY OF THE PRECIOUS BLOOD

CHAPTER II

THE NECESSITY OF THE PRECIOUS BLOOD

It is very difficult to feel as we ought to do about eternal things. We are surrounded by the sights and sounds of this short earthly life. We judge of things, if not by appearances, at least by their earthly importance. We cannot disentangle ourselves from the impressions which earth makes upon us. We are forced to measure things by a standard which we know to be untrue, but which we are so accustomed to that we cannot even think by any other standard. Eternity is simply a word to us; and it is exceedingly hard to make it more than a word. Thus, when we try to bring home to ourselves or to others the immense importance of eternal things, and the extreme triviality of all temporal things which are not simply made to minister to eternal things, we find ourselves in a difficulty. If we speak of them in common words, we convey false ideas. If we use high-sounding language and deal in superlatives, a sense of unreality comes upon ourselves, and still more upon our hearers; and we seem to be exaggerating, even when what we say is far below the mark. Time alone enables us in some degree to realize the importance of eternal things. A striking expression may rouse our attention. But eternal things, in order to be fruitful and practical, must grow into us by frequent prayer and long familiarity. Even then we fall far short of the mark. Even then we get false ideas, and, becoming used to them, are unable to substitute true ones in their place. It is almost impossible for us truly to realize the fact that lifelong pain or exuberant health, ample riches or bitter poverty, unintermitting success or incessant failure, are matters of perfect unimportance and of absolute indifference, except so far as they concern the salvation of our souls. We recognize the impossibility by seeing how men who talk and believe rightly fall far short both of their faith and their words, even when they are acting up to the highest standard in their power. We are placed in the same difficulty now, when we want to realize truly the necessity of the Precious Blood. It is more necessary than we can say or think. What would come of being without it is inconceivable by us. When we have said that, we have said all we can say. So, as time alone will make it familiar to us, we must say it in many different ways, and look at it from many different points of view, and repeat it to ourselves as if we were learning a lesson. This will enable us to gain time, and will answer better than big words or unusual metaphors.

The most recollected saint and the most thoughtful theologian, do what they will, live in the world all day without being able to realize how much, and in what ways, they are indebted to God, receiving from him, living upon him, using him, and immersed in him, nor how indispensable he is to us. So is it in the spiritual world with Jesus. It is a wonder that he ever came among us. Yet he is simply indispensable to us. We could in no wise do without him. We want him at every turn, at every moment. It is the wisdom of life, as well as its joy, to be always feeling this great need of Jesus. A true Christian feels that he could no more live for an hour without Jesus, than he could live for an hour without air or under the water. There is something delightful in this sense of utter dependence upon Jesus. It is our only rest, our only liberty in the world. It is the bondage of our imperfection that we cannot be directly and actually thinking of Jesus all day and night. Yet it is astonishing how near we may come to this. Our very sleep at last becomes subject to the thought of Jesus, and saturated with it. It is part of the gladness of growing older, not only that we are thereby drawing nearer to our first sight of him, but that we feel our dependence upon him more and more. We have learned more about him. We have had a longer and more varied experience of him. Our love of him has become more of a passion, which, by a little effort, promises at some not very distant day to be dominant and supreme. The love of Jesus never can be an ungrowing love. It must grow, if it does not die out. In our physical life, as we grow older, we become more sensible to cold and wind, to changes of place and to alterations of the weather. So, as we grow older in our spiritual life, we become more sensitive to the presence of Jesus, to the necessity of him, and to his indispensable sweetness. A constantly increasing sensible love of our dearest Lord is the safest mark of our growth in holiness, and the most tranquillizing prophecy of our final perseverance.

What would the world be without Jesus? We may perhaps have sometimes made pictures to ourselves of the day of judgment. We may have imagined the storms above and the earthquakes underneath, the sun and the moon darkened, and the stars falling from heaven, the fire raging over the face of the earth, men crying to the mountains and rocks to fall upon them and hide them, and in the masses of the eastern clouds Jesus coming to judge the world. We think it appropriate to add to the picture every feature of physical tumult and desolation, every wildest unchaining of the elements, although doubtless the catastrophe of that day of horrors will follow the grand uniformity of a natural law, even amidst the impetuosity of its convulsions. Yet the misery and confusion of earth at that day will have less of real horror in it than the earth without Jesus would have, even though the sun were shining, and the flowers blooming, and the birds singing. An earth without hope or happiness, without love or peace, the past a burden, the present a weariness, the future a shapeless terror— such would the earth be, if by impossibility there were no Jesus. Indeed, it is only in such a general way that we can conceive what the world would be without him. We can make no picture to ourselves of the real horror. His Five Wounds are pleading forever at the Right Hand of the Father. They are holding back the divine indignation. They are satisfying the divine justice. They are moving the divine compassion. Even temporal blessings come from them. They are bridling the earthquake and the storm, the

pestilence and the famine, and a thousand other temporal consequences of sin, which we do not know of, or so much as suspect.
Besides this, Jesus is bound up with our innermost lives. He is
more to us than the blood in our veins. We know that he is indispensable to us; but we do not dream how indispensable he is.

There is not a circumstance of life, in which we could do
without Jesus. When sorrow comes upon us, how should we bear
it without him? What feature of consolation is there about the
commonest human grief, which is not ministered by faith, or hope,
or love? We cannot exaggerate the utter moral destitution of a
fallen world without redeeming grace. With the apostate angels
that destitution is simply an eternal hell. Let the child of a few
weeks lie like a gathered lily, white, cold, faded, dead, before the
eyes of the fond mother who bore it but a while ago; and how
blank is the woe in her heart, if the waters of baptism have not
passed upon it! Yet what are those waters, but the Blood of
Jesus? Now she can sit and think, and be thankful even while
she is weeping, and there can be smiles through her tears, which,
like the rainbows, are signs of God's covenant with his people;
for she has volumes of sweet things to think, and bright visions
in her mind, and the sounds of angelic music in her soul's ear; and
these things are not fancies, but faiths, knowledges, infallible as-
surances. Even if her child were unbaptized, dismal as the thought
is that it can never see God, its eternal destiny is for the sake of
Jesus shorn of all the sensible pains and horrors which else would
have befallen it. It owes the natural blessedness, which it will one
day enjoy, to the merits of our dearest Lord. It is better even for
the babes that are not his, that he himself was once the Babe of
Bethlehem.

Sorrow without Christ is not to be endured. Such a lot would
be worse than that of the beasts of the field, because the possession
of reason would be an additional unhappiness. The same is true
of sickness and of pain. What is the meaning of pain, except the
purification of our soul? Who could bear it for years, if there were
no significance in it, no future for it, no real work which it was
actually occupied in doing? Here also the possession of reason

would act to our disadvantage; for it would render the patience of beasts impossible to us. The long, pining, languishing sick-bed, with its interminable nights and days, its wakeful memories, its keen susceptibilities, its crowded and protracted inward biography, its burdensome epochs of monotony—what would this be, if we knew not the Son of God, if Jesus never had been man, if his grace of endurance had not actually gone out of his Heart into ours that we might love even while we murmured, and believe most in mercy when it was showing itself least merciful?

In poverty and hardship, in the accesses of temptation, in the intemperate ardors of youth or the cynical fatigue of age, in the successive failures of our plans, in the disappointments of our affections, in every crisis and revolution of life, Jesus seems so necessary to us that it appears as if he grew more necessary every year, and were more wanted today than he was yesterday, and would be still more urgently wanted on the morrow. But, if he is thus indispensable in life, how much more will he be indispensable in death! Who could dare to die without him? What would death be, if he had not so strangely and so graciously died himself? Yet what is death compared with judgment? Surely most of all he will be wanted then. Wanted! Oh, it is something more than a want, when so unspeakable a ruin is inevitably before us! Want is a poor word to use, when the alternative is everlasting woe. Dearest Lord! the light of the sun and the air of heaven are not so needful to us as thou art; and our happiness, not merely our greatest, but our only, happiness, is in this dear necessity!

Nobody is without Jesus in the world. Even the lost in hell are suffering less than they should have suffered, because of the ubiquity of his powerful Blood. Yet there are some nations who are so far without him, as to have no saving knowledge of him. Alas! there are still heathen lands in this fair world. There are tribes and nations who worship stocks and stones, who make gods of the unseen devils, who tremble before the powers of nature as if they were at once almighty and malicious, or who live in perpetual fear of the souls of the dead. There are some, whose sweetest social relations are embittered by the terrors and panics of their own false religions; and the innocent sunshine of delightful climates is not unfrequently polluted by human sacrifices. Yet these people dwell in some of the loveliest portions of man's inheritance. Amidst the savage sylvan sublimities of the Rocky Mountains, on the eastern declivities of the magnificent Andes, in the glorious gorges of the Himalayas, in the flowery coral-islands of the Pacific, or in those natural Edens laved by the warm seas of the Indian archipelago, human life is made inhuman by the horrors of a false religion. Let us take a picture from the banks of the Quango, in the interior of Africa. In speaking of the people, Dr. Livingstone says, "I have often thought, in travelling through their land, that it presents pictures of beauty which angels might enjoy. How often have I beheld, in still mornings, scenes the very essence of beauty, and all bathed in a quiet air of delicious warmth! Yet the occasional soft motion imparted a pleasing sensation of coolness as of a fan. Green grassy meadows, the cattle feeding, the goats browsing, the kids skipping, the groups of herdboys with miniature bows, arrows, and spears; the women wending their way to the river with watering-pots poised jauntily on their heads; men sewing under the shady banians; and old gray-headed fathers sitting on the ground, with staff in hand, listening to the morning gossip, while others carry trees or branches to repair their hedges; and all this, flooded with the bright African sunshine, and the birds singing among the branches before the heat of the day has become intense, form pictures which can never be forgotten."* Nevertheless, he tells us that they cannot "enjoy their luxurious climate," so completely and habitually do they fancy themselves to be in the remorseless power of the disembodied souls. Around our daily path, on the other hand, are strewn the memorials and blessings of Jesus. There is the morning Mass and the evening Benediction. Three times a day the Angelus brings afresh its sweet tidings of the Incarnation. Our early meditation has left a picture of Jesus on our souls to last the livelong day. Our beads have to be told, and they

---

*Travels, p. 441.

too tell of Jesus. When we sink to rest at night, his own commendation of his Soul upon the Cross prompts the words which come most natural to our lips. Think of those poor heathen, wandering saviorless over their beautiful lands—what if we were like to them? And what perchance would they have been if they had had but half our grace?

There are many who call themselves after the name of Christ, who are yet outside the Church of Christ. Theirs is in every way a woeful lot. To be so near Jesus, and yet not to be of his blessed fold—to be within reach of his unsearchable riches, and yet to miss of them, to be so blessed by his neighborhood, and yet not to be savingly united to him—this is indeed a desolation. Their creed is words: it is not life. They know not the redeeming grace of Jesus rightly. They understand not the mysterious dispositions of his Sacred Heart. They disesteem his hidden Sacraments. They know God only wrongly and partially. Their knowledge is neither light nor love. Every thing about Jesus, the merest accessory of his Church, the faintest vestige of his benediction, the very shadow of his likeness, is of such surpassing importance, that for the least of these things the whole world would be but a paltry price to pay. The gift of being in the true Church is the greatest of all God's gifts which can be given out of heaven. We cannot exaggerate its value. It is the pearl beyond price. Hence also the woefulness of being out of the Church is not to be told in words. I doubt if it is even to be compassed in thought. What, then, if we had so far lost Jesus, as to be out of his Church? Unbearable thought! yet not without some sweetness, as it makes us feel more keenly how indispensable he is to us, and what a merciful good-fortune he has given us to enjoy.

But even inside the Church there are wandering Cains, impenitent sinners who have gone out from the presence of God and wilfully abide there. They have lived years in sin, and the chains of sinful habits are heavy upon them. They have resisted grace a thousand times, and it looks as if the divine inspirations were weary of whispering to hearts so deaf. Nothing seems to rouse them. They never advert to God at all. Their conversion must be a perfect miracle. They are obdurate. They are living portions of hell moving up and down the earth. It is only by God's mercy, and through the merits of Jesus, that we are any better than these obdurate sinners. Yet we rightly thank God, even while we tremble at the possibility, that he has prevented our falling into such a state. What then if we were like to these? What if we were numbered among the hardened and impenitent? What if we were now even what we ourselves may have been in past years, before the strong arm of the Sacraments was held out to us, and we had the grace to lay hold of it and let it draw us safely to the shore? Yet if we were any of these, heathens, or heretics, or obdurate sinners, we should still be far better off than if there were no Jesus in the world; for all these classes of men are blessed by Jesus, are visited by his grace continually, and are for his sake surrounded by hopeful possibilities of which they themselves are not aware. How unspeakably dreadful then our life would be without Jesus, when to be a heathen or a heretic is a misery so terrible!

But surely we have said enough to show the necessity of Jesus. Let us look at the world without his Precious Blood. In the early ages of the earth, while the primitive traditions of Eden were still fresh and strong, and when God was from time to time manifesting himself in supernatural ways, the world drifted so rapidly from God that its sins began to assume a colossal magnitude. There was a complete confusion of all moral laws and duties. There was such an audacity in wickedness, that men openly braved God and threatened to besiege heaven. He sent strange judgments upon them, but they would not be converted. Scripture represents to us very forcibly by a human expression the terrific nature of their iniquity. It says that the Eternal repented of having done what he had eternally decreed to do, repented of having made man. At length the divine justice opened the floodgates of heaven, and destroyed all the dwellers upon earth, except eight persons; as if the issue of evil could not otherwise be staunched. This is a divine manifestation to us of the nature and character of evil. It multiplies itself. It tends to be gigantic, and to get from under control. It is always growing toward an open rebellion against the majesty of God. Everywhere on the earth the Precious Blood is warring down this evil in detail. Here it is obliterating it: here it is cutting off its past growths, or making its future growth slower or of less dimensions. There it is diluting it with grace, or rendering it sterile, or wounding and weakening it, or making it cowardly and cautious. Upon all exhibitions of evil the action of the Precious Blood is incessant. At no time and in no place is it altogether inoperative. Let us see what the world would be like, if the Precious Blood withdrew from this ceaseless war with evil.

It is plain that some millions of sins in a day are hindered by the Precious Blood; and this is not merely a hindering of so many individual sins, but it is an immense check upon the momentum of sin. It is also a weakening of habits of sin, and a diminution of the consequences of sin. If then, the action of the Precious Blood were withdrawn from the world, sins would not only increase incalculably in number, but the tyranny of sin would be fearfully augmented, and it would spread among a greater number of people. It would wax so bold that no one would be secure from the sins of others. It would be a constant warfare, or an intolerable vigilance, to preserve property and rights. Falsehood would become so universal as almost to dissolve society; and the homes of domestic life would be turned into the wards either of a prison or a madhouse. We cannot be in the company of an atrocious criminal without some feeling of uneasiness and fear. We should not like to be left alone with him, even if his chains were not unfastened. But without the Precious Blood, such men would abound in the world. They might even become the majority. We know of ourselves, from glimpses God has once or twice given us in life, what incredible possibilities of wickedness we have in our souls. Civilization increases these possibilities. Education multiplies and magnifies our powers of sinning. Refinement adds a fresh malignity. Men would thus become more diabolically and unmixedly bad, until at last earth would be a hell on this side of the grave. There would also doubtless be new kinds of sins and worse kinds. Education would provide the novelty, and refinement would carry it into the region of the unnatural. All highly-refined and luxurious developments of heathenism have fearfully illustrated this truth. A wicked barbarian is like a beast. His savage passions are violent but intermitting, and his necessities of sin do not appear to grow. Their circle is limited. But a highly-educated sinner, without the restraints of religion, is like a demon. His sins are less confined to himself. They involve others in their misery. They require others to be offered as it were in sacrifice to them. Moreover, education, considered simply as an intellectual cultivation, propagates sin, and makes it more universal.

The increase of sin, without the prospects which the faith lays open to us, must lead to an increase of despair, and to an increase of it upon a gigantic scale. With despair must come rage, madness, violence, tumult, and bloodshed. Yet from what quarter could we expect relief in this tremendous suffering? We should be imprisoned in our own planet. The blue sky above us would be but a dungeon-roof. The greensward beneath our feet would truly be the slab of our future tomb. Without the Precious Blood there is no intercourse between heaven and earth. Prayer would be useless. Our hapless lot would be irremediable. It has always seemed to me that it will be one of the terrible things in hell, that there are no motives for patience there. We cannot make the best of it. Why should we endure it? Endurance is an effort for a time; but this woe is eternal. Perhaps vicissitudes of agony might be a kind of field for patience. But there are no such vicissitudes. Why should we endure, then? Simply because we must; and yet in eternal things this is not a sort of necessity which supplies a reasonable ground for patience. So in this imaginary world of rampant sin there would be no motives for patience. For death would be our only seeming relief; and that is only seeming, for death is any thing but an eternal sleep. Our impatience would become frenzy; and, if our constitutions were strong enough to prevent the frenzy from issuing in downright madness, it would grow into hatred of God, which is perhaps already less uncommon than we suppose.

An earth, from off which all sense of justice had perished,

would indeed be the most disconsolate of homes. The antediluvian earth exhibits only a tendency that way; and the same is true of the worst forms of heathenism. The Precious Blood was always there. Unnamed, unknown, and unsuspected, the Blood of Jesus has alleviated every manifestation of evil which there has ever been just as it is alleviating at this hour the punishments of hell. What would be our own individual case on such a blighted earth as this? All our struggles to be better would be simply hopeless. There would be no reason why we should not give ourselves up to that kind of enjoyment which our corruption does substantially find in sin. The gratification of our appetites is something; and that lies on one side, while on the other side there is absolutely nothing. But we should have the worm of conscience already, even though the flames of hell might yet be some years distant. To feel that we are fools, and yet lack the strength to be wiser—is not this precisely the maddening thing in madness? Yet it would be our normal state under the reproaches of conscience, in a world where there was no Precious Blood. Whatever relics of moral good we might retain about us would add most sensibly to our wretchedness. Good people, if there were any, would be, as St. Paul speaks, of all men the most miserable: for they would be drawn away from the enjoyment of this world, or have their enjoyment of it abated by a sense of guilt and shame; and there would be no other world to aim at or to work for. To lessen the intensity of our hell without abridging its eternity would hardly be a cogent motive, when the temptations of sin and the allurements of sense are so vivid and so strong.

What sort of love could there be, when we could have no respect? Even if flesh and blood made us love each other, what a separation death would be! We should commit our dead to the ground without a hope. Husband and wife would part with the fearfullest certainties of a reunion more terrible than their separation. Mothers would long to look upon their little ones in the arms of death, because their lot would be less woeful than if they lived to offend God with their developed reason and intelligent will. The sweetest feelings of our nature would become unnatural, and the most honorable ties be dishonored. Our best instincts would lead us into our worst dangers. Our hearts would have to learn to beat another way, in order to avoid the dismal consequences which our affections would bring upon ourselves and others. But it is needless to go further into these harrowing details. The world of the heart, without the Precious Blood, and with an intellectual knowledge of God and his punishments of sin, is too fearful a picture to be drawn with minute fidelity.

But how would it fare with the poor in such a world? They are God's chosen portion upon earth. He chose poverty himself, when he came to us. He has left the poor in his place, and they are never to fail from the earth, but to be his representatives there until the doom. But, if it were not for the Precious Blood, would any one love them? Would any one have a devotion to them, and dedicate his life to merciful ingenuities to alleviate their lot? If the stream of almsgiving is so insufficient now, what would it be then? There would be no softening of the heart by grace; there would be no admission of the obligation to give away in alms a definite portion of our incomes; there would be no desire to expiate sin by munificence to the needy for the love of God. The gospel makes men's hearts large; and yet even under the gospel the fountain of almsgiving flows scantily and uncertainly. There would be no religious orders devoting themselves with skilful concentration to different acts of spiritual and corporal mercy. Vocation is a blossom to be found only in the gardens of the Precious Blood. But all this is only negative, only an absence of God. Matters would go much further in such a world as we are imagining.

Even in countries professing to be Christian, and at least in possession of the knowledge of the gospel, the poor grow to be an intolerable burden to the rich. They have to be supported by compulsory taxes; and they are in other ways a continual subject of irritated and impatient legislation. Nevertheless, it is due to the Precious Blood that the principle of supporting them is acknowledged. From what we read in heathen history—even the history of nations renowned for political wisdom, for philosophical speculation, and for literary and artistic refinement—it would not be extravagant for us to conclude that, if the circumstances of a country were such as to make the numbers of the poor dangerous to the rich, the rich would not scruple to destroy them, while it was yet in their power to do so. Just as men have had in France and England to war down bears and wolves, so would the rich war down the poor, whose clamorous misery and excited despair should threaten them in the enjoyment of their power and their possessions. The numbers of the poor would be thinned by murder, until it should be safe for their masters to reduce them into slavery. The survivors would lead the lives of convicts or of beasts. History, I repeat, shows us that this is by no means an extravagant supposition.

Such would be the condition of the world without the Precious Blood. As generations succeeded each other, original sin would go on developing those inexhaustible malignant powers which come from the almost infinite character of evil. Sin would work earth into hell. Men would become devils, devils to others and to themselves. Every thing which makes life tolerable, which counteracts any evil, which softens any harshness, which sweetens any bitterness, which causes the machinery of society to work smoothly, or which consoles any sadness—is simply due to the Precious Blood of Jesus, in heathen as well as Christian lands. It changes the whole position of an offending creation to its Creator. It changes, if we may dare in such a matter to speak of change, the aspect of God's immutable perfections toward his human children. It does not work merely in a spiritual sphere. It is not only prolific in temporal blessings, but it is the veritable cause of all temporal blessings whatsover. We are all of us every moment sensibly enjoying the benignant influence of the Precious Blood. Yet who thinks of all this? Why is the goodness of God so hidden, so imperceptible, so unsuspected? Perhaps because it is so universal and so excessive, that we should hardly be free agents if it pressed sensibly upon us always. God's goodness is at once the most public of all his attributes, and at the same time the most secret. Has life a sweeter task than to seek it, and to find it out?

Men would be far more happy, if they separated religion less violently from other things. It is both unwise and unloving to put religion into a place by itself, and mark it off with an untrue distinctness from what we call worldly and unspiritual things. Of course there is a distinction, and a most important one, between them; yet it is easy to make this distinction too rigid and to carry it too far. Thus we often attribute to nature what is only due to grace; and we put out of sight the manner and degree in which the blessed mystery of the Incarnation affects all created things. But this mistake is forever robbing us of hundreds of motives for loving Jesus. We know how unspeakably much we owe to him; but we do not see that it is not much we owe him, but all, simply and absolutely all. We pass through times and places in life, hardly recognizing how the sweetness of Jesus is sweetening the air around us and penetrating natural things with supernatural blessings.

Hence it comes to pass that men make too much of natural goodness. They think too highly of human progress. They exaggerate the moralizing powers of civilization and refinement, which, apart from grace, are simply tyrannies of the few over the many, or of the public over the individual soul. Meanwhile they underrate the corrupting capabilities of sin, and attribute to unassisted nature many excellences which it only catches, as it were by infection, from the proximity of grace, or by contagion, from the touch of the Church. Even in religious or ecclesiastical matters they incline to measure progress, or test vigor, by other standards rather than that of holiness. These men will consider the foregoing picture of the world without the Precious Blood as overdrawn and too darkly shaded. They do not believe in the intense malignity of man when drifted from God, and still less are they inclined to grant that cultivation and refinement only intensify still further this malignity. They admit the superior excellence of Christian charity; but they also think highly of natural philanthropy. But has this philanthropy ever been found where the indirect influences of the true religion, whether Jewish or Christian, had not penetrated? We may admire the Greeks for their exquisite refinement, and the Romans for the wisdom of their political moderation. Yet look at the position of children, of servants, of slaves, and of the poor, under both those systems, and see if, while extreme refinement only pushed sin to an extremity of foulness, the same exquisite culture did not also lead to a social cruelty and an individual selfishness which made life unbearable to the masses. Philanthropy is but a theft from the gospel, or rather a shadow, not a substance, and as unhelpful as shadows are wont to be. Nevertheless, let us take this philanthropy at its word, and see what the world would be like, with philanthropy instead of the Precious Blood.

We will take the world as it is, with its present evils. What amount of alleviation can philanthropy bring, supposing there could be such a thing without the example and atmosphere of the gospel? In the first place, what could it do for poverty? It would be dismayed by the number of the poor and appalled by the variety and exigency of their needs. All manner of intractable questions would rise up, for the solving of which its philosophy could furnish it with no simple principles. Men would have their own work to do, and their own business to attend to. It is not conceivable that mere philanthropy should make the administration of alms and the ministering to the poor a separate profession; and self-devotion upon any large scale is not to be thought of except as a corollary of the doctrine of the Cross. Thus, while the alms to be distributed would necessarily be limited, and the claims almost illimitable, there would be no means of proportioning relief. Unseen poverty is for the most part a worthier thing than the poverty which is seen: but who would with patient kindness and instinctive delicacy track shamefaced poverty to its obscure retirements? The loudest beggars would get most, the modest least. The highest virtue aimed at in the distribution of alms, and it is truly a high one, would be justice. Thus it would come to pass that those who by sin or folly had brought poverty upon themselves would obtain no relief at all: and so charity would cease to have any power to raise men above their past lives, or elevate them in the scale of moral worth.

Eccentricity is a common accompaniment of misery; and that which is eccentric would hardly recommend itself to philanthropy, even if it did not seem to be a proof of insincerity. Christian charity can only sustain its equanimity by fixing its eyes upon a higher object than the misery which it relieves. What is not done for God in this matter is done but uncertainly as well as scantily, and soon wearies of the unlovely and exacting poor. It is only the similitude of Jesus which beautifies poverty. Works of mercy are not attractive to hearts untouched by love. Moreover, no slight amount of the beneficence of Christian charity resides in its irregularity. Coming from the impulses of love, it has an ebb and flow which make it like the seeming unevenness and inequalities of outward providence; and this, which reason would account as a defect, turns out in practice a more real blessing than the formal equality and periodical punctuality of a merely conscientious and justice-loving benevolence. Philanthropy must have a sphere, a round, a beat. It must of necessity have in it somewhat of the political economist, and somewhat of the policeman. It must never allow individual sympathies to draw off its attention to the public welfare. Its genius must be legislative, rather than impulsive. Sudden misfortunes, a bad harvest, a commercial crisis, a sickly winter—these things would sadly interfere with the calculations of philanthropy. If the amount of self-sacrifice is so small, when we have the example of our Lord, and the doctrine that alms redeem souls, and the actual obligation under pain of sin to set aside a portion of our incomes for the poor, what would it be if all these motives were withdrawn?

Let us consider bodily pain, and the agency of philanthropy in alleviating it. An immense amount of the world's misery consists in bodily pain. There are few things more hard to bear. It is one of our unrealities that we write and speak lightly of it. We think it grand to do so. We think to show our manliness. But the truth is, there are few men who could not bear a breaking heart better than an aching limb. There are many points of view from which bodily pain is less easy to bear than mental anguish. It is less intelligible. It appeals less to our reason. If the consolations of moral wisdom are of no great cogency to hearts in sorrow, they are of none at all to those whose nerves are racked with pain. Mental suffering has its peculiar extremities. To the few probably they exceed the extremities of bodily agony; but in the majority of cases they are less intolerable; and in all cases most intolerable when they have succeeded in deranging the bodily health and so adding that suffering to their own. Moreover, the excesses of mental anguish, while they visit chiefly the rarer and more sensitive minds, are always of brief duration: whereas it is fearful to think of the heights to which bodily torture can rise, and of the time extreme torment can last without producing either insensibility or death. But what can philanthropy do for bodily pain? Every one whose lot it is to lead a life of pain knows too well how little medical science avails to alleviate this particular kind of human suffering. It may do much in the way of prevention. Who knows? For the pain we might have had, but have not had, is an unknown region. Let us give medical science the benefit of our ignorance. But, as to the pains which we have actually suffered, how often have they refused to abate one tittle of their severity at the bidding of science! When they have done so, how slowly have they yielded to the power of remedies, and how often have the remedies themselves brought new pains along with them! The pains which the human frame has to bear from various ailments are terrible in their number, their variety, and the horror which attaches to many of them: over this empire, which original sin has created, how feeble and how limited is the jurisdiction of medical science! Yet what could philanthropy do for bodily pain, except surround it with medical appliances and with physical comforts? Let us not underrate the consolation of the large-minded wisdom, the benevolent common sense, and the peculiar priestly kindness of an intelligent physician. It is very great. Neither let us pretend to make light of the alleviations of an airy room, of a soft bed, of well-prepared food, of a low voice and a noiseless step, and of those attentions which are beforehand with our irritability by divining our wants at the right moment. Nevertheless, when the daily pressure of bodily pain goes on for weeks and months, when all life which is not illness is but a vacillating convalescence, what adequate or abiding consolation can we find, except in supernatural things, in the motives of the faith, in union with Jesus, in that secret experimental knowledge of God which makes us at times find chastisement so sweet?

It is the characteristic of mental suffering to be for the most part beyond the reach of philanthropy. Every heart knows its own bitterness. That part of a mental sorrow, which can be expressed, is generally the part which rankles least. The suffering of it depends mainly on feelings which belong to individual character, feelings which can hardly be stated, and which, if stated, could not be appreciated, even if they were not altogether misunderstood. Who has not often wondered at the almost invariable irritation produced in unhappy persons by set and formal soothing? There is a pity in the tone of voice which wounds rather than heals. The very composure of features aggravates us by making us feel more vividly the reality of our grief. We have long since exhausted for ourselves all the available topics of consolation. Not in gradual procession, but all at once like a lightning's flash, all the motives and wisdoms, which occupy my unsuffering friend an hour to enumerate, were laid hold of, fathomed, and dismissed by my heart, which suffering had awakened to a speed and power of sensitiveness quite incredible. Job is not the only person who has been more provoked by his comforters than by his miseries. Even the daily wear and tear of our hearts in common life cannot be reached by outward consolation, unless that consolation comes from above and is divine. Philanthropy, with the best intentions, can never get inside the heart. There are sufferings there too deep for any thing but religion either to reach or to appreciate; and such sufferings are neither exceptional nor uncommon. There are few men who have not more than one of them. If we take away the great sorrow upon Calvary, how dark and how unbearable a mystery does all sorrow become! Kindness is sweet, even to the sorrowing, because of its intentions: it is not valuable because of its efficacy, except when it is the graceful minister of the Precious Blood.

I reckon failure to be the most universal unhappiness on earth. Almost everybody and every thing are failures—failures in their own estimation, even if they are not so in the estimation of others. Those optimists who always think themselves successful are few in number, and they for the most part fail in this at least, namely, that they cannot persuade the rest of the world of their success. Philanthropy can plainly do nothing here, even if it were inclined to try. But philanthropy is a branch of moral philosophy, and would turn away in disdain from an unhappiness which it could prove to be unreasonable, even while it acknowledged it to be universal. It is simply true that few men are successful; and of those few it is rare to find any who are satisfied with their own success. The multitude of men live with a vexatious sense that the promise of their lives remains unfulfilled. Either outward circumstances have been against them, or they have been misappreciated, or they have got out of their grooves unknowingly, or they have been the victims of injustice. What must all life be but a feverish disappointment, if there be no eternity in view? The religious man is the only successful man. Nothing fails with him. Every shaft reaches the mark, if the mark be God. He has wasted no energies. Every hope has been fulfilled beyond his expectations. Every effort has been even disproportionately rewarded. Every means has turned out marvellously to be an end, because it had God in it, who is our single end. In piety, every battle is a victory, simply because it is a battle. The completest defeats have somewhat of triumph in them; for it is a positive triumph to have stood up and fought for God at all. In short, no life is a failure which is lived for God; and all lives are failures which are lived for any other end. If it is part of any man's disposition to be peculiarly and morbidly sensitive to failure, he must regard it as an additional motive to be religious. Piety is the only invariable, satisfactory, genuine success.

If philanthropy turns out to be so unhelpful a thing in the difficulties of life, will it be more helpful at the bed of death?

Death is the failure of nature. There is no help then, except in the supernatural. Philanthropy cannot help us to die ourselves; nor can it take away our sorrow for the deaths of others. Without religion death is a problem and a terror. It is only by the light of faith that we see it to be a punishment commuted by divine love into a crown and a reward. The sense of guilt, the uneasiness in darkness, the shrinking from the unknown, the shapeless shadows of an unexplored world, the new panic of the soul, the sensible momentary falling off into an abyss, the inevitable helplessness, the frightening transition from a state of change to one of endless fixedness—how is philanthropy to meet such difficulties as these? Truly, in the atmosphere of death all lights go out except the lamp of faith.

But we have spoken of the actual miseries of life, and the condition we should be in, if we took the consolations of philanthropy instead of those of the Precious Blood. This however is in reality not a fair view of the case. Great as the actual miseries of life are, the Precious Blood is continually making them very much less than they otherwise would be. It diminishes poverty by multiplying alms. It lessens the evil of pain, and to some extent even its amount, by the grace of patience and the appliances of the supernatural life; not to speak of miraculous operations, occurring perhaps hourly upon the earth, through the touch of relics, crosses, and other sacred objects. The amount of temporal evil which would otherwise have come upon the earth, but is daily absorbed by the Sacrament of Penance and by the virtue of penance, must be enormous. In the case of mental suffering, besides the many indirect alleviations brought to it by the Precious Blood, we must remember the vast world of horrors arising from unabsolved consciences, horrors which the Sacraments are annihilating daily. Failure is indeed the rule of human enterprise, and success is the exception. Yet there are numberless counterbalancing blessings won by the interest of the Mother of God, by the intercession of the saints, by the intervention of angels, by the Sacrifice of the Mass, and by the sacramental residence of Jesus upon earth, which would not exist but for the Precious Blood.

Finally, as to death, whatever light is cast upon it is from the Blood of Jesus. Were it not for Jesus, the dark hour would be darkened with an Egyptian darkness. It has something of the glory of a sunset round it now, and the glory is the refulgence of the Saviour's Blood.

But, in this world, manner is often a more substantial thing than matter. We often care less for the thing done than for the manner in which it is done, less for the gift than for the way in which the gift is given. Now let us picture to ourselves an imaginary philanthropic city. Its palaces shall be hospitals, hospitals for every form of disease which is known to medical science. Its business shall not be politics, but the administration of benevolent societies. Its rich population shall divide and subdivide itself into endless committees, each of which shall make some human misery its specialty. Its intellect shall be occupied in devising schemes of philanthropy, in inventing new methods and fresh organizations, and in bringing to perfection the police, the order, the comfort, the accommodation, the pliability, of existing beneficent institutions. The strangest successes shall be attained with the blind, the deaf and dumb, and the insane. Moreover, in this city, which the world has never seen, the philanthropy shall be the most genial and good-humored of all the philanthropies which the world has had the good fortune to see. Yet who that has ever seen the most estimable, easy-going, and conscientious board of Poor-Law guardians can doubt but that, on the whole, considerable dryness, stiffness, woodenness, theoretical pugnacity, benevolent pertinaciousness, vexatious generalizations, and irritable surprise at the unmanageable prejudiced poor, would characterize this philanthropic city? Misery cannot be relieved on rules of distributive justice. Masses will not organize themselves under theories. Hearts will not attain happiness through clear convictions that they ought to be happy. Individual misery has an inveterate habit of dictating its own consolations. The most openhearted benefactors would be met by suspicion. A needy man can outwit most committees. Machinery for men gets soon choked up by multitudes, and for the most part blows up and maims its excellent inventors. There are few who can handle a large army; yet that is easy work compared to the question of the management of the poor. Moreover, when the best men have done their best, there always remains that instinct in the poor, which makes them see only enemies in the rich; and that instinct is too strong for the collective wisdom of all the philanthropists in the world.

I am far from saying that Christian charity is perfect, or that the duties of catholic mercy, whether monastic or secular, leave nothing to be desired. Everywhere the scantiness of the alms of the rich is the standing grievance of the priest. Everywhere the breadth and activity of human misery are baffling and outrunning the speed and generosity of charity. Nevertheless, I verily believe that one convent of Sisters of Charity, or one house of St. Camillus, would do more actual, more successful work, in a huge European capital, than would be done in the whole of such a philanthropic city as we have been imagining. Out of the love of Jesus comes the love of souls; and it is just the love of souls which effects that most marvellous of all Christian transformations, the change of philanthropy into charity. Jesus with the Samaritan woman at the side of Jacob's well, or with the Magdalen in the pharisee's house, inspires a spirit totally different from that which animates the most benevolent philosopher. It is a spirit of supernatural love, a spirit of imitation of Jesus, a spirit of gentle eagerness and affectionate sacrifice, which gives to the exercise of charity a winning sweetness and a nameless charm which are entirely its own. The love of individual souls is purely a Christian thing. No language can describe it to those who do not feel it. If men see it, and do not sympathize with it, they so mistake it that they call it proselytism. They attribute to the basest motives that which comes precisely from the very highest. Indeed, from a political or philosophical point of view those things which are the most Christlike in charity are the very things which men condemn as mischievous, if not immoral. In their view harm is done by treating men as individuals, not as masses. Alms are squandered. Unworthy objects get them. The misery which punishes vice is the object of love, as well as that which comes of innocent misfortune. Charity cares too little about being deceived: it is too impulsive, too irregular, too enthusiastic; above all, it does not make the tranquillity and well-being of the state its sole or primary object. Evidently, then, the manners and gestures of charity in action are wholly different from those of philanthropy in action. The one succeeds with men, and the other does not; and the success of charity is owing to the spirit which it imbibes from the Precious Blood of Jesus Christ.

Here are many words to prove a simple thing, and a thing which needed no proving. But it brings home to us more forcibly and more in detail the necessity of the Precious Blood. But, after all, the grand necessity of it is the necessity of having our sins forgiven, the necessity of loving above all created things our most dear God and Father. Let us think for a moment. The depth of summer silence is all around. Those tall chestnuts stand up, muffled down to the feet with their heavy mantles of dark foliage, of which not a leaf is stirring. There is no sound of water, no song of bird, no rustling of any creature in the grass. Those banks of white cloud have no perceptible movement. The silence has only been broken for a moment, when the clock struck from the hidden church in the elm-girdled field, and the sound was so softened and stifled with leaves that it seemed almost like some cry natural to the woodland. We do not close our eyes. Yet the quiet of the scene has carried us beyond itself. What are time and earth, beauty and peace, to us? What is any thing to us, if our sins be not forgiven? Is not that our one want? Does not all our happiness come of that one want being satisfied? The thought of its being unsatisfied is not to be endured. Time, so quiet and stationary as this summer noontide, makes us think of eternity, and gives us a shadowy idea of it. But the thought of eternity is not to be faced, if our sins be not forgiven. But an eternal ruin—is that a possible thing? Possible! yes, inevitable, if our sins be not forgiven. The loss of another's soul is a hideous thing to contemplate. It broadens as we look at it, until our head gets confused, and God is obscured. It is a possibility we turn away from: what then can we do with the fact? We think of the sorrows and the joys of a soul, of the beautiful significance of its life, of its manifold loveliness and generosity, and of all the good that glittered like broken crystals amidst its evil. How many persons loved it! How many lives of others it sweetened and brightened! How attractive often in its good-humored carelessness about its duty! God loved it: it was the idea of his love, an eternal idea. It came into the world with his love about it like a glory. It swam in the light of his love, as the world swims in radiance day and night. It has gone into darkness. It is a ruin, a wreck, a failure, an eternal misery. Sin! What is sin, that it should do all this? Why was there any sin? Why is sin sin at all? We turn to the majesty of God to learn. Instinctively we lift up our eyes to that noonday sun, and it only blinds us. Sin is sin, because God is God. There is no getting any further in that direction. That soul, some soul, is lost. What we think cannot be put into words. But our own soul! That soul which is ourself! Can we by any amount of violence think of *it* as lost? No! our own perdition is absolutely unthinkable. Hope disables us from thinking it. But we know that it is possible. We sometimes feel the possible verging into the probable. We know how it can be lost, and perceive actual dangers. We know how alone it can avoid being lost; and in that direction matters do not look satisfactory. But it must not be lost: it shall not be lost: it cannot be lost. The thought of such a thing is madness. See, then, the tremendous necessity of the Precious Blood. Those heartless chestnut-trees! how they stand stooping over the uncut meadows, brooding in the sunshine, as if there were no problems in the world, no uneasiness in hearts! They make us angry. It is their very stillness which has driven us on these thoughts. It is their very beauty which makes the idea of eternal wretchedness somewhat more intolerable. Yet let us be just to them: they have also driven somewhat further into our souls the understanding of that unutterable necessity of the Precious Blood.

How precious is every drop of that dear Blood! How far more wonderful than all that the natural world contains is each one of those miracles which it is working by thousands every day! How

would creation be enriched by one drop of it, seeing that infinite
creations could not attain to the value of it! and how would the
history of creation be glorified by one manifestation of its omnipotent mercy! What are we to think, then, of its prodigality? Yet
this prodigality is not a mere magnificence of divine love. It is
not simply a divine romance. It would indeed be adorable if it
were only so. But to my mind it is even yet more divine that this
prodigality should itself be an absolute necessity, and, therefore,
in the majestic calmness and equability of the divine counsels, no
prodigality at all.

We have thought of the world without the Precious Blood;
let us think of it now with only partial or intermitting access to
its saving fountains.

Man fell, and God's justice was blameless in his fall. God's
mercy strove to hinder man from falling, and yet he fell. God
did every thing for man, short of destroying his liberty. The very
act of creation was a magnificence of mercy. But the creation of
man, not in a state of nature, but in a state of grace, was a glorious
love, which could proceed only from a grandeur as inexhaustible
as that of God. Man fell, and God was justified. Adam's descend-
ants might have found themselves hanging over the dread abyss of
eternal woe. They might have felt in themselves a violent propension to evil which only just stopped short of an actual necessity. The prospect before them would have been terrible, and yet
they would not have one intelligent word to say against it. If
their minds were not darkened, they would have seen that not the
justice only, but even the love of God stood unblemished in the
matter. Nevertheless, how unbearable the prospect! Earth would
be almost worse than hell, because it would be hell without the
miserable peace of its irrevocable certainty. It would be worse,
in the same way that a hopeless struggle is worse than the death
which follows. Truly there might still be hope, but then it would
be such a hopeless hope! Now let us suppose that God in the
immensity of his compassion should tell men, in this extremity of
wretchedness, that he would assume their nature, die for them
upon the cross, and purchase for them by his Precious Blood the

inestimable grace of baptism. They should have another trial given to them. They, who had blamed Adam, should have a chance of their own. They should be regenerated, spiritually born again by the most stupendous of miracles. They should be justified, and sanctified in their justification. The guilt of original sin should be altogether remitted to them. Not a shadow of it should remain. Even their liability to temporal punishment for that sin in purgatory should be remitted. God's justice should be satisfied in full. But the grace of baptism is far more than this. It restores us to a supernatural standing. It makes us God's adopted children. It does not merely rescue us from hell, and leave us to spend an eternity of mere natural blessedness by the streams and among the fruit-trees of some terrestrial paradise. It entitles us to possess and enjoy God forever. Moreover, this Sacrament stores our souls with most mysterious graces. It infuses celestial habits into us, and endows us with those unfathomable wonders, the gifts of the Holy Ghost. No miracle can be more complete, or more instantaneous, or more gratuitous, than the grace of baptism.

This, then, should be the work of the Blood of God; and no more than this. Yet would it not seem to men to be an outpouring of the most superabounding love? Would it not open to the wisest of men new depths in the character of God, and be a new revelation of unsuspected goodness in him? The most ardent and expansive of the angelic intelligences might have contemplated God for ages and ages, and yet their unassisted science would never have dreamed of such a mystery as the Incarnation, of such a redemption as the price of the Precious Blood. Yet does it not make us tremble to think of no more grace after baptism? Munificent as is that justifying grace, an invention only possible to a goodness which is simply infinite, what, with our experience of ourselves and our knowledge of others, would be our dismay if that one glorious access to the Precious Blood were the only one allowed to us! Surely a more frequent access to it, while it is on God's side a marvellous extension of a gratuitous indulgence, is on our side nothing less than an imperious necessity.

Blessed be the inexhaustible compassions of the Most High, we have incessant access to the Precious Blood. Our seeking of our own interest is made to be the glory of God. Our eager supply of our own needs is counted as an act of sweetest love to him, the more sweet the more eager it shall be. Yet it is difficult to bring this gracious truth home to ourselves, unless we put imaginary cases of a more restricted use of the Precious Blood. It would be a great thing to be forgiven once more after baptism; whereas we are being endlessly forgiven, and with as much facility the thousandth time as we were the first. No greater amount of attrition is needed to make our thousandth absolution valid than was required for our first. It would be a huge mercy if almost all sins were capable of absolution, but some few were reserved as unpardonable after baptism. Even this would seem to the angels a wonderful stretch of the divine forbearance. What then must it be to have no sins, and no reiteration of sins, exempted from the jurisdiction of that dear ransom of our souls? At first sight it looks as if such an inveterate compassion lowered the character of God and impaired the lustre of his exceeding sanctity. In this matter, as in others, God must be loved in order to be understood. It is the heart which must illuminate the head. Accustomed as we are to the free participation of the Blood of Jesus, how terrible seems the idea of men going about the world, visible portions of hell, because they have committed some sin exempted from absolution! To have met Cain upon his passionate wanderings over the unpeopled earth would have been less terrible; since we are not forbidden to have hope for him. But here, again, this incessant pardoning, this repetition of absolution, this endless sprinkling of our souls with the Precious Blood—is it not a necessity to our happiness, a necessity to our salvation? Astonishing as is the prodigality of the Blood of Jesus, could any conceivable restriction have been endured? It would have been something more than a diminution of our privileges: it would have been a bar to our salvation.

But let us suppose no sins were exempted from the pardon of the Precious Blood, but only that that price of our redemption was hard to get. God might have willed that it should only be obtained in Jerusalem, and that distant nations must seek it by long and painful pilgrimage. Of a truth, it would be glad tidings to a sinner, that at the eastern end of the Mediterranean there was a mysterious guarded well, which contained some of our Saviour's Blood, the touch of which forgave sin to those who possessed certain inward dispositions, but only forgave it on the spot, in Jerusalem itself. Most willingly would the children of the faith undergo the toilsome pilgrimage, rather than endure the miserable weight of sin. Yet what would happen to the sick, who were too weak to go, or to the aged, who had delayed too long, or to the dying, who have nothing before them but despair? How would it fare with the sorely-tempted poor, if absolution cost so dear? Shall the rich, or the young, or the robust, only be forgiven? What misery and disturbance also would be there in the social relations of life, while multitudes were evermore impulsively pouring themselves out of their homes in caravans of pilgrimage! Or what an intolerable inhumanity would prisons be, if the law of man could secure the eternal as well as the temporal ruin of its offenders! Still, even this single well at Jerusalem would be a mercy of God so great, that it would be incredible, unimaginable, unless it were revealed. Or, again, we might have to gain access to the Blood of our Redeemer by going through considerable bodily pain, or passing some severe ordeals. No one could complain of this. It would be a mercy beyond the uttermost mercies of human law. Oh, does it not make us weep to think then of our own carelessness, and backwardness, and dilatory, lukewarm indifference to that most dear Blood which we can have always and everywhere? We have come to slight God's mercies because his amazing goodness has made them to be so common. We have not even to seek the Blood of Jesus. It comes to us: it pleads with us: it entreats us to accept it: it complains; it waits; it knocks; it cries out to us: it all but forces itself upon our acceptance.

But all this mysterious condescension of God is not the needless outburst of an excessive love. Alas for our shame that we should have to say it! it is a downright necessity for our salvation.

Look at the innumerable confessionals of the Church, at the hundreds of daily death-beds, at the countless retreats of suffering poverty. Is the seeking for the Precious Blood what it ought to be? Nay, do men's hearts soften at its tender, eloquent pleading? Have not sinners to be constrained to come to Jesus? and even of those who are constrained to come to him, how many are there who will not let him save them? One saint speaks of souls flocking daily to perdition like the flakes of a snowstorm, blinding from their multitude. Another tells us of visions, in which she saw souls trooping constantly into the gates of hell, like the rabble of autumnal leaves swept into thick eddies by the wind. Yet not a soul gets there before whom the Precious Blood has not stood again and again, like the angel before Balaam's ass, and tried to drive it back. If, then, when all access is so easy, and when persuasion mounts almost to compulsion, souls are so backward in having recourse to the Precious Blood, what would be the case if any of these imaginary difficulties of ours were allowed to come in the way? Alas! so it is, that it is necessary to salvation that our salvation should be easy.

Let us tease ourselves with one more imaginary case, and then we will have done. To many persons the great burden of life is the secret of predestination; and most men have at times felt the uncertainty of salvation as a weight upon their spirits. To a good man, whatever increases this uncertainty is a grave misfortune. Without a private revelation, no one can at any time say absolutely that he is in a state of grace, not even although he may just have received absolution in the best dispositions in his power. Nevertheless he feels a moral certainty about it, which for all practical purposes is as good as an assurance. We are not then always absolutely certain that the Precious Blood has been applied to our souls in absolution. But whence is it that we derive that moral certainty which is our consolation and our rest? From the fact that, when properly received, the operation of the Precious Blood is infallible. What an unhappiness it would be, if this were not so! The power of the Blood of Jesus is never doubtful, its work never incomplete. Moreover, God has gathered up its virtue in a very special way into certain Sacraments. He has made its application almost visible. He has tied its miracles as it were to time, and place, and matter, and form, so as to bring us as near to a certainty of our being in a state of grace as is compatible with his laws and our own best interests. If we could be no more sure that we had validly received absolution in confession, than we can be sure we have ever made an act of perfect contrition, we should be in a sad plight, and go through our spiritual exercises and our inward trials in a very downcast and melancholy way. Our state would be, at least in that one respect, something like the state of those outside the Church, who are not living members of Christ, nor partakers in his saving jurisdiction in the Sacrament of Penance. If the Precious Blood had been shed, and yet we had no priesthood, no Sacraments, no jurisdiction, no sacramentals, no mystical life of the visible unity of the Church—life, so it seems, would be almost intolerable. This is the condition of those outside the Church; and certainly as we grow older, as our experience widens, as our knowledge of ourselves deepens, as our acquaintance with mankind increases, the less hopeful do our ideas become regarding the salvation of those outside the Roman Church. We make the most we can of the uncovenanted mercies of God, of the invisible soul of the Church, of the doctrine of invincible ignorance, of the easiness of making acts of contrition, and of the visible moral goodness among men; and yet what are these but straws in our own estimation, if our own chances of salvation had to lean their weight upon them? They wear out, or they break down. They are fearfully counterweighted by other considerations. We have to draw on our imaginations in order to fill up the picture. They are but theories at best, theories unhelpful except to console those who are forward to be deceived for the sake of those they love—theories often very fatal by keeping our charity in check and interfering with that restlessness of converting love in season and out of season, and that impetuous agony of prayer, upon which God may have made the salvation of our friends depend. Alas! the more familiar we ourselves become with the operations of grace, the further we advance into the spiritual life, the more we meditate on the character of God, and

taste in contemplation the savor of his holiness, the more to our
eyes does grace magnify itself inside the Church, and the more
dense and forlorn becomes the darkness which is spread over
those outside. Yet not indeed to this state—God forbid!—but
to a painful partial resemblance of it, should we be brought, if
God's tender considerate love had not as it were localized the
Precious Blood in his stupendous Sacraments. Truly the Sacraments are an invention of love, yet are they not also as truly a
necessity of our salvation, not only as applying the Precious
Blood to our souls, but as enabling faith to ascertain its application? Would not the divine assurance of our salvation be a very
heaven begun on earth? Yet the Sacraments are the nearest approach to such a sweet assurance as the love of our heavenly
Father saw to be expedient for the multitude of his children.

The Precious Blood, then, is the greatest, the most undeniable,
of our necessities. There is no true life without it. Yet, and it
very much concerns us to bring this home to ourselves, all creation could not merit it. Necessary as it is, it is in no way due to
us. It is not a right. God's love toward us had been a romance
already. It was wonderful what he had done to us. It is almost
incredible even now when we think of it. We know the unspeakable tenderness of our Creator, how placable he is, how soft of
heart, how prone to forgive, how easy to be persuaded. We know
that the needs of his creatures plead with him more eloquently
than we can tell. Yet no necessities could have claimed the Precious Blood, no merits could have won it, no prayers could have
obtained it. In truth, no created intelligence of angel or of man
could have imagined it.

Were heaven to be filled with saints in endless millions, as
holy as St. Joseph, the Baptist, or the Apostles, and were their
holiness allowed to merit, not in millions of ages could their
united merits have earned one drop of the Precious Blood. If
all those starry spirits in the godlike realm of angels had consented to sink their grandeurs in the penalties of hell for thousands of revolving epochs, or even had they consented to be an-
nihilated in sacrifice to the justice of God, never could they have

merited the Precious Blood. If all the merits, graces, gifts, and powers of our dearest Mother had been possible without the Precious Blood, they might have ascended as sweet incense before God forever, and yet in no possible duration of time could they have merited the Precious Blood. Not all these together, saints, angels, and Mary, with all their glorious holiness, growing yet more glorious in endless ages, could have bought one drop of Precious Blood, or merited that mystery of the Incarnation whose wonderful redeeming power resides in the Precious Blood. Oh, how this thought overwhelms my heart with joy—to have to rest upon the free sovereignty of God instead of my own wretched littleness, to be always thus thrown upon the gratuitous magnificence of God, to be forever and forever owing all, and such an all, to Jesus! Merciful God! this is the joy of earth which is nearest to a joy of heaven!

CHAPTER III

THE EMPIRE OF THE PRECIOUS BLOOD

CHAPTER III

THE EMPIRE OF THE PRECIOUS BLOOD

THE life of God is very vast. It is a thing to be thought rather than to be spoken of, nay, to be seen in the mind rather than to be thought. It is very vast. It seems to grow vaster every day. We kneel down before it in our prayers, as a man might kneel to pray on a great seashore. God lies before us as an ocean of infinite life. We kneel upon the shore. But behind us rolls the same great ocean. Suddenly it is at our right hand and on our left. We look upward, but the sky is gone. An ocean rolls where there was sky when we first knelt down to pray. The boundless waters stretch above us like a living canopy. The shore on which we kneel gives way. It is no shore. We are kneeling on the waters. The same eternal ocean rolls beneath us. We are hemmed in on every side by this ever-blessed ocean of infinite being. How full it is of burning life, how masterful, how soundless, how unchangeable!

The life of God is very vast. I feel it overawing me more and more, as I go on thinking of it. God is very simple. He is simply God. He is to be adored in his simplicity. His perfections are himself, and he is simply all his perfections. His perfections are not manifold. They are but one. He is himself his only perfection. His attributes are our ways of looking at him, of speaking of him, of worshipping him. His perfections are not separate from each other, nor from himself. We cannot comprehend so simple a simplicity. We have not purity of understanding sufficient to apprehend so infinitely pure an idea. It is on this account that we take the idea of God to pieces in our own minds, and contemplate and

79

love and worship him from a thousand points of view. We have no other way of dealing with the incomprehensible. Speaking then of the divine perfections in this sense, it appears to me that none of his attributes call forth so much worship in my heart as his life. His life amazes me; and yet it melts me with love. He seems to me least like an infinitely perfect creature, when I contemplate him as life; and when he is least like an infinitely perfect creature, he is most like the indescribable God. That view of him is less distinct than many others; but it appears to my mind more true on that very account.

The life of God is very vast. This is the thought which comes to me when I put before myself the empire of the Precious Blood. The life of God is blessedness in his own self. It is the joy of his unity, the fact of his simplicity. Once he was without creatures; and the calm jubilee of his immutable life went on. There could be no impulses in that which had had no beginning. His life started from no point, and reached to no point; therefore it could have no momentum: that is a created idea. He was imperturbable bliss. What can be more self-collected than immensity? His infinite tenderness comes from his being imperturbable, though at first sight there seems to be contradiction between the two. When he was without creatures, they were not a want to him. His unbeginning life was unspeakably centred in himself, and so went on. He became, what he had not been before, a Creator. But no change passed upon him. All his acts had been in himself before: now he acted outside himself. But no change passed upon him. Hitherto all his acts, which were the Generation of the Son and the Procession of the Holy Ghost, had been necessary: now his creative acts were free. Still no change passed upon him. Still the calm jubilee of the unbeginning life went on. As it was before creation, so it was after it, a jubilant life of unutterable simplicity. These are things we can only learn by loving. Without love they are merely hard words. God worked, and then God rested. Yet creation had been no interruption of his everlasting rest. Nevertheless, that Sabbath of God, of which Scripture tells us, is a wonderful mystery, and one full of repose to toiling, seeking, straining creatures. What was that seventh day's rest? To the untoiling Creator preservation is as much an effort as creation, and quite as great a mystery. But even creation, the evoking of being out of nothing, was not suspended. Human souls are forever being created, created out of nothing. Perhaps new species of animals may be so also. What then was his rest? Perhaps it is only another name for that expansive love, which as it were arrested itself to bless its beautiful creation out of its extreme contentment and ineffable complacency.

Still the vast life of God goes on. He was free to create; and he made his creation free. Perhaps those two things have much to do with each other. He made himself an empire outside himself, and crowned himself over it, the kingliest of kings. God is very royal. Royalty is the seal which is set on all his perfections, and by which we see how they are one. He enfranchised his empire, and then began to reign. Still there was no change. His free people dethroned him. Oftentimes now in the depths of prayer the love of his saints beholds him sitting in dust and ashes an uncrowned king, as it were piteously. But all this is embraced within his vast life without a shadow of change. It was part of the eternal idea of creation, that one of the Divine Persons should assume a created nature. The Second Person did so. He has carried it to heaven, and placed it in the bosom of the Holy Trinity for endless worship. This has displaced nothing. The vast life goes on. No pulse beats in it. No succession belongs to it. No novelty happens to it. The Precious Blood of the Son's Human Nature would have been a pure beauty, a pure treasure of God, an unimaginable created life, if there had been no sins. But there was sin, and the destiny of the Precious Blood was changed. But there was no change in the divine life. The Precious Blood became the ransom for sin. The Precious Blood had to conquer back to God his revolted empire. It had to crown him again, and to be his imperial viceregent. What stupendous mutabilities are these! Yet there is no change in the vast life of God. Its very vastness makes it incapable of change. It has no experiences. It goes through nothing. It cannot begin, or end, or suffer. It works while it rests; and it rests while it works; and it neither works nor rests, but simply lives, simply is. O adorable life of God! blessed a thousand thousand times be thou in the darkness of thy glory, in the incomprehensible sweetness of thy mystery!

To us the Precious Blood is inseparable from the life of God. It is the Blood of the Creator, the agent of redemption, the power of sanctification. Moreover, to our eyes it is a token of something which we should call a change in God, if we did not know that there could not be change in him. It seems to give God a past, to recover for him something which he had lost, to be a second thought, to remedy a failure, to be a new ornament in the Divinity, a created joy in the very centre of the uncreated jubilee. The empire of the Precious Blood is due to its position in the history and economy of creation, or, in other words, to its relation to the adorable life of God. It seems to explain the eternity before creation, inasmuch as it reveals to us the eternal thoughts of God, his compassionate designs, his primal decrees, and his merciful persistence in carrying out his designs of love. It makes visible much that in its own nature was invisible. It casts a light backward, even upon the uttermost recesses of that old eternity. Just as some actions disclose more of a man's character than other actions, so the Precious Blood is in itself a most extensive and peculiarly vivid revelation of the character of God. The fact of his redeeming us, and, still more, the way in which he has redeemed us, discloses to us his reason for creating us; and when we get some view, however transient and indistinct, of his reason for creating us, we seem to look into the life he leads as God. The light is so light that it is darkness; but the darkness is knowledge, and the knowledge, love.

We are to speak of the empire of the Precious Blood. But we must first see in what its royal rights are founded. The Precious Blood ministers to all the perfections of God. It is the one grand satisfaction of his justice. It is one of the most excellent inventions of his wisdom. It is the principal feeder of his glory. It is the repose of his purity. It is the delight of his mercy. It is the participation of his power. It is the display of his magnificence.

It is the covenant of his patience. It is the reparation of his honor. It is the tranquillity of his anger. It is the imitation of his fruitfulness. It is the adornment of his sanctity. It is the expression of his love. But, above all, it ministers to the dominion of God. It is a conqueror and conquers for him. It invades the kingdom of darkness, and sweeps whole regions with its glorious light. It humbles the rebellious, and brings home the exiles, and reclaims the aliens. It pacifies; it builds up; it gives laws; it restores old things; it inaugurates new things. It grants amnesties; and dispenses pardons; and it wonderfully administers the kingdom it has wonderfully reconquered. It is the crown, the sceptre, and the throne of God's invisible dominion.

I said its rights were founded in its relation to the life of God; and its relation has to do especially with that which is kingly and paternal in the character of the Creator. The dominion of God is part of his invisible beauty; but the Precious Blood is the scarlet mantle of his eternal royalty. God became a king by becoming a Creator. It was thus he gained an empire over which his insatiable love might rule. We are obliged to speak of creation as if it were a gain to him who has all fulness in himself. He created because of his perfections, because he was God, because he was the infinitely blessed God that he is. Temporal things came into existence because there were eternal things. Time is a growth of the ungrowing eternity. Nature is very beautiful, whether we think of angelic or of human nature. Created nature is a shadow of the Uncreated Nature, so real and so bright that we cannot think of it without exceeding reverence. Yet God created neither angels nor men in a state of nature. This is, to my mind, the most wonderful and the most suggestive thing which we know about God. He would have no reasonable nature, even from the very first, which should not be partaker of his Divine Nature. This is the very meaning of a state of grace. He as it were clung to his creation while he let it go. He would not leave it to breathe for one instant in a merely natural state. The very act of creation was full of the fondness of maternal jealousy. It was, to speak in a human way, as if he feared that it would wander from him, and that his attractions would be too mighty for the littleness of finite beings. He made it free; yet he embraced it so that it should be next to impossible it should leave him. He gave it liberty, yet almost overpowered its liberty with caresses the very moment that he gave it. Oh, that Majesty of God, which seems clothed with such worshipful tranquillity in the eternity before creation, how passionate, how yearning, how mother-like, how full of inventions and excesses, it appears in the act of creation!

God lost nothing by the fall of angels or of men. Yet, in our way of thinking, how great must have been the loss to a love which had longed so passionately to keep his creation with him! It was gone now. That mysterious gift of liberty had been too strong for that other mysterious tenderness of creating us in a state of grace. There was nothing of failure, or of disappointment, or of frustrate love, in all this. But how there was not we cannot tell. We know that the vast life of God went on the same in its unshadowed, unimpeded gladness. Yet to our ignorance it seems as if the Creator would have to begin all over again, as if he would have to pause, to collect himself, to hold a council of his attributes, and either to retire into himself or begin afresh. None of these things are compatible with his everlasting majesty. They are only our ways of expressing those divine things which are unspeakable. But what is before us? By an excess of tenderness, which only grows more amazing the longer we think of it, God had cloistered his creation in the supernatural state of grace. The cloister was broken. Almost the first use of angelic and human freedom had been sacrilege. What will God do? Creative love has no mutabilities. Mercy itself shall find out a way to satisfy justice, rather than that this dear creation shall be lost. Time shall not be a grave in which eternal ideas shall be buried. The lost shall be found; the fallen shall be raised; the ruined shall be redeemed. The original idea of creation shall be reinstated, without the gift of freedom being withdrawn. The everlasting scheme of divine love shall be inaugurated again in all the plenitude of divine power, with all the splendor of divine wisdom, only illustrated now even more than before with the flames of divine love. The act shall be the act of God, the act equally of all the Three Divine Persons. Yet it shall be appropriated to One of Them, to the Second Person. The instrument shall be a created thing, not created only for the purpose, for it would have been even if sin had not been; but it shall be a created thing whose value shall be simply infinite, because of its belonging to an Uncreated Person. It was the Precious Blood.

One of the ways, in which God chiefly makes himself known to us, is by his choices. Choice reveals character; and, when we know the character and excellence of him who chooses, the choice enables us both to understand and appreciate the object chosen. Thus, when God chooses the weak things of the world to confound the strong, and the foolish things to confound the wise, he makes a very broad revelation to us of his character. He discloses principles of action quite alien from those of creatures, and never adopted by them except from supernatural motives and in conscious imitation of him. We know also that the things in question are in themselves weak and foolish, because he chose them on that account. In the same way, when he chooses persons for some great and high end, his very choice endows them with gifts proportionate to their work and dignity. We have often no other means of judging except his choice. It is thus that we measure the immense holiness of the Apostles. It is thus that we learn the incomparable sanctity of the Baptist. It is by comparing God's choice of him with the office he was to fill, that we come to see the glory and the grandeur of St. Joseph, and to contemplate with reverent awe the heights of a holiness to which such familiarity with God was permitted. We are astonished that familiarity should be the characteristic of devotion to a saint so high; and yet we perceive that it must be naturally the special grace of a devotion to one who outdid all others in the spirit of adoration because he outstripped all others in tender familiarities with God. It is thus also that we gain some idea of the beauty and splendor of St. Michael, one of the foremost jewels in the crown of God's glorious creation. Thus, also, the choice of God is the only measure by which we can approach to any knowledge of his Immaculate Mother. As her office was inconceivable either by angel or by saint, unless it had been revealed, so also is the immensity of her holiness. The choice of God lights up vast tracts of her magnificence, and shows us also how much there is left for us to learn and to enjoy in heaven. The grandeur of her office is infinite, as St. Thomas says, and the omnipotence of God could not create a grander office: what then must be the infinity of her grace? It is God who chose her, the God of numberless perfections, of illimitable power, and of lavish munificence. His choice tells us that the mighty empress of heaven was adorned with the utmost participation of the divine splendor of which a creature was capable. What regalia must they be which come out of the inexhaustible treasures of God, and which are chosen for her whom he chose eternally to be his blessed Mother? So, finally, we get our idea of the worth of the Precious Blood by seeing the end for which the Creator chose it. It is an idea which cannot be put into words, or be estimated by human figures. If we may dare so to speak, God chose it as the auxiliary by which he would save himself in the day of battle with the powers of darkness, when the battle was going against him, and when he vouchsafed to appear as if put to his last resource. I know not how else to state that choice of his, and the circumstances under which he made it, which cover with such dazzling splendor the redeeming Blood of Jesus. It had to save a falling creation, which God had hindered his own omnipotence from saving, because he had conferred upon it the gift of freedom.

It is hard to breathe in heights like these. We have climbed the mountains of God's primal decrees, and have penetrated to those first fountains of creation which lie far up in the solitude of eternity. It is difficult to breathe in such places, amid such lonely sublimities, in such divine wildernesses, where the features are so unlike those of earthly scenery. Let us then rest a while, and think of our own poor selves. Of what avail to us is all this magnificent election of the Precious Blood, its astonishing relation to the immutable life of God, its intrinsic dignity in the plans of the Creator, and the fearfulness of its resplendent beauty as the sole successful auxiliary of the God of Hosts, unless it is the one joy of our lives that we ourselves are its happy conquest? What use is it to us that it looks as if it had rescued the Creator from failure, if it does not ransom us from sin? What does it matter to us that it makes wonderful harmony between God's seemingly opposite decrees, if it does not make sweet peace between our heavenly Father and ourselves? The Precious Blood saved God an empire; and he has given it that empire for its own. It is the one thing needful for ourselves, that we should belong to its empire and be happy beneath its rule. One sin forgiven, one sinful habit brought into subjection, one ruling passion uniformly tamed, one worldliness courageously kept down—these are more to us than the theological glories of the Precious Blood. Indeed, these glories are chiefly glorious to us, in that they tell us more and more of our dear God, that they widen our minds and deepen our hearts to make room for him, and that they heat the furnace of our love seven times hotter than it was before. Theology would be a science to be specially impatient with, if it rested only in speculation. To my mind it is the best fuel of devotion, the best fuel of divine love. It catches fire quickest; it makes least smoke; it burns longest; and it throws out most heat while it is burning. It is the best fuel of love, until the soul is raised to high degrees of mystical contemplation; and then, as if to show how needful it was still, God infuses theological science even into the ignorant and youthful. If a science tells of God, yet does not make the listener's heart burn within him, it must follow either that the science is no true theology, or that the heart which listens unmoved is stupid and depraved. In a simple and loving heart theology burns like a sacred fire.

But, if this is the relation of the Precious Blood to Creation, in what relation does it stand toward the Incarnation? This also we must consider. The Incarnation of One of the Three Divine Persons was part of the original idea of Creation. It expresses in God the same mysterious and adorable yearning which was manifested in his creating angels and men in a state of grace. If there had been no sin, still the Second Person of the Holy Trinity would have been man. Jesus Christ was eternally predestinated to be King of angels and of men, the sovereign of all creation in right of his created nature, even if there had been no fall, and no redemption. I am repeating what I have said before; but I must do so in order to be clear. As God in his Divine Nature was the Sovereign Lord of all creation, so Jesus in his Created Nature was to be the King of kings and Lord of lords. He would have come and lived among us. He would have been born of the same blessed and most dear Mother. But his Bethlehem and his Nazareth and his Jerusalem would have been very different. He would have had no Egypt and no Calvary. He might perchance have dwelt longer with us than Three-and-Thirty years. But all the while, wherever he was, he would have been radiant as on the summit of Mount Thabor, the beauty and the glory streaming out from him incessantly. He would have had no Passion, no Resurrection; and perhaps he would not have ascended till the Day of Doom. He would have had the same Sacred Heart, the same Precious Blood. His Blood would have been a living joy to him, a beauty and a joy to all creation. Perhaps his Blood would still have been the wine of immortality to his elect. It might have been still the Blood of the Eucharist. There might have been the Sacrament without the Sacrifice. It might have been the chalice of his espousals with the soul. As some theologians say there might have been Communion before the Incarnation for the saints of the old covenant, if God had so willed, much more might it have been so with the impassible and glorious Incarnation, had there been no sin. The Precious Blood might still have been the sacramental fountain of eternal life. But it would not have had the office of ransoming the world from sin. Sin came; and by its coming it did to the Sacred Humanity of the Incarnate Word what it also did to the uncreated Majesty of God. It deprived it of its kingdom. It laid waste its empire. It miserably uncrowned it. It left him only the unfallen tribes of angels to rule over. It threatened to frustrate the Incarnation, and to take the chiefest jewel out of his Mother's diadem, the jewel of her sinlessness. As sin had dared to impede divine love in the matter of Creation, so did it dare to hinder divine love in the matter of the Incarnation. In one case it tried to infringe the eternal dominion of God; in the other case it strove to destroy the kingship of his created nature. As with Creation, so with the Incarnation, it was the Precious Blood which saved the kingdom. A change, as we are obliged to call it, came over its destinies. It should be created passible, and not impassible. It should be endowed with a suffering life. It should flow out of a suffering Heart, and should sustain a suffering Body. It should be selected by the Holy Trinity, for reasons inscrutable to us, inscrutable perhaps because we know so little about life, to be the solitary ransom for sin. If we knew the secret of life, we might perhaps know many new things about the Precious Blood. The wisdom of God beheld innumerable fitnesses in this mysterious choice. We can adore them, even though we do not know them. Thus the Precious Blood was to conquer back his kingdom for Jesus, and to secure the jewel of sinlessness for his Mother's diadem. Thus Jesus owed to his Precious Blood his kingdom and his Mother. Yet this Blood, what is it but the own life of Jesus? Thus was sin frustrated without the creature's liberty being forfeited. Thus did darkness war against light; and what came of it was, that, through the Precious Blood, the original idea of Creation was even beautified, without any change in the Unchangeable. These are the relations of the Precious Blood to Creation and the Incarnation. These are its titles to royalty—that it reinstated the dominion of God, and that it restored the kingdom of Jesus.

Let us pause for a moment to make an act of loving reparation to the immutability of God. We have had to speak of him with the infirmity of human words, as if his plans had failed, or his counsels had been altered. But we must not let any such idea rest on our minds. How it is that he did not change we cannot see: but we know that he did not; and we adore his blissful immutability. God changes his works without changing his counsels, says St. Augustine. But the change is in creatures, not in him. Time cannot change him, because he is eternal; nor place, because he is immense. He cannot change within himself, because he is perfect. He cannot be changed by any thing outside him, because he is almighty. His life is absolute repose, beatitude, simplicity: and in all this there can be no change. The very necessity, which compels us to speak of God as if he changed, only brings home to us more forcibly the perfection of his tranquillity. Let us then boldly offer to his love these ignorant words; and, while they enable us to understand somewhat of the peculiar office and grandeur of the Precious Blood, let us lovingly adore that unchangeableness of God, which has lain for all eternity more unwrinkled than a summer sea, and will lie to all eternity, with almost infinite worlds round about it, and yet have neither current, stream, or pulse, or tide, or wave, with no abyss to hold it and with no shore to bound it, with no shadow from without, and no throbbing from within.

Now that we have endeavored to show the place, which the Precious Blood holds in the counsels of God, with reference both to Creation and the Incarnation, let us, before we advance any further, see how the Holy Scriptures speak of it, and how completely their language is in harmony with our theology. We will content ourselves with putting the texts together, as we find from experience that many persons, when a special devotion to the Precious Blood is urged upon them, were not at all aware of the stress which the inspired writings lay upon it, but have rather regarded it as merely a convenient figurative expression to sum up and represent the mysteries of redemption.

Then Jesus said to them: Amen, Amen, I say unto you: Except you eat the Flesh of the Son of man, and drink his Blood, you shall not have life in you. He that eateth my Flesh, and drinketh my Blood, hath everlasting life: and I will raise him up in the last day. For my Flesh is meat indeed, and my Blood is drink indeed. He that eateth my Flesh, and drinketh my Blood, abideth in me, and I in him. In him, says St. Paul, it hath well pleased the Father that all fulness should dwell, and through him to reconcile all things unto himself, making peace through the Blood of his Cross, both as to the things on earth, and the things that are in heaven. Christ, being come an high-priest of the good things to come, by a greater and more perfect tabernacle not made with hand, neither by the blood of goats, or of calves, but by his own Blood, entered once into the Holies, having obtained eternal redemption. For, if the blood of goats and of oxen, and the ashes of an heifer being sprinkled, sanctify such as are defiled, to the cleansing of the flesh, how much more shall the Blood of Christ, who by the Holy Ghost offered himself unspotted unto God, cleanse our conscience from dead works, to serve the living God? Neither was the first testament dedicated without blood; and almost all things, according to the law, are cleansed with blood; and without shedding of blood there is no remission. It is necessary therefore that the patterns of heavenly things should be cleansed with these; but the heavenly things themselves with better sacrifices than these. We have, therefore, brethren, a confidence in the entering into the Holies by the Blood of Christ, a new and living way which he hath dedicated for us through the veil, that is to say, his Flesh. We are come to the sprinkling of Blood, which speaketh better than that of Abel. The bodies of those beasts, whose blood is brought into the Holies by the high-priest for sin, are burned without the camp: wherefore Jesus also, that he might sanctify the people by his own Blood, suffered without the gate. St. Peter speaks of us as elect, according to the foreknowledge of God the Father, unto the sanctification of the Spirit, unto obedience and sprinkling of the Blood of Jesus Christ. St. John says, The Blood of Jesus Christ his Son cleanseth us from all sin. This is he that came by water and Blood: not by water only, but by water and Blood: and it is the Spirit which testifieth, that Christ is the truth; and there are Three who give testimony in heaven, the Father, the Word, and the Holy Ghost; and these Three are One; and there are three that give testimony on earth, the spirit, and the water, and the Blood; and these three are one. The Ancients in the Apocalypse sung a new canticle, saying: Thou art worthy, O Lord, to take the book, and to open the seals thereof: because thou wast slain, and hast redeemed us to God in thy Blood, out of every tribe, and tongue, and people and nation, and hast made us to our God a kingdom and priests, and we shall reign on the earth. And one of the Ancients answered and said to me: These that are clothed in white robes, who are they? and whence came they? And I said to him, My lord, thou knowest. And he said to me, These are they who are come out of great tribulation, and have washed their robes and made them white in the Blood of the Lamb. Therefore they are before the throne of God; and the Lamb, which is in the midst of the throne, shall rule them. And I heard a loud voice in heaven, saying: Now is come salvation, and strength, and the kingdom of our God, and the power of his Christ; because the accuser of our brethren is cast forth, who accused them before our God day and night; and they overcame him by the Blood of the Lamb. And I saw heaven opened, and behold! a white horse: and he that sat upon him was called Faithful and True; and with justice doth he judge and fight; and his eyes were as a flame of fire, and on his head were many diadems; and he had a name written, which no man knoweth but himself; and he was clothed with a garment sprinkled with Blood; and his name is called The Word of God: and the armies that are in heaven followed him on white horses, clothed in fine linen white and clean; and he shall rule: and he hath on his garment and on his thigh written, King of kings and Lord of lords. Again St. Paul says, The Chalice of benediction, which we bless, is it not the communion of the Blood of Christ? Now in Christ Jesus, you, who sometime were afar off, are made nigh by the Blood of Christ. St. Peter says, We know that we were redeemed with the Precious Blood of Christ, as of a lamb unspotted and undefiled, foreknown indeed before the foundation of the world, but manifested in the last times. St. Paul also speaks of the God of peace, who brought again from the dead the great pastor of the sheep, our Lord Jesus Christ, in the Blood of the everlasting testament. To the clergy of Ephesus St. Paul speaks of the bishops who rule the church of God, which he hath purchased with his own Blood. To the Romans he speaks of the redemption that is in Christ Jesus, whom God hath proposed to be a propitiation, through faith in his Blood, to the showing of his justice, for the remission of former sins, through the forbearance of God. Christ died for us: much more therefore, being now justified by his Blood, shall we be saved from wrath through him. He speaks to the Ephesians of our being predestinated unto the praise of the glory of God's grace, in which he hath graced us in his beloved Son, in whom we have redemption through his Blood, the remission of sins, according to the riches of his grace. Similarly to the Colossians he speaks of the Father having delivered us from the power of darkness, and translated us into the kingdom of the Son of his love, in whom we have redemption through his Blood, . . . that in all things he may hold the primacy. St. John in the preface of the Apocalypse delivers his message as from Jesus Christ, who is the faithful witness, the first-begotten of the dead, and the prince of the kings of the earth, who hath loved us, and washed us from our sins in his own Blood, and hath made us a kingdom, and priests to God and his Father, to him be glory and empire for ever and ever! Amen.*

He who desires to attain to a deep and fervent devotion to the Precious Blood cannot do so more readily than by taking the foregoing texts of the Holy Scriptures for the subjects of his meditations. They will carry him, and very gently, far down into the mind of God. They will infuse into him a more tender and a more ardent love of the Person of the Eternal Word, while they will also increase his reverence for the Sacred Humanity. They, like all Scripture words, will bring forth fruit a thousandfold in his heart. Meanwhile, with reference to our present train of thought, the reader will observe how frequently and in what a striking way the mention of the Precious Blood is coupled by the Holy Ghost with the idea of kingdom, empire, and primacy, how carefully the eternal determination and foreknowledge of the Precious Blood is kept in sight, how it is put forward as the making of an offering, the restoring of his creatures, to God, and, finally, how it is to St. Peter, our Lord's Vicar upon earth, that we owe

---

*St. John vi. 54, 56. Col. i. 20. Heb. ii. 14; ix. 7; x. 19; xii. 24; xiii. 11. 1 Pet. i. 2. 1 John i. 7; v. 6, 8. Apoc. v. 9; vii. 14; xii. 11; xix. 13. 1 Cor. x. 16. Eph. ii. 13. 1 Pet. i. 19. Heb. xiii. 20. Acts xx. 28. Rom. iii. 25; v. 9. Eph. i. 7. Col. i. 14. Apoc. i. 5.

the title of Precious as applied to his Master's Blood. I cannot but believe that many men will feel their devotion to the Precious Blood increased as a special devotion when they see the wonderful teaching of the Bible on the subject brought into one view.

There are of course many ways in which the Precious Blood establishes the empire of Jesus. We may illustrate the matter sufficiently for our purpose by selecting three of them, Conversion, Sanctification, and the Building up of the Church. We shall have to speak more at length of Conversion in the next chapter. We shall treat therefore very briefly at present of these three things, and chiefly from one point of view, namely, the contrast and comparison between them and the act of Creation.

We have then to remember that it is the office of the Precious Blood to reconquer for God an empire which sin has wrested from him, and to govern and administer this empire in proportion as it reconquers it. Its royal rights, while they are the gratuitous appointments of God and flow from his eternal choice, are also based on the double relation of the Precious Blood to Creation and the Incarnation. Its relation to Creation makes it the rightful representative of the Dominion of God. Its relation to the Incarnation makes it the natural vicegerent of the Kingdom of the Sacred Humanity.

To us fallen creatures Conversion is the most interesting divine act of which we are able to take intimate cognizance. It is an act going on in the world at all moments, and which must happen to every one of us, either in the waters of baptism or out of them, if we are to be saved. Moreover, it is an act which may be repeated several times in each individual soul. It is to our supernatural being what Creation is to our natural being. The one calls us out of nothingness into life; the other out of darkness into light. The one makes us citizens of earth; the other citizens of heaven. By the one we are entitled to preservation, and all the numerous means, appliances, and consequences of life; by the other we have a right to claim sanctification, and all the numerous means, appliances, and consequences of grace. The creation of our souls was the work of an instant. God willed the existence of our souls, and exactly of such souls as he had fore-seen and chosen to be our peculiar selves from all eternity. There was no process. He willed, and it was done. Where there had been nothingness, there was now a human soul, a soul beautiful in its indestructible simplicity, beautiful in its complicated life. The sum of existence had been swelled by one; and that one had now to fulfil a strange, difficult, varied, romantic, destiny which would go on to be eternal. Conversion, on the other hand, is a process, and often a very long one. Sometimes whole years of life go to its preparation. Ten thousand circumstances, sweetly constrained by the paternal tenderness of God, gradually converge upon some predetermined hour and minute. Misfortunes are sent to prepare the ground, to plough it up with rude troubles, to soften it with silent weeping, or to break it to pieces through the kindly action of the frost. Happiness comes from God like an angel, to exorcise evil spirits from the mind, the temper, or the heart, and to clear the way for more supernatural operations. Accident, or seeming accident, also has its function in this work. Chance books, chance conversations, chance meetings, frequently accelerate the process, and not seldom hurry it at once to its conclusion. If only we could see them, we should discover that the graces which precede Conversion are, for number, variety, strangeness, unexpectedness, and kindliness, among the most wonderful works of God and the most touching ingenuities of his love. Yet, while the process of Conversion contrasts with Creation in that it is a process at all, it also resembles it in being really instantaneous. The actual justifi-cation of a sinner is the work of an instant. We see this in the baptism of infants. But also in grown-up people the transition from the enmity of God to his friendship, from a state of sin to a state of grace, takes place in a moment. One moment, and if the soul left the body it must perish eternally; another moment, and if sudden death came salvation would be secure. The change from the formless abyss of nothingness to the fresh, complete soul, is not more instantaneous than the justification of a sinner. What has gone before has been merely preparatory. It might weigh in judgment as ground for abating the severity of punishment; but it could not avail to alter that state of the soul which death has rendered fixed, certain, and irrevocable.

God condescends to put himself before us as effecting Creation by a word. He spoke, and it was done. Let light be, and light was. Thus Creation is effected by the most simple of all agencies, namely, by a single means, and that means, not a work, but a mere word. The Precious Blood, on the other hand, effects its creations in Conversion by a multiplicity of means, of means which are often repeated, often varied, often intensified, often newly invented for fresh cases, and often quite peculiar to the individual case. There is nothing in the world which the Precious Blood cannot make a means of grace. Even sin, though it cannot be a means of grace, can be constrained to do the ministries of grace, just as Satan is made the reluctant bondsman of the elect, and is forced to jewel their crowns with the very temptations he has devised for their destruction. Nevertheless in this respect also Conversion is like Creation. It is like it in its choice of means, though not like it in its simplicity. For the Precious Blood also chooses words for its instruments, as if in honor of that Eternal Word whose human life it is. The Sacraments are its ordinary modes of action, as we shall see later on; and words are the forms of the Sacraments, without which their peculiar miracles of grace cannot be wrought. Divine words are the chosen instruments of production in the supernatural as well as in the natural world.

It is one of the glories of the act of Creation, that there is no semblance of effort about it. It is the free act of God, but it is hardly an act in the sense in which we commonly use the word. It is an act in a much higher sense, a simpler and yet a more efficacious sense. It is an act without effort, without succession, without processes. It is an act such as befits the perfections of the Most High. His power did not rise up, as it were, to do it, nor his wisdom deliberate about it, nor his love grow to it. Nothing went out of him to the act, nor was the tranquillity of his life quickened by it. Conversion, on the contrary, has all the look of effort about it. Nay, effort is not the word: I should rather have said agony. The Precious Blood working its way out of our

Blessed Lord's Body in the sweat of Gethsemane, the slow, painful oozings from the Crown of thorns, the rude violence of the
sprinkling at the Scourging, the distillation of the Blood along
the streets of Jerusalem and up the slope of Calvary, the soaking
of his clinging raiment, the four wells dug by the cruel nails
ebbing and flowing with the pulses of his feeble life, the violation
of the silent sanctuary of his Dead Heart, to seek for the few
drops of that precious treasure that might be left—all these are
parts of the effort of Conversion. Neither is there less look of
effort in the Conversion of each single soul: more with some, and
less with others. In most instances the Precious Blood seems to
return to the charge again and again. Here it fails, there it succeeds. Now its success is hardly perceptible, now it is manifest,
striking and decisive. The Precious Blood tries to convert every
one, just as it was shed for every one. Multitudes remain uncon-
verted, and are never won back to the kingdom of God. With
them the battle has gone against grace. Even in defeat the Precious Blood triumphs. It gains glory for God; but it is in ways
which in this life we cannot even put ourselves into a position to
understand. It can boast also of decisive victories, of great strokes
of grace, of hearts carried by storm, of saints made at once out of
one heroic deed. But these are not the common cases. With most
hearts it strives, and pleads, and toils; then it seems to intermit its
labors, as if it were fatigued; it retires from the heart as if in
despair. Once more it returns to its task, and occupies itself with
incredible patience in minutest details, often working under
ground and in circuitous ways. Not seldom it retires again, as if
now completely baffled; and finally, when least expected, it leaps
upon its prey from afar, and triumphs as much by the suddenness,
as by the impetuosity, of the onslaught.

Look at that soul, almost the richest booty it ever won in
war, the soul of St. Paul. What long years there were of religious
antecedents, what a blind generosity of misdirected zeal, what a
fidelity to unhelpful ordinances, what a preparation for humility
in the cruel persecution of the faithful, what a prelude to apostolic
fervor in that furious partisanship of the conscientious pharisee,

what an insensible drawing nigh to the Gospel through the very perfection of his Judaism! Then follow St. Stephen's prayers, and things are coming to the best with Saul when they are at their very worst. Yet Stephen's prayers are not so much attacking him as circumventing him. Then the heavens open at noonday, and the glorified Redeemer overwhelms him with sudden light, and blinds him, and flings him to the ground; and the blood of Stephen, which had cried aloud to the Blood of Jesus, is sweetly avenged by the heart of Paul being cleansed by that atoning Blood, and sent out unto all nations to be the especial preacher of that Blood which had so glorified itself in his Conversion. Yet, while there is such a seeming contrast between Creation and Conversion in this matter of effort, there is also a close comparison between them. There is in reality no effort in the operation of the Precious Blood. It only needed to let itself be shed. It only needs now to let itself be outpoured. Its touch is health, life, resurrection, immortality, and glory. Its sole touch is its sole work. It never touches but it changes. It needs but to touch once in order to make its spiritual change complete. If it seems to add, to repeat, to re-touch, to deepen, to broaden, to improve on itself, all that comes from another part of its character. It is no sign of want of power, no necessary expenditure of artistic labor, no demand of experience, no consequence of more mature reflection.

The absence of contrivance is another splendor of the divine act of Creation. No plan was laid. No gradual train of thought reached the grand conclusion. No provisions were made, no preparations finished, no materials collected. There were no preliminaries. There was no change in the Ever-blessed Agent. Without any prelude, and yet with a tranquillity which admitted not of suddenness, God created. There was no model for him to go by. There was no law to constrain him. He had never done a free act before. This was his first. Yet it affected not his immutability. From all eternity the Son was being born of the Father; from all eternity the Holy Ghost was proceeding from the Father and the Son. But these were necessary actions. They were the inward life of God. Creation was a free act, an act which he was free to do, or to leave undone, without altering his perfections. He acted. He created. The consequences are stupendous. They are endless. They are beyond the comprehension of the highest angels. With all these consequences God himself is most mysteriously mixed up. There is his concurrence with all created actions and movements, the intricacies of his never-halting providence, the Incarnation, the Divine Mother, the Fall, the Precious Blood, the Church, the Sacraments, the Economy of grace, the Doom, the Wail of hell, the Jubilee of heaven. Yet he acted out of his adorable simplicity. He put himself in no attitude to create. He made no movement. He contrived nothing. He spoke, but his utterance broke not the everlasting silence; and at his voiceless word all was done. There is no calm in the universe like the calmness of the act by which the whole universe was created. There was not a stir in the life of God when a million times ten million angels sprang into beautiful existence, and a million times ten million material worlds leaped up like fires out of a void abyss, where a moment before neither abyss nor void had been. Thus there was no history in the act of Creation, whereas in each Conversion there is a marvellous, orderly, yet entangled history. There is a look of contrivance about the Precious Blood. It was to be got from Mary's heart. Her heart was to be hindered, by a strange miracle of anticipation, through the very virtue of the unformed Precious Blood itself, from coming under the law of sin. It had to pass into the life of Jesus, and to multiply in his veins to the full supply of manhood. The methods by which it was to be shed were all to be contrived, with times, places, quantities, and circumstances befitting them. It had to be looked after during the triduo of the Passion, and its restoration to the Body of our dearest Lord contrived. After all this, further contrivance was needed concerning the methods of applying it to the souls of men. Its impetuosity had to be in order. Its prodigality had to submit to law. What an immensity of divine contrivance went to all this machinery! Yet in itself the Precious Blood operates with as little contrivance as effort. In the matter of contrivance, as in the matter of effort, Conversion emulates the simplicity of Creation. The brief word of a Sacrament is enough to work its huge miracle upon the unresisting soul of the infant at the Font. Nay, with the most obdurate sinner it can by its first grace accomplish the entire work of sanctity, and raise him into a saint at once without any of the sweet insidious contrivances with which the gentleness of redeeming love so often surrounds the operation of the Precious Blood. Conversion can be masterful as well as tender.

He that is eternal grows not weary. Eternity itself is endless, unbeginning rest. Eternity before Creation is but the name of the life of God. But the Eternal rested after Creation. He had an unimaginable sabbath, in which he rested from the works that he had made. There is no sabbath yet for the Precious Blood. Its creative work upon the earth is incessant, increasing as the multitudes of the tribes of men increase. There is no end to its activity, day and night. It starts each epoch and each century with renewed ardor and redoubled vigor. It becomes more abundant and more energetic in the Church on earth, in proportion as the Church becomes more populous in heaven. Yet it has a sabbath too, even while it toils. It rests in the glorified Heart of Jesus in heaven. It rests upon that mediatorial throne whereon the Sacred Humanity has been exalted. The souls of the righteous worship it on high with everlasting lauds; and the angels, prostrate in adoration, sing canticles in its honor all through the nightless day of that radiant land above. It rests in Jesus. It is his life, his love, his jubilee, and his repose. This is its sabbath-life in heaven, while its industry is so divinely vigorous and fertile upon earth. But the sabbath of Creation is also a time of working, while it is a time of rest. Not only is the continuous preservation of all things and the fulfilling of all created things with the divine concurrence an almost illimitable extension and on-going of Creation, but new souls of men are literally created out of nothing every moment of time. Yet still, in some mysterious sense, God's sabbath is unbroken. Thus Conversion, like Creation, has its sabbath, even while it works. When the Grand Doom has come and gone, who can tell into what a sabbath the rest of our dearest Lord shall deepen?

If Conversion is the conquest of the empire of the Precious Blood, Sanctification is its government of that which it has conquered. Sanctification is to Conversion what Cosmogony is to Creation. It is the dividing up, and dispensing, and setting in order, and adorning, what has already been created out of nothing. Or, again, it is to the work of justification what, in natural things, the preservation of life is to the evolving of life out of nothing. It was the Holy Ghost who fashioned the Precious Blood out of the immaculate blood of Mary. He was the Fashioner of the Sacred Humanity. To him that work is specially appropriated. He also is especially, and by appropriate office, our Sanctifier. It was to him that Jesus left his Church. What our Lord himself had been during the Three-and-Thirty Years, the Holy Ghost began to be in some peculiar manner from the day of Pentecost. Jesus himself has returned to abide in his Church in the Blessed Sacrament; but he abides in it as it were beneath the administration of the Holy Ghost, which he himself appointed. The Precious Blood, which the Holy Spirit fashioned, is now the same Spirit's instrument in the great work of sanctification. As that Blood was the love of the Son's Sacred Humanity, by which he offered his atonement to the Father, so is it the love of his Sacred Humanity, by which with sweetest affectionate ministries he subserves the sanctifying office of the Holy Ghost. By the Precious Blood the Son himself became Redeemer, while by the same dear Blood reparation was made to the Father's honor as Creator, and to the Holy Spirit's tender love as the Sanctifier of Creation. He who in the Holy Trinity was produced and not producing became fertile by the Precious Blood.

Was there ever any such fertility as that of the Holy Ghost? The leaves of the trees, the blades of the grass, the matted entanglement of tropical herbs in the moist forest, the countless shoals of the living inhabitants of ocean, the swarms of insects which in hot regions blacken the sun for miles as if they were sandstorms—these are but types of the fecundity of the Holy Ghost in the operations of grace. We never can do justice to the magnitude of the world of angels. The poor child, who has no notion of money but in pence, would be bewildered if he were called upon to deal with gold and to count his gold by millions. So we in earthly things are accustomed to dimensions, and to numbers, on so dwarfish a scale, that even our exaggerations will not raise our ideas to the true magnitudes and multitudes of the world of angels. The countless myriads of individual spirits, the countless graces which are strewn all over the breadth of their capacious natures, the colossal size of those graces as compared with those of human souls, the inconceivable rapidity, delicacy, and subtlety of the operations of grace in such gigantic intelligences and such fiery affections — these considerations, if well weighed, may give us some idea of the fruitfulness of the most dear sanctifying Spirit. Every one of those graces was merited for the angels by the Precious Blood. Converting grace they never had; for they never needed a conversion; and to those who fell no conversion was allowed. If we think also of the multitude of souls, the sum of successive generations from Adam to the uncertain Doom, if we try to bring before ourselves the variety of vocations in the world, the strictly peculiar needs of each single soul and the distinctive characteristic shape of the holiness of each single soul, then the multiplicity of the processes of grace prolonged perhaps over half a century or more, we shall see that the arithmetic of even human graces is amazing. Through the instrumentality of the Precious Blood, the Holy Ghost is everywhere and always making all things productive of sanctity in some measure and degree. Sanctification may be called the production of heavenly beauty in the world. It is the filling of nature with the supernatural. It is the transforming of the human or angelic into the divine. It is the engraving of the image of God upon every piece and parcel of the rational creation. It is the brightening and the beautifying of creation. It is the empire of light stealing upon the realm of darkness, swiftly, slowly, variously, with beams and splendors, with transformations and effects, more marvellous than those of any lovely dawn upon the mountains and forests of the earth. It is the especial and appropriate office of the Holy Ghost, with the universal and invariable and inseparable agency of the Precious Blood. Thus, every process of Sanctification, while it is an outpouring of exquisite love upon creatures, is also a passage of mutual love between Jesus and the Holy Ghost. Our Lord's words in the Gospels indicate to us something of the unspeakable jealous love of the Sacred Humanity for the Eternal Spirit our dearest Saviour, whose very office and occupation it was to forgive sin, was unlike himself when he excepted from this amnesty the sin against the Holy Ghost: unlike himself, yet true to some depth of holiness and love within himself. On the other hand, it was to be the office of the Paraclete to bring Jesus to mind, to fill the memory with the sweet words he had said, to keep the Thirty-Three Years alive on earth forever, to be forever testifying of Jesus, and forever completing and adoring the work which he had come on earth to do. Thus, as in theology the Holy Ghost is named the Kiss of the Father and the Son, the Son and the Holy Ghost kiss Each Other in the Precious Blood. All Sanctification is the love of the Holy Ghost for the Sacred Humanity; and every operation of the Precious Blood is a tender adoration of the Holy Ghost by the Created Nature of our Blessed Lord.

But we should soon sink out of our depths in mysteries like these. We will pass on to the third of the principal ways in which the Precious Blood reconquers for God the empire of his own Creation, and establishes the kingdom of Christ—the Building up of the Church. To continue our comparison with Creation—as Conversion represents the act of Creation, and Sanctification the work of Cosmogony, so the Building up of the Church is parallel to those changes in the face of Creation made by the lapse of time and the agency of the natural laws of the universe. The alterations of the bed of ocean, the deposits of mighty rivers, the crumbling of the rocks, the devastations of the earthquake and volcano, the elevation and subsidence of the earth, the spreading of the sandy deserts, the mutations of climate from other and less normal catastrophes—all these things have altered the face of the earth, made it more habitable, and by deciding its physical geography have gone far to decide its history and to locate the centres of its civilization. So is it with the spiritual earth through the vicissitudes of the Church. The Church is the work of the Precious Blood. It was made by it, cleansed by it, adorned by it, propagated by it, and kept glorious by it. The Church is that portion of Creation purchased by the Precious Blood out of alien possession, recovered from unjust holding, redeemed from slavery, conquered from enemies. The salvation of individual souls is dependent upon the Church. Hence the Building up of the Church is one of the grandest works of the Precious Blood. The conversion of nations, the history of doctrine, the holding of councils, the spread of the episcopate, the influence of the ecclesiastical upon the civil law, the freedom of the Holy See, the papal monarchy of past ages, the concordats of the present day, the filial subordination of catholic governments—all these things alter the face of the spiritual world. Every one of them is a vast fountain of God's glory, an immense harvest of souls, a prolific source of human happiness, and the antidote to a thousand evils. Above all things, the honor, the freedom, and the empire of the Holy See are the works of the Precious Blood. The Church is the Body of Christ; and nowhere are the lineaments of our dearest Lord, his beauty, his persuasiveness, his strange commingling of gladness and of woe, so faithfully expressed as in the Head of his Church. Hence it is that the joyousness of the saints ebbs and flows with the vicissitudes of the Holy See. Hence it is that the most secret mystics are affected by the fortunes of distant Rome, like the wells that dry and fill again in hidden sympathy with an earthquake in some remote quarter of the world.

In quiet times good men can love the Vicar of Christ, and look at him as their venerable father and monarch, ruling over all the best affections of their hearts, with a loyalty which the hereditary sovereigns of the earth can never obtain, and which is a far more heavenly thing than a patriot's love of the land which gave him birth. But when the clouds gather round the Sacred City, when the pressure of self-seeking potentates again begins to crucify our Lord afresh in the person of his Vicar, when the coils of diplomacy twist themselves round Peter's throne, when wellnigh all the world, schism, heresy, unbelief, ambition, injustice, and catholic states world-tainted, league together against the Lord's Anointed, then to the saints the face of Christ's Vicar becomes like the countenance of his Lord. It grows more majestic in abjection. The anguish on it is divine. It is more worshipful than ever, at the very moment when it is calling out our tenderest love and our keenest sympathies. This too is a time rife in victories to the Precious Blood. Rome is saved, and man has not saved it. They were bearing the papacy out to burial, and lo! a glorious resurrection! When deliverance was furthest off, then it came.

But these great historical triumphs are not the only victories of the Precious Blood in evil days. It wins many in the secrets of hearts. The spirit of the age is forever tainting the minds and hearts of the elect. There are few who do not end by going with the multitude, few who are not imposed upon by the pompous elation of science, by the juvenile pronouncements of an improved literature, by the complacent self-glorifications of temporal prosperity, and by the pretensions to an unparalleled grandeur which each generation makes as it struts out upon the stage of life. It is fine to innovate: it is refreshing to be audacious: it is a cheap victory to attack: it is comfortable to be on the same side with the loud-voiced world around us. Few men have clearly ascertained their own principles. They admit into their inconsequent minds wandering ideas of the times, without seeing that they are in reality hostile to the holy things which occupy the sanctuary of their hearts. Hence they get upon the wrong side, specially in middle life. It is not youth so much as middle life that falls in this way. While the generosity of youth makes early life to err in questions of degree, the same generosity keeps it incorrupt in questions of kind. It is the egotistical self-importance of middle life, which makes apostates, reformers, and malcontents. It is then that men get upon the wrong side. They fight under wrong banners. They frustrate the promise of their better years. They become out of harmony with the Church. From that hour their lives are failures. They grow querulous and contentious, peevish and captious, bitter and sour. Their old age is extremely solitary; and it is a great grace of God if they do not die on the wrong side, they who seem to have been raised up to be the very foremost champions of the right. Now it is bad times which open men's eyes. They see then how the spirit of the age has been nigh to deceiving them, how they mistook its loudness for wisdom, and how near they were to losing the simplicity of their devotion in the unhelpfulness of an intellectual demonstration, which has passed away, and has done as little, and is remembered as much, as the popular novel of a season. Many are the victories of disenchantment which the Precious Blood gains in times like those. Souls, that are won back to the old ways and the antique fashions, may yet be saints, whose promises of holiness must soon have been withered, cankered, or dispersed in the vanity of modern attempts and innovations.

Nay, though we may be unable to see it, we cannot doubt that there are triumphs of the Precious Blood in the spread of heresies, in the schism of kingdoms, and in similar catastrophes of the Church. Souls seem to perish, and it is hard to bear. But the life of the Church is very vast, and is ruled by immense laws; and when her Spouse comes at the end, the Precious Blood must needs present her to him "a glorious Church, not having spot, or wrinkle, or any such thing."* We must remember always, therefore, that the Church is the empire of the Precious Blood, and that that Blood will be the law of its life, and will govern it, not at all in the world's way, not at all in the spirit of an age, but altogether after its own spirit and altogether in its own way. Souls soon lose themselves who chafe because the Church is not wise with a worldly wisdom.

But we should have a very imperfect notion of the empire of the Precious Blood if we did not take into account the chief methods by which it does its work. We have seen some of the principal ways in which it spreads its empire; let us now see the means by which it spreads it. These means are the Sacraments.

It is difficult to describe the Sacraments. If an angel were to bear us from this globe which we inhabit, and carry us to some

---

*Eph. v. 27.

distant star, which God may have adorned as a dwelling-place for some other species of reasonable creatures, we should be struck with the novelty and peculiarity of the scenery around us. Some of its features might remind us of the scenery of earth, although with characteristic differences; while other features would be entirely new, entirely unlike any thing we had ever seen before, either in color, form, or composition. This is very much the effect produced upon us when we come to learn the catholic doctrine about the Sacraments. It introduces us into a new world. It gives us new ideas. It is more than a discovery; for it amounts to a revelation. The Sacraments are part of the new world introduced into creation by the Incarnation of the Eternal Word, and therefore are an essential part of creation as it was eternally preordained by God. Yet they are quite distinct from any other province in creation. The Sacraments of the Old Law were but shadows of the Sacraments of the Gospel. The Sacraments of the New Law are created things which have been devised and fabricated by our Blessed Lord himself. The Eucharist was foreshadowed by the Paschal Lamb: the Sacrament of Order by the consecration of priests; and Penance by the legal purifications of the tabernacle. There was no shadow of Confirmation, because it is the Sacrament of the fulness of grace, and so can belong only to the Gospel dispensation. Neither was there any shadow of Extreme Unction, because it is the immediate preparation for the entrance of the soul into glory; and there was no entrance into glory for any human soul till Jesus had risen and ascended. Neither could Matrimony be a Sacrament under the Old Law, because the Word had not yet actually wedded our human nature; and the sacramentality of Marriage consists in its being the figure of those transcendent nuptials of the Sacred Humanity.

What then shall we call these Sacraments? They are not persons, yet they seem to be scarcely things: I mean that they seem to be something more than things. We want another word for them, another name, and cannot find one. They are powers, lives, shrines, marvels, divine hiding-places, centres of heavenly power, supernatural magnificences, engraftings of heaven upon earth, fountains of grace, mysterious efficacies, marriages of matter and spirit, beautiful complications of God and man. Each Sacrament is a species by itself. Each has some specialty, which is at once its excellence and its mystery. The pre-eminence of Baptism consists in its remission of original sin and of the pains due to it. The pre-eminence of Confirmation resides in the vastness of the succors of actual grace which it brings with it, as we see in the fortitude which it conferred upon the Apostles, and which the Eucharist had not conferred. The Sacrament of Penance can claim the privilege of being the most necessary of all Sacraments to those who have been baptized, and of the capability of reiterated remission of mortal sin, which Baptism cannot claim. Extreme Unction excels Penance in the greater copiousness of its graces. The excellence of Order consists in its placing men in the singularly sublime state of being domestic ministers of Christ. Matrimony has a glory of its own in its signification of the union of our Lord with the Church. The pre-eminence of the Eucharist resides, as St. Thomas says, in the very substance of the Sacrament, seeing that it is as it were the Sacrament of all the other Sacraments, the centre of them, the cause of them, the end of them, and the harmony of them. All are because of it, and are subordinate to its amazing supremacy.

These Sacraments were designed by our Lord himself, and were instituted by him with varying degrees of detail as to matter and form in various Sacraments; and yet, saving their substance, he has given his Church very extensive power over them, because they are so intimately connected with its unity. We see the exercise of this power in the bread of the Eucharist, in the impediments of Marriage, and in the varieties of Order in the Latin and Greek Churches. The Sacraments are institutions which illustrate at once the magnificence of God's dominion over his creation, and also the capability of creatures to be elevated by him to astonishing sublimities far beyond the merit and due of nature; and this elevability of creatures is one of the most glorious manifestations of the liberty of God.*

---

*There are certain differences of opinion in theology which seem to keep quiet in their own subject-matter, and not to control other opinions in separate departments of theology. But there are, on the contrary, opinions, often of seemingly little or merely local importance, which draw along with them a man's whole theology. Among these, hardly any is more remarkable than the opinion we may form on the subject of what theology calls "potentia obedientialis." I mention this here, because in the exposition of the doctrine of the Sacraments given in the text, I have taken pains to use no expressions which shall be unfair to those who hold the moral operation, and not the physical operation, of the Sacraments. Amicus has beautifully shown that both the theories equally, though differently, magnify the grandeur of the Sacraments. If the physical theory attributes to them a more marvellous operation on the recipient, the moral theory attributes to them a more mysterious action upon God himself. I wish to observe also that, although there is a manifest sympathy between the Scotist doctrine of the Sacraments and the Scotist doctrine of potentia obedientialis, the connection is not necessary. It is a matter of sympathy rather than of logic. A man who holds the moral theory of the operation of the Sacraments lies under the same obligation of explaining his potentia obedientialis as one who holds the physical theory. This Amicus has candidly pointed out. The doctrine of potentia obedientialis is to me the part of Scotus's system which is most hard to receive. St. Thomas's doctrine of potentia opens out a view of creation much more deep and philosophical, from this point of view, while, when we come to look at creation from the point of view of the Incarnation, Scotus seems to be much more deep and philosophical than St. Thomas. Perhaps the views of the later scholastics on potentia obedientialis are still more philosophical. I would venture to recommend a special study of this question to students of theology, as one which particularly gives unity and consistency to the multitude of a man's theological tenets. See Ripalda, De Ente Supernaturali, lib. ii. and especially Disputations 40 and 41. Haunoldus, Controversiæ Theologicæ, lib. iv. tract ii. cap. 1, controversia 2. Amicus, the latter part of Disp. iv., de Causalitate Sacramentorum, and all Disp. v., de Potentia Obedientiali, and Disp. vi., Quæ entia et ad quos effectus elevari possint. Viva, the whole of Disp. ii., de Causalitate Sacramentorum; and the other great theologians in loco. But in connection should be read also in the different writers de Angelis the treatment of the question, An creatio communicari possit creaturæ obedientialiter, and its cognate questions, which are to be found under the de principio productivo Angelorum: or, in some theologians, under de Deo, especially de Dei cognoscibilitate, or de Beatitudine, or de Hominis creatione, or de Opificio sex dierum. I would especially mention the De Deo of Francis de Lugo, Disp. vii., De ente supernaturali in communi, and Disp. viii., De variis divisionibus entis supernaturalis: and likewise the 10th and 11th Disputations in Arriaga de Sacramentis. There are also some interesting things in the huge work of Castaldus the Dominican, de Potestate Angelica, and in Arriaga's Physics.

The Sacraments are not mere signs of grace, but causes of it. They cause grace in us physically by the omnipotence of God which exists in them as if it were their own proper virtue and energy; for the omnipotence of God exists so specially in the Sacraments that if, by impossibility, God were not omnipresent, he would nevertheless be present in the Sacraments. The Sacraments cause grace physically, just as our Lord's Blood, shed long ago, cleanses us from our sins physically, not morally only, and just as his Resurrection and Ascension cause our resurrection and ascension physically, by an energy and a force which God has appropriated to them.* The Sacraments also cause grace in us morally, by representing to the Father the merits of Christ's Passion actually accomplished, and so doing a sort of holy and irresistible violence to God, and thereby procuring for us more abundant, and at the same time very special, succors of grace. Both these methods of causing grace bring vividly before us the unspeakable majesty of the Sacraments, and enable us to estimate the grandeur of the merits of our dearest Lord; but perhaps of the two methods the honor of Jesus is most concerned in the Sacraments causing grace physically, because it is more intimate to him so to cause it,† and in many other respects more divine and more excellent. But these are questions too difficult for us to enter upon here. It is enough to say with St. Chrysostom that the way in which the Sacraments confer grace is above the power of an angel to tell, or with St. Gregory Nyssen that the grace of Baptism transcends human understanding. Such language could hardly be used of the merely moral efficacy of the Sacraments;

---

*Viva Pars., vii. Disp. ii. q. 2.

†Sicut Caro Christi habuit virtutem instrumentalem ad faciendum miracula propter conjunctionem ad Verbum, ita Sacramenta per conjunctionem ad Christum crucifixum et passum. *S. Thomas, Quodlibet.* 12, *art.* 14. Theology suggests three ways in which the Sacraments may confer grace physically—per virtutem obedientialem cum concursu omnipotentiæ, per qualitatem supernaturalem intrinsecam, per omnipotentiam specialiter inexistentem. In the text the third method has been adopted, in harmony with the views of Viva; but the theological discussion of the question has been avoided as unfit for the popular character of this Treatise.

and, as Viva observes, if the fires of Purgatory and Hell act upon the soul physically in real and marvellous ways, it is at least congruous to suppose that the instruments of the Divine Mercy shall enjoy the same privileges as the instruments of the Divine Justice. But the Sacraments not only confer sanctifying grace and infuse habits of virtue, both physically and morally: they also confer a certain special sacramental grace, which is peculiar and distinct in each Sacrament. It is difficult to explain this sacramental grace; but it seems to be a special power to obtain from God, by a certain right founded upon his decrees, particular assistances and kinds of grace in order to the fulfilment of each Sacrament. Moreover, it belongs to the grace of the Sacraments that certain of them impress what is called a *character,* or seal, or signet, on the soul. The nature of this *character* is involved in mystery; but the most probable interpretation of it is that which describes it as a natural similitude of the Soul of Jesus, likening our souls to his, and imparting hiddenly to our souls a resemblance of his, hidden in this life, but to be divulged with exceeding glory hereafter. This is a beautiful thought, and fills us full of a peculiar love for the dear Human Soul of Jesus. Lastly, the grace of Sacraments suspended or dormant has a marvellous power of revival, which enhances the mystery and the magnificence of these strange and unparalleled works of God.

But our clearest idea of the Sacraments is that which we gain from Hugh St. Victor and the elder theologians. They are the making visible of invisible grace. In them the Precious Blood has clothed itself in visible forms. In the matter and form of the Sacraments it has put on its priestly vestments, of unearthly fashion, and of manifold significance. Indeed, the grace of the Sacraments is the very physical grace which was in the Soul of Jesus, replicated, as theology speaks, that is, repeated again and again in us, and repeated in us by means of the Precious Blood. Many theologians have held that all the grace, which is in any of us, was first, physically, really, and locally, in the Soul of Christ; so that our grace is, most literally and most affectingly, a derivation from the abundance of his grace. How near does this exquisite doctrine seem to bring us to our dearest Lord!* Do the forms, the fashions, and varieties of these sevenfold sacramental garments, in which the Precious Blood clothes itself, tell us of its mysteries, its nature, or its character? Doubtless they have deep meaning, and are symbolical of its genius; but we are unable to decipher them. They are hieroglyphics of some hidden wisdom of God. But we see so much as this: that the Sacraments are the actions of Christ. He instituted them as Man; and thus *they are the going-on of the Thirty-Three Years upon earth.* This is the clearest and the truest view of these marvellous portions of creation. Let us now see if we have not learned enough of their theology to meditate practically upon them in connection with our subject.

The Sacraments are then, as we see, in a very special sense the vases of the Precious Blood. They are the means by which the Precious Blood is ordinarily applied to the souls of men. They are the most characteristic features in the economy of grace. They are the most striking memorials of the love of Jesus; and a knowledge of them is most necessary to a right understanding of redemption. This is not the place for entering further upon the doctrine and definition of the Sacraments. My readers are doubtless sufficiently familiar with the teaching of the Church upon a subject of such constant practical importance, and what has been said in the foregoing pages will enable them to call to mind at least its most prominent features. But it is very needful for our present subject that we should make some reflections upon the Sacraments, rather in the way of meditation than of doctrine. We cannot do justice to the Precious Blood of our dearest Lord, unless we have a true spiritual discernment, a loving admiration, and an immense esteem of the grandeur, riches, and sweetness of the Sacraments. In an ascetical point of view, I hardly know any thing upon which I should lay greater stress in these days, than a fervent devotion to the Sacraments.

---

*Some eminent theologians have even held that of two Communions of equal fervor, one by a layman, and one by a priest, the priest's Communion would merit more, because of his conjunction with our Blessed Lord as his domestic minister. In like manner the special efficacy of our Lady's prayers is attributed precisely to her conjunction with our Lord as his Mother.

The Sacraments are the inventions of God himself. No creature could have devised them. I do not believe that without revelation the most magnificent intelligence of the angels could have imagined such a thing as a Sacrament. It is a peculiar idea of God. It represents a combination of his most wonderful perfections. It conveys to us in itself quite a distinctive notion of God. We already know God as the unbeginning God. We know him also as the God of nature and as the God of grace. These are two different disclosures of him to us. So the knowledge of him as the God who devised the Sacraments is another disclosure of him. It adds many new ideas of him to the other ideas of him which we possessed before. We should in some respects have thought differently of God, if there had been no Sacraments, from what we think now. This is a great deal to say. It confers upon the Sacraments a most singular dignity, or rather it expresses in an intelligible manner that singular dignity which belongs to them. Moreover, God not only invented them, but he invented them for the most magnificent of purposes. He invented them, that by their means especially he might impart his Divine Nature to created natures, that he might justify sinners, that he might sanctify souls, that he might unite to himself the race whose nature he had condescended to single out and assume to himself. If they are his own invention, they must be works of unspeakable excellence; for the least of his works is excellent: but, if they were meant also for purposes so dear to him and of such an exalted character, who shall be able rightly to imagine the excellence of these Sacraments? Furthermore, they are very peculiar inventions. They do not follow the laws of nature. They even superadd to the laws of grace. They are things apart, almost belonging to an order of their own. They are apparently without parallel in all creation. I know of nothing else to which I could liken them. They come out of some depth in the unfathomable wisdom of God, which does not seem to have given out any other specimens of itself. They are emanations of some abyss of his magnificence, which has only opened once, to give them forth, and then has closed, and rested. As matter and spirit, as nature and grace, are samples of

God's beauty, tokens of ineffable realities in him, manifestations of his invisible treasures, so likewise are the Sacraments. They invest God with a new light in our minds. They are some of his eternal ideas, the more imperiously demanding our devout study, because we have no others like them, no others which we can use as similitudes or as terms of comparison. My knowledge of God is not only increased in degree, but it is extended in kind, by my knowledge of a Sacrament.

Strictly speaking, we do not call the Sacraments miraculous. They have laws of their own. So perhaps have miracles. But the laws of the Sacraments are revealed to us. Their action follows rules, and is, under fitting circumstances, invariable. Their order and immutability are two of their most striking features; and this distinguishes them from miracles. They are processes; and in this also they are unlike what we popularly term miracles. But so far as they are wonder-working, so far as their results call forth our astonishment, so far as their effects are beyond the power of nature, so far as their completeness and their instantaneousness are concerned, so far as the revolutions they accomplish and the transmutations they make are beyond the strength of common grace, so far as their success is in their secret divinity—so far we may call their operation miraculous. It is certainly in the highest degree mysterious. Their use of matter seems to point to a philosophy of matter and spirit far deeper than any which has yet been taught. It awakens trains of thought which carry us rapidly into speculations which are too high for us, yet which give us now and then unsystematic glances into the secrets of creation. The forms of the Sacraments betoken a mysterious grandeur in language, reminding us of God's peculiar way of working by efficacious words, a characteristic which doubtless is connected in some hidden manner with the Eternal Generation of the Word. The invisible sacerdotal power which is necessary to the validity of so many of the Sacraments is another of their splendors, while the Sacraments which do not need it imply that latent priesthood which abides in all Christians, and which is an emanation of our Saviour's own priesthood "after the order of Melchisedec." The jurisdiction required for the administration of so many of the Sacraments, and especially for valid absolution, is a participation in those regal powers which belong to the kingdom of Christ, to the Church in its character of a monarchy. The power of the Church itself to limit the validity of a Sacrament, as in the case of reserved sins in Confession, and of impediments in Matrimony, is another feature in the Sacraments, which enhances their mysterious character, while it exalts that lordship of the Sacred Humanity of Jesus which has been so copiously imparted to the Church. All these things are points for meditation, which cannot fail to fill the soul with reverence and love, and to unite it more closely with God, by making us feel how the natural is hemmed in with the divine, and with what awful reality we are always lying in the arms of God, with our liberty held up, secured, and at once imprisoned and set at large, by all this exuberance of supernatural interventions.

The grace of the Sacraments is another subject for pious wonder. The special grace of each Sacrament, peculiar to itself and accomplishing a peculiar end, is a marvel in itself. Just as the sun brings out the blossoms, and paints their variegated leaves in parti-colored patterns, though the whole leaf is supplied with the same sap through the same veins, so does the Sun of justice work in the special graces of the Sacraments. How he determines them to such various effects is a secret hidden from us. The Sacraments have probably spiritual laws of their own, which are neither gratuitous nor arbitrary, but founded in some intrinsic fitness of things, which results from the character of God. The special grace of each Sacrament seems to be almost a visible approach of God to the individual soul, to accomplish some particular end, or confirm some definite vocation, or interfere in some distinct crisis. It is not his usual way of working. It is not merely a general augmentation of sanctifying grace, an infusion of livelier faith, of keener hope, or of more burning charity. It is something more intimate between God and the soul, more personal, more full of reference to the individual case. Again, we must not omit to reflect on the inexhaustibleness of the grace of the Sacraments. It takes an immense heroism like martyrdom to come near to the grace of a Sacrament. Even martyrdom does not supersede Baptism or Confession, if they can be had. No one can tell how much grace lies in a single Sacrament. In a single Communion lies all grace; for in it is the Author and Fountain of all grace; and, if the theological opinion be true, that there is no grace in any of his members which has not actually been first in our Lord himself, then all the grace of all the world lies in one Communion, to be unsealed and enjoyed by the degree of fervor which we bring. The saints have said that a single Communion was enough to make a saint. Who can tell if any created soul has ever yet drained any single Sacrament of the whole amount of grace which was contained in it simply by virtue of its being a Sacrament? I should be inclined to think, from manifold analogies both of nature and of grace, that no Sacrament had ever been duly emptied of its grace, not even in the Communions of our Blessed Lady.

No Sacrament is content to confine itself to the conferring of its special grace. There is always an exuberance about it, giving more than is asked, doing more than is promised, reaching further than was expected. This is a characteristic of all God's works. His magnificence is confined in every one of them, and is forever bursting its bounds, and carrying light, and beauty, and fertility, and blessing, far beyond the shrine in which it had been localized. But the Perfection of God, which above all others the Sacraments appear to represent, is his magnificence. They belong to this Attribute in a very special and peculiar way. Hence there is about them a redundancy of grace, a prodigality of power, a profuseness and lavishness of benediction, which go beyond the ordinary laws of the world of grace. Moreover, besides this exuberance, there is an agility about the Sacraments which is most worthy of note. Sometimes, if need be, one will do the work of another. Those, which have no office to communicate first grace and justify the sinner, will do so under certain circumstances. Communion will forgive. Extreme Unction will absolve: not ordinarily, but when there is necessity for it, and the fitting dispositions. We cannot think without surprise of this power of transforming themselves, and of passing into each other and supplying for each other, which within certain limits the Sacraments possess. Furthermore, the rivers of grace in the Sacraments never run dry. Consider the multitude of Sacraments administered daily in the Church. Picture to yourself the wonderfulness of grace and its supernatural excellence, and then imagine the quantity of it drawn out of the eternal fountains for the well-being of the world. It is an overwhelming thought. Grace is not only more abundant in the Sacraments, and more nimble, but it is also more sure, more invariable, more victorious. It is also more patient. Grace waits longer inside the Sacraments, than out of them. They seem to detain it, to hold heaven down upon earth with a sweet force, and so to multiply the occasions and prolong the opportunities of men.

The character, which some of the Sacraments confer, also belongs to their grace. It is a revelation to us of the divine impetuosity and energy of the Sacraments. Amid the ardors of heaven, and in the dazzling splendors of the Beatific Vision, the mystic signets, the inexplicable characters of the Sacraments, three in number, as if adumbrating the Three Divine Persons, shine forth as distinct beauties, and brighten through eternity. The character of Baptism is as it were the finger-mark of the Eternal Father on the soul. The character of Order glistens like the unfailing unction of the priesthood of the Eternal Son. The character of Confirmation is the deep mark, which the fires of the Holy Ghost burned in, the pressure of his tremendous fortitude, which was laid upon us, and yet we perished not, so tenderly and so gently did he touch us. In the wild fury of the tempestuous fires of hell the same characters glow terribly. They are indestructible even there, fiery shames, intolerable disgraces, distinct fountains of special agony forever and forever.

To these reflections on the grace of the Sacraments we must not fail to add a due consideration of the doctrine of intention. What things can be more purely divine than these Sacraments? Yet see how sensible they are to human touch! It is as if the very delicacy of their divine fabric made them more liable to human impressions. They are jealous of their powers. They do not need our active co-operation, so much as our permission. They require obstacles to be removed, but not assistance to be conferred. They work, as we say in theology, by the force of their own work, not by the energy of the recipient. This is their peculiarity. It is this which distinguishes them from other means of grace. They have reason to be jealous of so magnificent a distinction. Yet, in spite of all this, they are so sensitive to the touch of our fervor, that they unlock fresh and fresh graces according as we press them, as if in their love and their likeness to God they were delighted to be pressed, to be solicited, and to be importuned. They are also so delicate and so susceptible that they are at the mercy of our intentions. The very thought of this makes us tremble. We could almost wish it were not so. To be so fragile, while they are so exceedingly strong, is not this a surprise and a perplexity, not seldom too a sorrow and a dread? It seems to show that they are purely things of heaven, exotics upon earth, or weapons of omnipotence becoming brittle when they are plunged suddenly among human actions. Baptism can justify the child whose reason has not dawned. Extreme Unction can deal with the relics of sin in a sinner who lies insensible. Such independent power have these masterful Sacraments. Yet are they in bondage to our intention. They must be human acts, if they are to be divine ones also. They are not mere charms, or spells, or sleight of hand. They have magic about them, but it is only that magic of incredible love in which God has clothed them with such resplendent beauty. Nothing, as I think, demonstrates the divinity of the Sacraments more evidently than this exquiste sensitiveness to human touch.

Now look out upon the great laboring world, the world of human actions and endurances. It is not possible to measure the influence which is being exercised upon the world at this moment by the Sacraments. They are penetrating the great mass of mankind like the network of veins and arteries in a living body. They are being the causes of millions of actions, and they are hindering the consequences of millions of other actions. They are weaving good, and unweaving evil, incessantly. The roots of

great events, which grow up and tower in history, are perhaps
fixed in some secret Sacrament or other. The silent and orderly
revolutions of the Church are often moulded in them. Society
would hardly credit to what an extent it is held together by them.
The influence of a single reception of a Sacrament may be handed
down for generations; and the making of the destinies of thousands may be in its hands. At this instant by far the greatest
amount of earth's intercourse with heaven is carried on, directly
or indirectly, through the Sacraments. There is a vast wild world
of sorrow upon earth. But over great regions of it the Sacraments
are distilling dews of heavenly peace. In the underground scenery
of hidden hearts they are at work, turning wells of bitterness into
springs of freshness and of life. They are drying the widow's tears,
raising up unexpected benefactors for the orphan, nerving the
pusillanimous, softening the desperate, rousing the torpid, crowning those who strive, and doing all things for those who die. As the
animals came trooping to Adam to be named, so mortal sorrows
are coming in herds at all hours to the Sacraments to receive the
blessing of the second Adam. Somewhere or other at this moment
a Communion may be giving a vocation to some youthful apostle
who in after-years shall carry the Gospel to populous tribes in the
Asian uplands, or throughout the newly-opened river-system of
neglected Africa. Crowds in heaven shall owe their endless bliss
to that one Communion.

But the world of human joys is not much less vast than the
world of human sorrows; and the Sacraments are there also, puri-
fying, elevating, sanctifying, multiplying, supernaturalizing multitudes of these blameless delights. Yet there is a difference between
their action upon sorrows and their action upon joys. They make
no sorrows. They cause no mourning. They create no darkness.
Whereas they are forever creating gladnesses. Splendors flash from
them as they move, and their splendors are all jubilees. They are
fountains of happiness to all the earth. They cover even the monotonous sands of life with verdure, and make the desert bloom,
and crown the hard rocks with flowers, and beautify with their
softness the sternest solitudes. Who can tell what songs of human

goodness are being sung this hour in the ear of God, because of the joyous inspirations of the Sacraments? Of a truth human joy is a beautiful thing, a very worship of the Creator. Out of himself there is no beauty like it, unless it be the jubilee of angels. But the joys which the Sacraments have sanctified, and, still more, the joys which the Sacraments have gendered, who can tell how sweet they are to the complacency of our heavenly Father?

It is to be thought of, also, how the Sacraments embrace and compass human life in their mysterious number seven. Man's life is a pathetic thing. There is no dulness in any biography of earth. Each life has many turns. Within the soul common vicissitudes are not without romance. Supernatural things greatly increase the romance of life. Even calmness and uniformity are like sunset skies, full of noiseless plays of light, and scarce perceptible shiftings of gold-red clouds, which change the splendor we know not how. Yet is there in all human lives a like recurrence of like vicissitudes. It is this which blends them into one, although they are so various. It is like the burden of the song, which chimes in with equal fitness whether the verse be one of gladness or of sorrow. The things that are common to all men are more touching than those which happen only to some. They are fountains of deeper feeling. They are more touching because they are more natural. They are diviner visitations, because they are more general. It is these things upon which the Sacraments fasten with their instincts of love. The times, the vocations, the states, the crises of human life, these are all clasped together by the sevenfold band of Sacraments. If we think of all these things, we shall own that it is no exaggeration to say that their mere existence makes all creation different from what it would have been without them.

But who can speak worthily of the Sacraments? The Eucharist gives us a measure of their grandeur; and is it not an immeasurable measure? Would that men would study more the science of the Sacraments! Devotion would be greatly increased thereby. The peculiar hatred, with which the author of heresy pursues what may be called the sacramental principle in our holy faith, is a token to us of the stress which we ourselves ought to lay upon it. Hardly anywhere is theology more deep than in the matter of the Sacraments. They give us more intimate glimpses of God than almost any thing else, and especially of the ways of God, those ways by which we seem to know him, to recognize him, and to realize him. We should know much less of the capabilities of human actions, their limit and their reach, the point at which grace is grafted on them, and their comportment under the pressure of divine things, if it were not for our knowledge of the Sacraments. That human actions can be the matter of a Sacrament is surely a truth full of philosophical import as well as of theological significance. The union of freedom with sustaining and impelling grace—where is it so marvellously illustrated as in a Sacrament?

Moreover, a devotion to the Sacraments is very needful for the times in which we live. The spirit of the age must necessarily affect both our theology and our asceticism. Under its depressing constraints we shall be tempted to sacrifice the supernatural to the natural, the passive to the active, and the infused to the acquired. Theology will be allured to merge into metaphysics. Devotion will be considered a vocation, priests a caste, and theology a private professional training. The substance of the old Condemned Propositions about spiritual direction will be adroitly renewed. Men will sneer at perfection in the world. Education will be bidden to throw off what it will be taught to consider the last relics of its monastic trammels. Men will chafe at the condemnation of books, and indeed at all acts of *intellectual* authority on the part of the Church. The study of dogmatics will be discouraged. The whole theory of Condemned Propositions will be disliked. A discontent with the existing Church, or at least a want of cordial forward sympathy with it, will grow up, while the wickedness of "the respectful silence" of Jansenism will be renewed. The sovereignty of the Church, the pope's temporal power, and the hallowed truths enshrined in canon law, will provoke impatience as obstinate things which will not die although their hour of death has come. The mystical side of the

Gospel will become more distasteful while it grows less intelligible. Heroism will have to rank lower than the ordinary attainments of conscientious piety. The privileges of the Church will be less esteemed, and heresy less hated. The Sacraments will count almost for nothing in a man's system. The influence of the Incarnation will be far less recognized and acknowledged in the world; and a modern mixture of Judaism and Pelagianism will take possession of many minds, to the grievous disadvantage of Christian perfection. Such is the spirit which will try to waylay souls on their road to Calvary or to Thabor. Such was not the temper or genius of the saints. Such, by the blessing of God, will not be ours, if we foster in ourselves a deep, a tender, and an intelligent devotion to the Sacraments. I repeat, as I said before, that, in an ascetical point of view, I hardly know any thing upon which I should lay greater stress in these days, than a fervent devotion to the Sacraments.

Now, these Sacraments are simply the machinery of the Precious Blood. They are the means by which it first conquers, and then keeps what it has conquered. They are, under ordinary circumstances, the conduits by which it is conveyed to the souls for whom it was shed. They are God's system for dispensing it. We should have not only an inadequate but an absolutely wrong notion of the empire of the Precious Blood, if we did not see it as working and circulating through the Sacraments. They are the grand features of its empire. They are its method of government, which expresses its character and suits its disposition. It is the Sacraments which hinder it from being a past historical expiation for sin. By them it is always truly flowing in the Church. Nay, by them it is forever being shed afresh within the Church. Possibly, there might have been Sacraments even if man had needed no redemption. But it seems as if there would hardly have been Sacraments if there had been no Incarnation. The Sacraments, while they express a most wonderful part of the Divine Mind, seem also to imply the Precious Blood. They might have carried the glorious life of the Incarnate Word into the lives of his fellowmen in mysterious comminglings and engraftings, even if there had been no fall. But, if there had been no Precious Blood, we cannot conceive of the Sacraments. The nuptials of matter and spirit might have been celebrated in other ways, yet not in these particular ways which now make up our idea of Sacraments. Anyhow, according to the economy of redemption, the Sacraments form the system by which the Precious Blood traverses the whole Church, gifts it with unity, and informs it with supernatural energy and life. We cannot, even in thought, disjoin the Sacraments from the Precious Blood, or the Precious Blood from the Sacraments, without changing in our minds the order and establishment of God.

But we have not spoken sufficiently of the vastness of the empire of the Precious Blood. Let us look for a moment at its extremes. On the one hand, it includes the first-fruits of creation, and on the other hand, the refuse of creation. The first-fruits of creation are those flowers whom our Lord gathers in the pure fragrance of their first blooming. They are the souls of infants, in whom as yet reason has not dawned, but whom the water of Baptism, our Saviour's Precious Blood, has justified and crowned. These are the successors of the Holy Innocents, those first Christians who, baptized in blood, went to adorn with their infancy the Church Triumphant, first in Abraham's Bosom, and then in the heaven of heavens—the first martyrs, whose blood was at once the prophecy and the prey of the Precious Blood of Jesus, which had already preluded its shedding in the mystery of the Circumcision. Those, who form the refuse of creation, are they whom God has cast off forever. They lie in outer darkness. Their exile is eternal. Yet even there we find the energy of the Precious Blood. Inconceivable as are the severities of hell, they are less than rigorous justice would exact. They are so, precisely because of the Precious Blood. Before the days of Peter Lombard the generality of theologians held that, as time went on, there were some mitigations of the fierce punishments of hell. They sank after a while to a lower level. There were expiations which were only temporal and not eternal. There were condonations within certain limits. Peter Lombard, as St. Thomas himself says, innovated upon this teaching, and St. Thomas followed in his steps. In recent times Emery of St. Sulpice revived the older traditions, but without making much impression upon the schools. Suffice it to say that, if, independent of all hell being below the rigor of justice because of the Precious Blood, there were any such mitigations as the elder theologians believed, they also came without a doubt from the empire of the Precious Blood. To it alone can they be due, if they exist at all.

There are saints in heaven. They are the heights of the Church of Christ. There are newly-converted sinners upon earth. These are the lowest depths in the happy land of redeeming grace. But the light upon those mountain-tops is the glory of the Precious Blood, and the sunshine in those valleys is the kindness of the selfsame Blood. There are sufferers in purgatory, dwelling in a mysterious region of pain and quietude, of patience and of love. They live beneath the earth, yet are upon their road to heaven. Their land is vast and populous. It is a territory won from hell by the Precious Blood, and its pain made uneternal. It is a detention, not an exile—a detention which is a marvellous artifice of mercy, one of the many compassionate devices of the Precious Blood. There are sufferings on earth, sufferings by which hearts are cleansed, sins swiftly expiated, merits rapidly accumulated: sufferings in which grace comes, sufferings which are likenesses of Jesus, sufferings which are secret loves of God. These earthly sufferings also the Precious Blood alleviates, illuminates, sanctifies, crowns, glorifies, and knows how to render so delectable that they who have drunk deep of the Precious Blood get a strange new nature, and thirst for more suffering still. Thus both these extremities of suffering, beneath the earth and on it, belong to the empire of the Precious Blood. If we look outside ourselves, we see everywhere the empire of the Precious Blood stretching away in interminable vista. The whole Church is its legitimate inheritance. Her jurisdiction is the law and order of the Precious Blood. The priesthood is its army of officials. The catholic hierarchy is its venerable administration. The lofty tiara, that most sovereign thing on earth, gleams with it like the polar star of nations. The Blessed Sacrament, multiplied a hundred thousand times, is its own adorable self, its Heart-fountain, and its Five Free Wells, worshipful in its union with the Godhead, the beautiful amazing Created Life of the Uncreated Word. If we look within ourselves, there is still the self-same empire of the Precious Blood. There is the character of Baptism, its still inexhausted grace, its titles unforfeited or re-conferred, its infused habits, its heroic Spirit-gifts. There are the footprints of so many Absolutions, the abiding fragrance of such reiterated Communions, perhaps the character of Order and its fearful powers, perhaps the mysterious traces of Extreme Unction, certainly the signet of the Holy Ghost in Confirmation, and nameless graces, nameless vestiges where Divine Feet have gone, and where Divine Virtue still resides. There also is that most innermost sanctuary of the soul, which so few reach on this side of the grave, the secret cabinet where the Holy Trinity dwells blessedly, in the very centre of our nature, up from whose secret recesses joys shall one day break and flow, such as we never dreamed of, such as would look to us now far beyond the possibilities of our nature. All this, outside us or within us, is the empire of the Precious Blood.

But it is only in heaven that its supremacy is tranquil and complete. We must mount thither in spirit, where we hope one day to mount in all the jubilee of an incredible reality, if we would see in its full grandeur the royalty of the Precious Blood. Countless saints are there, various in the splendors of their holiness. They are all kings now, who once were serfs, but were redeemed by the Precious Blood. They are the children of many generations, the natives of many lands. They were of all degrees on earth, and in their fortunes the diversity was endless. But they were all bought by the same Blood, and all own the lordship of that Blood in heaven. When they sing their songs of praise, songs of a human sweetness which the angels greatly love, they sing of the Lamb slain and of the triumphs of his Blood. When their potent intercessions win hourly graces for their clients who are still struggling upon earth, it is their desire to spread the empire of the Precious Blood, which throws such loyal intensity into their prayers. Shall they forget their Ransom, whose freedom is their endless joy?

Cast your eye over that outspread ocean, whose shores lie so faintly and far off in the almost infinite distance. It gleams like restless silver, quivering with one life and yet such multitudinous life. It flashes in the light with intolerable magnificence. Its unity is numberless. Its life is purest light. Into the bosom of its vastness the glory of God shines down, and the universe is illuminated with its refulgence. It is an ocean of life. Who can count the sum of being that is there? Who but God can fathom its unsearchable caverns? What created eye but is dazzled with the blazing splendor of its capacious surface? It breaks upon its shores in mighty waves; and yet there is no sound. Grand storms of voiceless praise hang over it forever, storms of ecstatic lightning without any roll of thunder, whose very silence thrills the souls of the human saints, and is one of their celestial joys—that deep stillness of unsounding worship. This is the world of angels. There too the Precious Blood reigns supreme. The angels have needed no ransom. Amid their almost countless graces there is no redeeming grace. But there is not a grace in all that sea of grace which was not merited for them by the Precious Blood. They too owe all they are, and all they have, to its blissful royalty. They too sing anthems in its praise, though not the same anthems as the Redeemed. Jesus is Head of angels as well as men; and it is as Man that he is Head of angels. Thus the whole of that marvellous world of glorious intelligence, profound gladness, gigantic power, and beautiful holiness, is a province of the empire of the Precious Blood.

Who can doubt its sweet constraints over the immaculate heart of Mary? She is queen of heaven and earth. Far and wide her empire stretches. Its boundaries are scarce distinguishable from those of the Precious Blood itself: so closely and so peacefully do the two sovereignties intertwine. Mary holds sway over the Precious Blood. It does her bidding, and she commands with a mother's right. Yet she too is a subject of the Precious Blood, and rejoices in her subjection. Out of her very heart that Blood first came; and out of that Blood came also her

Immaculate Conception. It was the very office of her Divine Maternity to minister that Blood; and it was that Blood which from all eternity had merited for her the Divine Maternity. It was the Precious Blood which made her suffer; but it was the Precious Blood also which turned her suffering into dignities and crowns. She owes all to the Precious Blood, to whom the Precious Blood owes its very self. Yet the river is greater than its fountain. The Precious Blood is greater than Mary; nay, it is greater by a whole infinity, because the waters of the Godhead have assumed its uncommingled stream unto themselves. Mary sits upon her throne to magnify the Precious Blood. Her power is used for the propagation of its empire. Her prayers dispense its grace. Her holiness, which enchants all heaven, is the monument and trophy of that victorious Blood.

Shall it rule also over the Divine Perfections? Behold that inexorable justice, which an infinite holiness stands by as assessor! Can endless worlds of mere creatures satisfy those claims, or appease that adorable wrath? Yet the Precious Blood has done it. A mercy that is limitless, and a justice that is insatiable—will not sin set these attributes at strife? Who shall be peace-maker in such unspeakable debate? The Precious Blood! Justice and mercy have met together, and have kissed each other in the Precious Blood. How shall the decrees of the Creator comport with the continued liberty of the fallen creature? The Precious Blood, heavenliest of inventions! has found out a way. The unchangeableness of God shall condescend to wait upon the mutabilities of the fickle creature, and yet its own repose be all the more glorified the while; for this too shall be one of the secrets of the Precious Blood. If greater good comes out of evil, it is through the alchemy of the Precious Blood. If all the Divine Perfections combine in some resplendent work of the Most Holy Trinity, whether it be Creation, Redemption, or the Blessed Sacrament, it is the Precious Blood in which the combination has been made, and which the attributes of God delight to magnify, while it with its adoring ministries is magnifying them. If any of the Divine Perfections will come down from heaven, and walk amidst the nations of men, and give light and scatter peace and healing as it goes, it first puts on the vesture of the Precious Blood, in order that it may not slay but make alive. Justice is occupied in crowning saints. Mercy is forever traversing its empire as if in pure delight at its immensity. Holiness is adorning its infinite purity with the little sanctities of feeble and imperfect souls. Immutability is hourly adapting itself to the changeful needs of innumerable hearts. Omnipotence is putting itself at the disposal of created weakness, as if it were some generous beast of burden serving a master whom it could so easily destroy. Eternity is busy commuting time into itself. Love changes its eternal name, and only calls itself by the name of the Precious Blood. All these marvels belong to the empire of the Blood of Jesus. The peace of God is all activity to do the work of that dear Blood. The self-sufficiency of God is toiling as if nothing could suffice it, except the salvation of its creatures. All this is the sovereignty of the Precious Blood. Nay, the dread sovereignty of the Everlasting King seems to be forever passing into the created Kingship of the Precious Blood.

Inside the Unity of God, within the life of the Threefold Majesty, even there we find the tokens of the Precious Blood; even there it seems to rule. The Son, who has assumed it, owns the gladness of its love. The Holy Ghost, who fashioned it at first, and now works with it his sanctifying work, broods dovelike with complacency upon its deeps. The Eternal Father chose it as the one thing to appease him; for he too owns the mastery of its exceeding beauty. It seems, if with becoming reverence we may say so, to have widened his Fatherhood. It has added fresh treasures to those inexhaustible treasures which he had in his Eternal Son. But these are thoughts for silence rather than for words. May his infinite Majesty pardon the freedoms which the ignorance of our love has been taking with his perfections! It is of his own goodness that we cannot help loving, even while we tremble.

There is one corner of creation, where the empire of the Precious Blood is not what we would have it be. It is our own hearts. Yet is it not our one work to subject ourselves to it in all things? We desire to have no instincts, but the instincts of the Precious Blood. We wish to esteem nothing, but as the Precious Blood esteems it. It desires nothing so much as to be loved. We desire nothing so much as to love it. Why then is it that our weakness and our want of courage so sadly keep our grace in check? Alas! we are inverting the right order of things. We are ruling the Precious Blood by limiting its empire. It longs to rule over us; it longs with a masterful sweetness. The day shall come, when its longing shall be satisfied. Neither shall it be a distant day. For we will begin this very day to love and serve our dearest Lord as we have never loved and served him heretofore. Always and in all things shall his Blood rule and guide us. Its rule is blessedness even upon earth. It shall rule, not our spiritual life only, but all our temporal circumstances. It shall rule our love of those we love, and it shall make our love of them a doing to them spiritual good. How shall we die unless at that moment the Precious Blood is reigning in our hearts? If it rules us not then, we are lost forever. But how shall we better secure its empire at our deaths, than by establishing it over our lives? The past will not do. Jesus must be more victorious in our souls, more a conqueror, and more a king. Oh that the Precious Blood might so work in our hearts that life should seem to have only one possible gladness, the gladness of having Jesus to reign over us as King! Oh Grace! Grace! would that we were altogether conquered! But we will be of good cheer; for the time is coming when we shall be completely and eternally vanquished by victorious love.

CHAPTER IV

THE HISTORY OF THE PRECIOUS BLOOD

CHAPTER IV

THE HISTORY OF THE PRECIOUS BLOOD

WHY is it so hard to be at peace in life? Why do little things, and such very little things, trouble us? We came forth from God, who is the Father of peace: why then are we so restless? We are but winging our flight over this narrow gulf of time, and the great eternity is already in sight: why are we so full of volatile distractions? Ever in our flight God still holds us in his Hand: why then do we flutter so? It is strange we cannot lie still even in the Hand of God. It is because our minds are at once so active and so wandering. They need continual occupation. They require to be fed incessantly with images, which they consume rapidly, and are insatiable. It is this which makes a contemplative life so difficult. It is this need of images. Our minds are restless if they do not see a thousand varying objects before them in constant motion, with light and color upon them. They are fatigued with stillness. They pine when they are kept to one thought, to one object. They sicken even of one range of thought, one class of objects. The weary sea with its monotonous clash of waves is not more restless or more mobile than our minds. Here is the grand difficulty of prayer, the fixing of our minds on the object of our worship. Most of the things which are hard in the spiritual life, are hard because of the unity, the simplicity, the concentration of mind, which they require or imply. The chief power of the world over us arises from our having given it possession of our minds. It would be a much less difficult task to dislodge it from our hearts, if we could only once expel its images from our minds.

Satan's power over the heart comes from his power over the mind. Here then is the universal work of everybody's spiritual life, either the getting rid of images or the changing of them.

Now, the first of these processes is a very difficult one, and belongs to a high region of the spiritual state, with which we have nothing whatever to do just now. The second, the changing of our images, is more within our reach. In fact, we must absolutely reach it, if we are to be devout at all. Our hearts will be what our minds are. If our minds are full of images of the world, we shall never be weaned from the world. If they are full of images of self, we shall never conquer our self-love. If our minds will never rest, unless endless processions are forever winding their way across them, then let us have our processions religious; let our images be of God, of Jesus, of Mary, and of heavenly things. I do not say this is altogether easy to do; but it is comparatively easy; and moreover it must be done. Let me refer to childish things for our example. When sleep was coy and would not visit us, when the pains, or the sorrows, or the excitements of childhood banished slumber from our eyes, they used to tell us, at least among the hills of the north, to make a picture in our minds, and to count the very white sheep as they passed across the very green slope of the mountainside: and so of a truth sleep was often won; and the opiate at least was innocent. In later years, when the sense of pain was keeping the mind awake, sleep has been wooed after a somewhat similar fashion. We filled our minds with images; only, books and travels made them of a more ambitious and complicated sort. We bent our minds on placid objects such as we knew to be somewhere on earth that night. We looked down the golden green vistas of tropical forests, or on the calm shores of very solitary shining seas, or on the perfumed shrubby tangles of islets in the ocean, or on some dusky glen which a cataract fills with silence by deadening all other sounds except its own: and so also sleep has come. It were better to have thought of God, and so have rested. Still we may learn a lesson from our success. It is even so with the restlessness and perturbation of our minds in the spiritual life. If we will shut our eyes to the world, and make pictures of heavenly things, and watch the Thirty-Three Years of Jesus, or the Mysteries of Mary, or the flights of angels, or the panoramas of the Four Last Things, or the figurative pageants of the Divine Perfections, pass studiously before our inward sight, then that sweet, facile, rapid, undistracted prayer, which is the soul's sleep, the soul's renewal of its vigor, will soon come to us. An oblivion of the world, less and less disturbed by dreams, will steal over us, and we shall taste the gift of peace.

This is not the highest of spiritual ways; I know it well. Yet is the highest one fittest for you and me? Are we yet in such a state that we should strive to banish all images from our minds, and think only of the indistinct and formless majesty of God? We know not what God may do with us in time. One thing, by his help, we have resolved upon. It is that we will not stand still, neither will we be contented with any grace, with any degree of love. All life long we will advance. Daily will we climb higher. Constantly will we trim the fires of our love, and make them burn more ardently. We know not, therefore, what God may do with us in times to come. But for the present we must endeavor to cast one set of images out of our minds by introducing another set. So shall we fill our minds with God continually, and be delivered from the burden of self and from the thraldom of the world.

Our present task, then, is to marshal a Procession of the Precious Blood, with all its various yet kindred images, through our minds. It shall be to us like the defiling of soldiers over the mountain-passes. The bravery of war shall add to the beauty of the scenery, and the scenery shall set off the bravery of war. Far off we shall see the glittering pomp, and then again so near that the martial music shall strike upon our ears. Here the light shall fall upon it in all its beautiful array, and there the clouds shall obscure its path, and the crags appear to swallow up the pageant. Much we may see which we cannot understand; but much also which we can both understand and love. From first to last it all tells of Jesus. From first to last it is a thing of God. Nay, we must not be strange to it ourselves. We too must fall in with the Procession. We must climb with it, as part of its life, its beauty, and its music, until we are lost to sight among the cloud-covered mountains of eternity. Our soul longs for rest. It would fain seek some peaceful solitude, where the sights and sounds of the world cannot intrude. It yearns to repose itself on God in the vigilant sleep of prayer. How shall it attain its end? We read in the Book of Esther that, when King Assuerus could not sleep, "he commanded the histories and chronicles of former times to be brought him," and they read them before him. So may we have the history and chronicle of the Precious Blood brought to us. It will make music in our ears, like the reading of a famous ancestry to the high-born and the royal. It will be a picture before our eyes, like a procession emerging out of that first dark eternity of God, winding over the picturesque inequalities of time, and re-entering the second illuminated eternity of God, up which we see in a vista of confused gorgeousness, as those who look through the doorway of some vast cathedral, and behold the banners waving, and the masses of gold and color all tinted with the hues of the painted windows, moving slowly in indistinct progress to the distant starry altar. If with this pageant we can fill our minds, for a time at least the hold of the world upon us will be loosened. The things of God will interest our hearts, and many acts of divine love will flow from us, as from a fountain. Let us then turn aside from the images of earth, and rest a while, and watch this venerable Procession.

To what shall we dare to liken the Mind of God? With what shapes of allegory shall we venture to clothe that infinite eternal object, which is the fountain of all our destinies? To us it looks like some tremendous chain of mountains, whose sublimities are inaccessible, whose heights are hidden always in the darkness, whose shapes are not the shapes of earthly scenery, whose sound and silence are alike terrible, and yet whose sides are always clad in the beautiful repose of radiant light. But it is a chain of mountains which has only one side, one descent. None has ever climbed those heights, nor ever shall. But we know that, if they were surmounted, there would be no descent upon the other side.

A vast tableland stretches interminably there into the boundless distance, an unbeginning, uncreated land, of which faith alone, itself a supernatural virtue, can report; and it reports only, together with some few facts, the unchanging peace of awful sanctity which is the life and joy of God. That is the land of the Divine Decrees. There is the cradle of Eternal Purposes, which were never younger than they are today, and needed no cradle, because they had neither beginning, growth, nor change. In the trackless distances of that nameless upland have we ourselves been hidden from all eternity: so that, in some sense, our nothingness is clothed in the robes of God's eternity. In those untravelled, unimaginable plains, the Divine Perfections have been tranquilly occupied with us in unbeginning love, an unbeginning love which does the work of everlasting justice. In those fastnesses, round which a glory of impenetrable darkness hangs, lie the living mysteries of Predestination, of the Divine Permissions, and of that unnamed perfection out of which the gift of Freedom to creatures came. It is a land before whose misty regions we bend our knees in breathless adoration, in prayer which ventures not to clothe itself with words. A sacred horror fills our souls as we think of the irresponsible power which reigns there, of the mightiness and the celerity of that all-absorbing will, of the resistless march of that all-devouring glory, of the unfathomable abysses of that incomprehensible secrecy, of the unswerving exactions of that appalling sanctity, and of that amazing plenitude of life, to which no creations have been able to add, and which no incarnations could intensify. If the mysteries which we know to lie there undivulged are so tremendous, what may we not conceive of other grander mysteries which are simply unimagined? Yet one thing we know of that pathless world of the Mind of God, pathless because neither reason of man nor intelligence of angel has ever wandered there, pathless because God himself traverses it not by any process of remembrance or discourse but always possesses it in simple act—one thing we know of it, and cling to: it is, that everywhere its vastest solitudes, its farthest-withdrawn recesses, are all resplendent with the most tender justice, and are all beautified by the omnipotence of love. Nothing is small to a God so great. It is this thought which renders so vast a majesty, not tolerable only, but so sweetly intimate and so intensely dear.

Over then those fertile deserts, fruitful though nothing grows there, unpeopled but where all is life, coming out of the interminable dark distances, we behold the Procession of the Precious Blood emerging. We could not see its starting-point, if it had had one. But it never had. In the Mind of God it was an unbeginning Procession of created things. It went forth from his power, and it returns into his love. The Precious Blood is the crowned king of all his decrees. All other creation sprang from it in prolific, multitudinous diversity, and it is forever fetching creation back to the Creator. We see it only as it were through dazzling mists. Yet it seems to come with banners flying, whereon the names of the Divine Perfections are emblazoned. The Divine Decrees hover above it like glorious clouds, which are dark from their exceeding luminousness. All the Types of created things appear to follow in its train. Onward it comes, so like an uncreated splendor, that it is hard to think it a created thing. We kneel to worship, because faith, like a herald, proclaims it as it comes, as the Created Life of an Uncreated Person. Ages of epochs hang like shapeless mists about the long Procession, as if there were even in eternity some divisions which would seem to us like time, or as if eternity were thus striving to make its length and its endurance visible to mortal eyes. The whole of that illimitable country is somehow covered with the Precious Blood. It is like the spirit of the place, or at least the atmosphere which hinders its being mere darkness to our view. The light is colored by it. The darkness is thickened by it. The silence makes it felt; and, if there be any sound, it is the sound of that Blood lapsing in its channels.

Now it has reached the edge of that boundless upland. Now it stands revealed upon the heights, which face down upon creation. It passes from the region of bright bewildering mists, mists which bewilder the more because they are so bright; and it emerges into light amidst created things. Or rather, to speak more truly, it comes, the Procession of Divine Decrees, the pageant of the Precious Blood, to that invisible, imperceptible point in eternity, when time should fittingly begin. At once a whole universe of fairest light broke forth, as if beneath the tread of those Decrees, as if at the touch of that Precious Blood. It was but an instantaneous flash, the first visibility of the invisible God; and there lay outspread the broad world of angels, throbbing with light, and teeming with innumerous and yet colossal life. The brightness that silvered them was the reflection of the Precious Blood. From it and because of it they came. Out of it they drew their marvellous diversity of graces. Their sanctities were but mantles made of its royal texture. They beautified their natures in its supernatural streams. It seemed as if here the Procession halted for a moment; or perhaps it was only that the sudden flash of light looked like a momentary halt. The new creatures of God, the first created minds, the primal offspring of the Uncreated Mind, were bidden to fall in, and accompany the great Procession. Oh, it was fearful—that first sight outside the immense serenity of God! Then truly, too truly, there was a halt, as if homage and obedience were refused. There is a gleam as of intolerable battle, and a coruscation of archangelic weapons, and Michael's war-cry, echoing, the first created cry, among the everlasting mountains. A third of that creation of purest light has refused to adore the Human Blood of the Incarnate Word, and is flung speedily into the dread abyss; and the ranks close in, and the unfallen light now beams more resplendently with its thinned array than ever it beamed before the fallen fell; and onward the Procession moves.

To our eyes it has a firmer footing when it comes among material things. It is a material thing itself. It has passed the world of angels, who are now following in its train. Suddenly, on its advance, or even before it has advanced at all, another universe springs up to life, the immense universe of matter. Perhaps there was hardly any gulf between this creation and that of spirit. But it was a new manifestation of the Divine Perfections. In some

respects it was more wonderful than the creation of spirit, because
its product was less like any thing in God. It was a wider thing
than spirit, and perhaps more various. It carried God further out
of himself. It was a longer reach of his perfections. It was a more
unexpected thing than spirit. Yet it was in some way older in the
decrees of God. It was the creation in which his predilections lay.
It was here that he had selected the created nature which he
would assume to himself. It should be a nature neither wholly
material or wholly spiritual, but which should bridge the interval
between the two. It was a creation also which should be more
under the dominion of time. It should be left to ripen through
long epochs for human habitation. Material life should be tried
in a gradually ascending scale. The laws of physical nature should
be allowed to operate for long successions of periods upon the
huge masses of matter. Moreover, God himself, by a series of
secondary creative acts, would set in order and adorn in a sequence of six divine days the matter, which in one instant, without succession, he had evoked from nothingness. Moreover,
alongside the secular mutations of matter, God would move in a
series of unresting creative acts. Age after age, every hour of
every day, would he call up from nothing beautiful souls to
tenant the new bodies perpetually budding forth and growing
upon the earth. So that this creation of matter was in all respects a very peculiar and notable creation, not to be thought
meanly of because of its manifold imperfections, but to be
deeply studied and reverently admired as the locality and material of the Incarnation. It was now to this point that the Precious Blood had come, to a world which was as it were its natural
home. The Types of created things, which had surrounded it
from the first, now suddenly as if at some divine command
spread themselves out in front. With lightning's speed they flew
in showers of golden fire into the vast realms of space created to
contain them. It was like a vast swarm of locusts gleaming, now
lonely, now in troops, in the distinct blackness of space. Orbs, and
pairs of orbs, and brotherhoods of orbs, and hosts of brotherhoods of orbs, sprung off exultingly on their immense careers. It

was a scene that looked to be one of wild terrific power, of ruin rather than of creation: only that on closer view there was such unstriving peace, such harmony among the unimpeded crowds of worlds, such a magnificent gentle self-confidence of order, that it was amazing to behold. Minerals and vegetables, solids and fluids, shone in families with hitherto uncovered types, which had come from the exhaustless beauty of the Maker. It was all so ponderous and yet all so light, so multiplied and yet so simple, so profuse yet so economical, so free and yet loving law so strangely, that we could never weary of admiring this spectacle of the material creation. It was created also expressly as the equipage of the Sacred Humanity. It was formed upon its model. It was in intimate relations with it. The Precious Blood was beneath the jurisdiction of its laws, even while it was advancing like a lawful king and like a heavenly conqueror. Verily the Divine Decrees are coming now in sight of their magnificent conclusion.

For a long while the road of our Procession has lain over lonely worlds, now in lifeless chaos, in heaps of mineral ruin or in fantastic crystal shapes, now clamorous with life which, to our eyes used to other types, seems portentous and uncouth, now through periods of glacial cold when life died out, and then again through epochs of streaming heat when life was almost strangled in the green density of colossal verdure. Order grows beneath the feet of the Procession, as if the earth were beautified by its advance: when, all at once, in a mountain-girdled garden of this uncentral planet there are seen amid the shades two startling shapes, shadows to the angels they would seem, shadows of Jesus and Mary whom those blessed spirits had been allowed to gaze upon in the Divine Decrees. Now from out eternity that beautiful patient pomp has reached so near to us, has reached the father and the mother from whom we ourselves are sprung. But why does it linger on the banks of Eden's fourfold river? Why does it not rather come on with quickened step, quickened by love to meet us, the children of centuries still far on, who are so yearning for its coming? Alas! there are mists covering the mountains. There are rude winds waving the boughs of Eden, and displacing its quiet foliage. The powers of evil, through mysterious permission, are breaking up out of their dark imprisonment. There is a stir among the angels. The faces of the Divine Decrees are clouded. The Procession has halted, not in confusion, yet abruptly. Man also has sought himself, and has used his liberty against the divine dominion. The beautiful paradise is overcast with shades. The rivers brawl more hoarsely in their beds. There are sounds of tempests among the mountains. The quiet beasts are seized with a panic which they do not comprehend. Yet there is no suddenness of God's glorious anger now, as with the angels. It is as if there were heavenly deliberations, as if mercy were pleading against justice, and staying the uplifted arm. Those two human faces, the likenesses of Jesus and of Mary, are sweet to the eye of God even in their fall. That look of human sorrow and of human penitence, why should it be so availing? Why should he pause to look at it, and as if to let it work upon him, when he dashed in pieces with so summary a wrath the surpassing beauty of those countless angels? It is the Precious Blood itself which seems to interfere. It glows with unusual light. The splendor of it appears to clothe the justice, and the mercy, and the sanctity of God with a glory which to our eyes makes those perfections softer, while it also makes them more resplendent. A kind of glorified sadness, yet also of well-pleased love, comes over all countenances in that Procession; and it looks even more divine. Now angels join the ranks, bearing new banners in their hands, emblazoned with mysterious symbols. They are the emblems of the Passion. The vision of the blissful Mother passes into the Queen of dolors; and the Incarnation forsakes the white brightness of Thabor for the unutterable gloom of Calvary. Yet the human sadness beautifies it all. That Precious Blood was human from the first; and now that those two human faces of Adam and of Eve have joined it, and have not only joined it but called forth new possibilities in its nature, there seem, if we may dare to say it, a more congruous loveliness, a more harmonious unity, in the wonderful Procession. But it turns away from the mountainous frontiers of Eden, and advances slowly over the expanses of the untilled earth.

Men built cities for themselves, because they had instincts of the heavenly city which was above; and Damascus was the first city which they built, the first Jerusalem of the Precious Blood. Then for four thousand years the ever-widening and ever-lengthening Procession wended on. They were four thousand years of those grand vicissitudes which form the traditions and religions of all the nations of the earth. There was a murder and a martyrdom just outside the gates of paradise. The first brother shed his brother's blood, and the hitherto unpolluted earth cried aloud to God. Yet, rightly considered, that elder brother was not the first to shed fraternal blood; Adam had already shed the Blood of his Elder Brother, who should also be his Son, in Eden itself: and now Abel, like another St. Stephen, was the martyr of the Precious Blood, and went to dwell, himself the first inhabitant, in the peaceful expectation of the limbus of the Fathers. They were wild scenes, amidst which the Procession had now to move. The glorious science of Adam faded from the minds of men. The patience of God seemed at last worn out, and the deluge came. But the Precious Blood, with its retinue of angels, was everywhere on the face of the angry waters. It was not only in the ark with the chosen eight. It was cleansing countless souls among the drowning. It was shriving them upon the high hilltops. It was uttering brief but victorious prayers out of their souls, as they sank like stones into the depths. That Flood was a stern mission. Yet the Precious Blood was a marvellous missionary, and a glorious harvest of souls was garnered, with Abel and the primeval saints, into the limbus of the Fathers. But the new earth grew colossal sins. It was like the time when the steaming soil had grown the gigantic ferns of the coal-beds. The cries of the hunters filled the glens, and the animals fell off from human-kind in terror and alarm. Had God's judgments only quickened the fertility of sin? Truly a singular portentousness of sin answered to a singular immensity of mercy. Multitudes banded together to build a high tower to reach to the low-seeming heavens; but their tongues were confounded, and they could no longer sing the same songs in the Procession. Still everywhere that Procession was reflected; for their religion and their worship were nothing but blood-shedding and prayer.

It would take too long to tell all the travels of the Precious Blood during those wistful ages, while it was at once a pilgrim and a warrior, an explorer and a king, a conqueror going up to take possession and a victim led forth to sacrifice and to be slain. We know of it by the tents of Abraham on the Chaldean plains. It was Isaac's evening meditation in his pastoral fields. Jacob dreamed of it in the dark nights upon the lonely wolds of Mesopotamia. Job sang of it wonderfully amid the ruddy cliffs of the Stony Arabia. Moses shed the glory of it over the gravelly desert and round the haunted sanctuaries of Sinai. It shone like moonlight over Palestine, and it was the dim but sufficient light of all the rest of earth. The time of sunshine was not come. It was a voice of minstrelsy in the heart of David, ravishing the world. It was the sun behind the clouds of prophecy, making them to glow with such a crimson glory. The temple of Jerusalem was its wellhead; but its tricklings reached to the newest-peopled island in the far Pacific. It had made the limbus of the Fathers populous with the accumulated generations of the saints. Angels cannot tire. Yet there was a look of weariness about the long Procession. It went slowly, was often silent, and was manifestly travel-stained. Sighs took the place of songs. Hearts made faces beautiful by the intensity of their desires. Yet on many countenances there was an air of doubt which mingled sadly with their wistfulness. Everywhere there were bands of brave Maccabees, whose hearts could be unmanned by no captivity. But the greater part of men marched on like slaves going toward the land of their foreign bondage, rather than pilgrims to their homes. Nevertheless, in the foresight of the shedding of that Blood, grace took possession of those four thousand years, and delighted itself in incessant victories, victories that were not confined to the chosen race of Israel.

But now a great and sudden change comes over the aspect of

our Procession. It is not so much a change in the retinue of the Precious Blood, as it was in the case of Adam and Eve: this time it is a marvellous change in the Precious Blood itself. It has prepared all things for itself in secret; but its preparations have been hidden mysteries. The souls of Joachim and Anne have been adorned with unusual graces. The yearnings of the saints in Israel have burned within them, until their hearts have hardly been able to endure the fire. The instincts of all the earth have grown uneasy, as if some unwonted thing were coming upon nature. In secret the Precious Blood has done a work which may vie with the great work on Calvary. It has effected the Immaculate Conception, wherein heaven was opened, and such abysses of grace poured out upon the earth, that the accumulated graces of the four thousand years of human history, and even the worlds of grace with which the angels were so munificently endowed, were as drops to the ocean compared with the grace of the Immaculate Conception. Beautiful as an unexpected sunrise seen suddenly as we turn out of the dark defiles of a mountain-pass, was the Nativity of Mary, as the Procession of the Precious Blood came all at once into its visible effulgence. Perhaps there is not among the divine mysteries one of such unblemished gladness, of such unmixed joy, as the Nativity of our Blessed Mother. It was like Bethlehem, without those grave foreshadowings of Calvary which give to Bethlehem such pathetic solemnity. The birth of Mary was like a mystery of the unfallen world. It was the sort of mystery unfallen worlds would have, and its feast the sort of feast unfallen souls would keep. Swiftly the Procession advances. The shapes, the figures, and the symbols of the pageant seem to furl themselves one by one, while the Precious Blood assumes the distinct features of an actual Human Life. It is more heavenly now, because it is more earthly. Its actual creation renders yet more visible those uncreated perfections out of which it sprang. It is more manifestly a glory to be worshipped, now that it can be seen in the Face of the Infant Jesus.

But who can tell the beauty of that Precious Blood, as it moved about the earth with slow human movement during the Three-

and-Thirty Years? Saints rapt in ecstasy may see, and haply may in part understand a spiritual loveliness, which they cannot express in words. Like other artists, their conceptions are mostly above the level of language. But to us the Thirty-Three Years are an indistinct wonder, distinct enough to fix us in admiration, and to make our hearts burn with love, but indistinct so far as understanding goes. There is something in our Lord's mysteries, which is akin to the Divine Perfections. They are best seen in indistinctness. An indistinct view seems to teach us more than a distinct one. We see more truthfully, if not more clearly, when our view is less defined. When our view is distinct, it is like a beautiful picture or a beautiful poem. It pleases and soothes; it elevates and chastens; it sobers and refines. It fills us full of sweet thoughts, noble sympathies, and heavenly imaginations. But it is not the repose of prayer. It is not the heat of the mystical life. It is not the swiftness of spiritual growth. It only unites us to God in a distant or a circuitous way. The saints perhaps may see these mysteries clearly, and yet at the same time with such a view as transforms their souls and unites them to God in the crowning grace of the divine espousals. To them, a spiritual beauty may be always a spiritual grace. Yet even to contemplatives there is for the most part more of heavenly and supernatural operation in an indistinct view of the Divine Perfections and of the Mysteries of Jesus, than in a distinct one. We only desire to know, in order that we may increase our love. To love is better than to know. Indeed, it is itself a higher knowledge.

Here, then, at the point of Bethlehem, the Procession of the Precious Blood comes out into a light too strong for us to see the details of its magnificence. It is too near to us to be seen except in detail, and its details are too bright to be distinct. Like all the works of God, it hides itself by coming close up to us. We must speak of it hereafter from a different point of view, rather as of a Life, than as of a Procession. Nevertheless it moved in fairest pomp along those Three-and-Thirty Years of visible, earthly, human life. Now and then it appeared upon the highways of the world and in the streets of cities; but for the most part it haunted sequestered retreats of its own, and it haunted them with mysterious delays. It bore its banners furled. No voice of song, but the low strains of the Mother's Magnificat, were heard in its encampments. A saint, whose very soul was part of the silence of heaven, alone guarded it for nearly all its appointed years. For thousands of years the world had looked for its manifestation; and now, behold! that manifestation was a concealment. Before it came, it was a palpable pageant of history. When it came, it melted, as a cloud melts in the sunshine, into the more substantial reality of a divine mystery. It hid itself in Mary; and we see it for an instant passing in unwonted haste over the uplands of Judea. We hear it in the tones of Mary's voice. We taste it in the sweetness of her chosen words. By the light of Joseph's lantern we catch a glimpse of it at midnight on the floor of a cave at Bethlehem, where shepherds gaze in silence, and Oriental kings are kneeling to adore, while the angels, who that night could not be so silent as their God, sing high up in heaven as if they feared lest their jubilee should wake the earth and divulge the secret of their King. In the courts of the great temple we see the humble pomp of its dear Candlemas, a sort of childish anticipation of its second triumph on Palm Sunday more than thrice ten years hereafter. It moves along the sandy depressions and stone-sprinkled troughs of the desert, not in a glorious caravan of merchants laden with the gold and jewels of India or with the drugs and gums of Araby, but in a timid pilgrimage with Joseph and with Mary. It hides amidst the bulrushes of the Egyptian river, as the cradle of the Hebrew lawgiver had hidden centuries ago. Once more it wound its way across the desert. Its pilgrimage was one of three now, whereas seven years before it seemed only to be of two, itself being nothing more than the alternate burden of the foster-father and the mother. The Boy can walk now, though the sands weary his Feet with their burning, and the pebbles bruise him with their hardness. But the thorns of the acacias and the prickles of the salt-plants pierce him, and his Feet leave a faint line of red behind them, which angels adore and recognize as the veritable Procession of the Precious Blood.

As if impelled by its kingly instincts, it drew near its own lawful palace in Jerusalem; and then, as if glad of an excuse to hide itself afresh, it turned aside through fear of a usurping king, and sank, like a bird whom the hawk has been pursuing, into that hidden bowl of mountain-meadows which men call Nazareth. Here it disappeared, like a river which has gone under ground. There was a long halt of three-and-twenty years. Occasionally, when the crowding of the feasts gave greater facilities for its disguise, it went over the steep paths to its sacred metropolis, and worshipped in the temple amidst the multitude. Once very notably it appeared there, five years after the return from Egypt; and its voice was heard in the Jewish schools; and its beauty looked out of boyish eyes into the hearts of old men and wise scholars and profound interpreters, and puzzled them with its loveliness, which needed a more spiritual interpreting than they could give. This was a moment in the Procession of the Precious Blood, of all moments the most difficult to understand; for it seemed to turn away from that fountain in Mary's heart, round which it had been flowing in rings which seemed to draw nearer at every circuit. But it had this time only fetched a wider circuit, that it might better turn, and flow straight back into its fountain, and live hidden there in indistinguishable distinctness for eighteen years of another childhood, which the strength of size and age only adorned with more tender ministries and only graced with a more beautiful docility. Even the appearances, the looks, the outward shows of divine mysteries are full of significance. In this staying behind at Jerusalem it *seems* as if the Eternal Father and the mortal Mother were beckoning the Procession of the Precious Blood different ways, and as if in the end the Creator had given way to his chosen creature. This is the look of that secret parting of the Boy of twelve at the gate of Jerusalem.

But now, as through some gateway on which the sun is brightly shining, or some triumphal arch hung round with braided flowers, the Procession of the Precious Blood issues out of the pastoral solitude of Nazareth at Cana of Galilee in the unexpected light of a marriage feast. It was as if the multiplying of the human family was a joy to its love of souls. With how exquisite a fittingness, and with how much disclosure of his own character, did our Lord make that first of his public mysteries a triumph to his Mother! We know not how to express the glory of that feast to her. The eternal counsels were anticipated at her word. The time, which in our Lord's mind had not come, came at his Mother's will; and the first refulgence of his miracles shone forth on her, and at her bidding. Through her he had entered on the earth: through her he entered on his Ministry. With her he went up Calvary: with her he mounted the Hill of the Ascension. All the mysteries of Jesus are glories of Mary. The Ministry is not less full of her fragrance than the Childhood or the Passion. As the Father's work was deferred for Mary when her Son was twelve, the same work was precipitated for her when he was thirty.

Through this portal, then, of Cana in Galilee, this Gate of Mary, as we may call it, the Precious Blood issued forth from its concealment. The low white houses gleamed with their flat roofs among the pomegranate-trees, and the broad-leaved figs, and the shrubby undergrowths, while the plain below was all waving with the billowy corn. The corn below, even if it bore a thousandfold, was but a poor figure of the harvest that Blood should gather now, that Blood which shone more ruby-like than the ripest pomegranate in Cana. A little water from the village well was turned into generous wine; but that Blood, which men will spill like water, shall be the wine of immortality to all the world. Now for three years the Procession of the Precious Blood moved to and fro within the precincts of the Holy Land. One while it was upon the hill-tops, which look down upon the lake, the lake of the Great Vocations, as we may fitly name it. Another while it was winding along the paths which clove the tall corn in the fields. The day saw it in the temple-courts; the moonlight disclosed it in the gray hollows of the stony mountains. It went to carry blessing to the houses of the poor; and it crossed the inland sea in the boats of fishermen. Yet it did not move at random. Its very journeys were a ritual. It was like the procession in the consecration of a church. Its movements have a meaning, and make up a whole. Whether it goes round the walls with the bunch of hyssop, or writes alphabets on the ash-strewn floor, or clusters in seeming confusion round the yet unconsecrated altar, there is a symbol and a law in every posture. So was it with the sinuous wanderings of the Precious Blood in Palestine. Like the course of the Israelites in the desert, it had a pattern to the eye of God, and betokened some hidden wisdom, which we are unable to decipher. It was beautiful beyond words, beautiful beyond our comprehension. It had no ornaments. Its figurative pageantry was gone. The words of life were its only music. It was now neither like a pilgrimage nor a march. There was nothing to which it could be compared. It was a Countenance which moved to and fro, intensely human because it was more than human, smiling, weeping, looking downcast, adoring, speaking, clad in wonderful anger, bound in placid sleep, pale, weary, meek, submissive, yet unspeakably commanding. All human expressions gathered there, save one; and that was the expression of surprise. Sometimes in his words there was what sounded like a tone of surprise, escaping plaintively from some wounded love within his Heart. But on the vastness of his mind nothing like surprise could dawn, nor any perplexity pass upon the serenity of his Face. To see that Face was a heaven to the pure and good; and when the heart came to fear too much, because the beauty of the Face was so reverend, its likeness to the Mother's face confused it sweetly with earthly things, and enabled the heart to respose on its divinity. Thus the Procession came to Olivet and Calvary.

Who can gaze steadily on the intolerable brightness of that Procession now, all flashing with a crimson light which blinds the eye of the beholder? As, when we gaze upon the sun, we seem to see it double, and the two orbs quiver in our wounded eyes with a vermilion haze, so is it with the Precious Blood amid the mysteries of the Passion. It appears double. There are two Processions instead of one. One is all shame, and suffering, and defeat. We might almost have said disorder; but there is something so venerable in its disgrace, something so imposing in the tranquillity of that Countenance, that there is order and self-mastery in its abasement. The other Procession is all triumph and exultation. Eager mercy hurries to and fro. Hidden counsels of the Eternal open their banners for the first time, and wave them joyously; and the jubilant silence of the angels is so intense that we might almost dream we heard it, as some strain of music in which the complainings of blameless envy mingled with the impassioned notes of self-forgetting victory. How dark the stains looked in the moonlight that silvered the olive-tops of lone Gethsemane! How the red rain spotted the pavements of Jerusalem, like those portentous showers of blood which pagan history records with fright! How red the streams looked upon the white Body, and then how black! and how the eclipse, which came on and hid it all, made the spectre of it burn with a fiery reality in our eyes, because we knew so certainly and so exactly what the darkness contained! At the foot of the Cross also the Blood itself looks double; for, if the Face of Jesus was like the face of Mary, now the tears of Mary are like the Blood of Jesus. They were tears of blood, and of the very blood which had been the fountain of the Precious Blood.

Then a change comes over our Procession. The Blood goes alone. It is no longer in the Sacred Heart as in its living tabernacle. It is no longer mantling in the Mary-like Face. It is apart and uncompanioned now, and by itself is absolutely adorable. The souls of men have got the Soul of Jesus to themselves beneath the earth, where it is brightening the caverns with the Beatific Vision. The love and piety of men have tended the Body, embalmed it, and laid it in the tomb. To whom shall the Blood belong? Even to those for whom only it was not shed in expiation, to those for whom only it was not a ransom, to the multitudes of the delighted angels! Who can tell their jubilee in that brief but sole possession of the ransom of mankind? They are sentinels over it, where it lay. On the hard stones of the street and on the stained plants of Calvary, on the accoutrements of the soldiers and on the garments of the great Mother, in the dry dust of Olivet and on all the instruments of the Passion, they kept watch and ward, and adored the Precious Blood. Mary saw them, and blessed them in their deed. Through the Friday night, and the Saturday, and till the Sunday dawned, they sang their voiceless songs in those low-lying crevices of earth, finding their heaven amid the dust of men's feet. Then they raised each drop with touch of reverent fear and tremulous abasement, and set it up as a grand thing of beauty and of worship, and went in unimaginable procession to the sepulchre. Who can tell how they marshalled that pomp upon the earth, nor how like it was to that simultaneous order of the Incarnation, of which theology teaches such marvellous things, nor how like it was to the Chalice which Jesus himself had consecrated, as it were an external Sacred Heart, on the Thursday night, nor how like it is now to the daily separation of the Blood in the Chalice of the Mass? Alongside of the Soul returned from limbus, and enjoying the same Divine Union as the Soul, the Precious Blood re-entered the Sacred Heart, filled with the sounds of life its silent halls, and poured the glorified beauty of an immortal human life over every sacred Limb, effacing all vestige of the Passion, save where it gathered itself up and burst forth into five roseate suns in the Hands and Feet and Heart, suns whose exuberant radiance is causing unsetting day this hour in the farthest extremities of heaven. But that separate procession, that exclusive keeping of the Precious Blood, is a glory and a pride of the angelic kingdom, which their songs will tell of to all eternity.

Green Nazareth was not a closer hiding-place than the risen glory of the Forty Days. As of old, the Precious Blood clung round the sinless Mother. Like a stream that will not leave its parent chain of mountains, but laves them incessantly with many an obstinate meandering, so did the Blood of Jesus, shed for all hearts of men, haunt the single heart of Mary. Fifteen times, or more, in those Forty Days, it came out from under the shadow of Mary's gladness and gleamed forth in beautiful apparitions. Each of them is a history in itself, and a mystery, and a revelation. Never did the Sacred Heart say or do such ravishing things as during those Forty Days of its Risen Life. The Precious Blood had almost grown more human from having been three days in the keeping of the angels. But, as it had mounted Calvary on Good Friday, so now it mounts Olivet on Ascension Thursday, and disappears into heaven amidst the whiteness of the silver clouds. It had been but a decree in heaven before, a divine idea, an eternal compassion, an inexplicable complacency of the life of God. It returns thither a Human Life, and is throned at the Right Hand of the Father forever in right of its inalienable union with the Person of the Word. There is no change in the Unchangeable. But in heaven there had never been change like this before, nor ever will be again. The changes of the Great Doom can be nothing compared to the exaltation of the Sacred Humanity of the Eternal Word. The very worship of the glorious spirits was changed, so changed that the angels themselves cannot say how it is that no change has passed on God. Somehow the look of change has enhanced the magnificence of the divine immutability, and has given a new gladness to their adoration of its unspeakable tranquillity.

For a moment nothing on earth is visible. The white light of the Ascension has dazzled our eyes. We see a confused splendor, and nothing more. It is but for a moment; and then, more wonderful than ever, the Procession lies outstretched before the vision of our minds. It is no longer single. It is not even double, as it was on Calvary. It is treble now. Girdled with amazing refulgence, it fills all heaven. Upon earth, breaking away beyond the confines of Palestine, it is visible in all nations of the globe, and crossing the broadest seas. Everywhere it is traversing the plains, scaling the mountains, and penetrating the sanctuaries of the wilderness. The Procession in repose above is like the Procession Blood. The Procession below is the omnipresence of its power, of the Thirty-Three Years. It is the actual life of the Precious the outstreaming of grace from its treasuries, faith's veritable application of the Precious Blood to the souls of men. This last is like the Procession of the four thousand years before the Incarnation, only that it has now sacramental realities of its own, and looks backward to the past, not, as that other Procession, forward to a future. The third Procession is not one, but manifold, and multiplied incessantly. Swifter than the sunbeam, from out the opened heavens the Precious Blood is flowing upon the altars of the Church. It is filling innumerable chalices at the same moment in the most distant places. The Sacred Heart, which is its natural tabernacle, is halting in countless tabernacles of human artifice, or is being borne about the fields and streets to the dying by the anointed servants of our Lord. This last Procession is not less actual than the one which is in heaven. It lives the same glorified life. It is but one life, and the same life. This is the threefold vision of the Precious Blood, which we see when the radiance of the Ascension has passed away. The one in heaven ministers in unknown mysteries to the Majesty of the Father. The one that moves over the earth is the minister of the Holy Spirit, who guides and rules the Church. The mingled activity and rest of the Blessed Sacrament is the human life of the Eternal Son himself, haunting the earth which he loved so dearly as to redeem it with his Blood. So the glory of the Holy Trinity satiates itself upon the Precious Blood.

The Upper Room of Pentecost is another Bethlehem. It is the birthplace of the Church. There is the same Mother as in the midnight cave. But, instead of Joseph, there are apostles. Instead of angels' songs in the quiet midnight, there is the rushing wind of the Eternal Spirit; and his fiery tongues, instead of the wintry brightness of the stars. From that Upper Room the Procession seems to start again. Not that the Precious Blood had left the earth, even at the Ascension. The whole of those ten days it lay, in real sacramental presence unconsumed, on Mary's immaculate heart as on a reposoir. But it is not our present purpose to dwell upon the analogies between Bethlehem and the Room of Pentecost. We must still follow our Procession. From the day of Pentecost we can see its course onward for ages. The scenery of history is more varied than even that of geography. It has its bleak mountains and its cultivated lands, its valleys and its plains, its forests and even its deserts, its cities and its solitudes, its beautiful maritime borders and its gray expanses of melancholy wold.

Across all this various scenery the Procession of the Precious Blood moves on, sometimes in single pomp, sometimes multiplied into many pomps, then again reuniting in one, or again sending forth a branch which shines for many a league and then disappears gradually or at once, as if the earth had drunk it up, as the sands drink the rivers of the desert. Still its course is plainly onward, from the east to the west; and its metropolis is changed, from Jerusalem to Rome. Its pageantry is more magnificent than ever. The choirs of angels still attend it; but its sacred vessels are borne by a resplendent human hierarchy, which is a copy of the hierarchies of heaven, and an emanation of the eternal priesthood of Jesus. At its head moves the never-dying Peter, the prince of the apostles and the vicar of his Lord, while by his side moves evermore the glorious St. Michael, the captain of the hosts of God and the famous zealot of his honor. So multiplied are the symbols and the blazonries of Mary, that we might sometimes take it for a procession of our Lady. But then again, from its more solemn pomp, and more austere observance, we perceive that it is in truth a Procession of the Blessed Sacrament. Above it all, in a glory of sweetest light, hovers the Eternal Dove, who has come to be to the Church what Jesus was to his disciples during the Three-and-Thirty Years. Beautiful Spirit! He has clothed the Procession with his beauty. He has shed over it the whiteness of his holiness. He, who fashioned the Sacred Humanity after his own model of Mary's loveliness, has imprinted the thousandfold expression of the likeness of Jesus upon the Church. So the Procession moves on, bearing on high the strange heaven-invented vessels of the Sacraments, and attended with this amazing equipage.

It fits all times. It harmonizes with all scenery. Its bravery does not flaunt the twilight of the catacombs, while it is in equal keeping with imperial courts. It illuminates ages which else were dark, and the eye rests reposefully upon its placid glories when false glitter all around at once deludes and fatigues the sight. With appropriate magnificence it adorns institutions venerable for their long antiquity, while with equal fitness it inaugurates the unprecedented novelties of daring epochs, as calmly as if it had been used to them for centuries. In the desert of the Thebais and amidst the temples of Athens, in the white squares of Iconium and by the thousand runlets of Damascus, amidst the swamps of Bulgaria and the mosques of Granada, in the oak sanctuaries of Scandinavia or the colleges of Paris, in the market-places of the Flemish towns or by the missionary rivers of La Plata, it is at once the light of the supernatural ennobling nature, and at the same time a beauty which seems as natural as the gray ruin which an aged wood so well knows how to incorporate with its quiet self. We have seen all this; for the light of history falls clearly upon it. But we trace the Procession far onward, toiling over the unborn ages, where the starry indistinctness of prophecy reveals it to our eyes. There are times to come, which shall be very different both from the times that have been, and from the times that are. The later ages of the Church will be portentous epochs. The times of Antichrist will never have been paralleled, although they may have been foreshadowed chiefly by the primeval centuries of Scripture history. But even amid those monstrous novelties the Procession of the Precious Blood, with its miraculously-preserved Sacraments, will move on with the same ready gracefulness, the same instinctive pliability, the same tranquil consciousness of its mission, which have distinguished it since Pentecost. Oh, happy we, who shall see that marvellous future in peaceful admiration from out the Bosom of our heavenly Father, and may have to help it with our prayers!

But this Procession is not to be always a splendor of the earth. Its eternal sanctuary is heaven. It will pass from earth to heaven through the dark portal of the Valley of Josaphat, the Valley of Universal Doom. That will be the day of his earthly triumph, the crown of that other day of shame and outpouring upon Calvary. The lone trumpet of the archangel, which shall wake the dead, is part of the pageantry of the Precious Blood. The union of the souls and bodies of the just is its work. The transfiguring of all glorified bodies into the likeness of the Body of Jesus is due also to the energy of its merits. Out of the Human Life, which is in that Blood, all judgment will proceed. The Blood itself will be the measure of justice, and the immeasurableness of mercy. All that will be magnificent in the vindictive sanctity of God that day will be a glory of the Precious Blood. In all that will be sweet, and gentle, and compassionate, it will seem as if the Precious Blood led the very love of God captive through its own greater capacities of love. Then too will all its difficult secrets be told, and its honor gloriously restored. Its mysteries of election, its seeming inequalities of grace, the irregularities of its patience, its varying prodigality, the apparent caprices of its impetuosity, its predilection for particular races and climates, its choice of favorite epochs, its look of waywardness with each individual soul, the amazing revelations of the saving grandeur of the Seven Sacraments—all these things will then be made plain, all will magnify its justice and its lovingness, all will illustrate the God-like equality of its beneficence, and all will redound to its eternal praise. The Universal Doom will be nothing else than a grand Feast of the Precious Blood, a Feast solemnized by the most marvellous functions, ushered in by the archangel's trumpet at the dead of night. The rendering of their dead by land and sea, the jubilee of countless resurrections, the leading in chains of Satan and the rebel populace of hell, the superb gathering of the angels, the radiant Advent of the Judge and his Mother from heaven, the silent pomp of the all-holy judgment, the ascent at eventide back to the palaces of heaven with very worlds of material beauty won to God by the resurrection of the just—these are the sacred pageants of that supreme Feast of the Precious Blood.

After this, what shall we dream of the history of the Precious Blood in heaven? Will it still be like a Procession, though gathered round the High Altar of creation? Will it still have new works to do, new glories to contribute to the Uncreated Majesty? What means that mysterious laying down of the kingdom by the Sacred Humanity, of which the apostle speaks to the Corinthians? What side are we to take in that thrilling controversy of theologians about the eternity of the priesthood of our Lord? Will not the repose of heaven be more energetic than the

activity of earth, and be the more energetic because its peace
is so profound? At least we may say so much as this: No work of
God is a work done; but rather it is eternally a grand work, being
grandly, and always more and more grandly, done. It seems to
my ignorance that, with God, all his works will be, now that they
have once begun, like the Generation of his word and the Procession of his Spirit; they will not be done, but will be being done
forever. So perchance there will be in the Precious Blood eternal
novelties eternally to magnify the glory of the Uncreated Trinity.
All works of God are completed as soon as they are begun; and
yet they are also endless in the unity of their accomplishment: and
which of his works is invested with such royal rights as is the
Precious Blood?

Our object in this chapter was to get a clear idea of the history of the Precious Blood. There are some subjects in which
clearness is every thing. If we can make a definite picture in our
minds, we have done every thing. This is the case with the history
of the Precious Blood. The price of our redemption is full of unfathomable mysteries. We cannot hope to understand them all, or
indeed any of them, fully. That single divine law, that without
shedding of blood there is no remission of sin, is beyond our
grasp. It only clothes for us with dim magnificence that gift of
God, which of all his natural gifts we least understand, the gift
of life. What we want is to understand so far as to be able to
worship and to love. Our best understanding of the Precious
Blood is the sight of what it has done, the enumeration of its
deeds, the narration of its history. So far we have endeavored to
get a clear idea of its history under the figure of a Procession.
Most divine works liken themselves better to processions than any
thing else. Any one, who has tried to make theology clear to
those who are not theologians, must have discovered this; and a
great deal that is very remarkable is implied in the fact. All that
is outside of God has an inveterate likeness to that which is within.
It is the genius of creative acts to put on the semblance of processions. At the same time we look upon a procession from without.
Things seen from without are seen more definitely. Their form

and figure are more palpable. Hence we gain in clearness. But the outside is never more than a partial manifestation. Besides this, it is liable to erroneous impressions which can only be corrected by some knowledge of what is within. Having asked you, then, to look at the history of the Precious Blood as a Procession, I must now, at the risk of some repetition, ask you to look at it as a Life, or as a series of lives. We shall thus complete our study of this marvellous history, and do our best to guard against any such misapprehensions as might interfere with our devotion.

All God's works are in a certain sense part of the life of God. It is this which gives to creation its interest as well as its significance. It is in this way that time participates in eternity. The life of the Precious Blood may be divided into seven epochs; or it would be more true to call them seven lives, both because they do not follow each other in order of time, and also because they are not all actual periods of its existence. These seven lives are as follows: the life of the Precious Blood in the Mind of God before creation; its life of efforts in the world from creation to the Incarnation; its life upon earth during the Thirty-Three Years; its life of energy in the Church afterward, up to the day of Doom; its contemporaneous life all that time in heaven; its contemporaneous life on earth in the Blessed Sacrament during that same time; and finally its eternal life in heaven, when the Doom is past. In all these lives of the Precious Blood there is a hidden life which we cannot reach, and whose mysteries are not only above our comprehension but beyond our imagination. Its union with the Divinity is inexplicable. Its peculiar redeeming value, in that it is blood, is also a secret hidden from our intelligence. It represents abysses of the divine wisdom, which are not only unfathomable but nameless. It bears upon itself the imprint of unsuspected perfections in the broad majesty of God. The jubilee of its life is a height of creation lost to our eyes in the burning vicinity of the uncreated. To this innermost inward life we cannot penetrate; but we can see, and understand, and love much of an inward, though less secret, life, which we could not see when we regarded the Precious Blood under the figure of a Procession. It is of this inward life we must now endeavor to get some idea.

The life of the Precious Blood in the Mind of God from all eternity is in one sense a real life, and in another sense an unreal one. It was not an actual life. It was a life of predestination, of foreseen beauty, of multiplied divine intentions. It was a specially divine invention, if we may use such a word. It was an idea which could not have come to any mind but that of God, and therefore the complacency which it caused in the Divine Mind was immense. It was a sort of second Word to God, a created expression of his uncreated perfection. It was part of the most grand and glorious thought of God, the Incarnation. It was a most important part of it. It was also a specially chosen part, selected for the accomplishment of our redemption, and for the restoring of a revolted creation to the dominion of its Maker. In the most dear and dread Mind of God it was a fountain always flowing. The beauty of its flowing had been one of his unbeginning gladnesses. It was the fountain which gave forth, multitudinous and beautiful as the creation of the radiant angels, the countless predestinations of the infinitely varying souls of men. The mystery of all election was from the first glassed in its beaming depths. It was its spray, which caught the golden light of eternal things, and fell down before the throne, even as it is still falling now, in starry showers of splendor. It was a mirror too in which the manifold countenances of the divine perfections looked always, and loved to make their beauty bearable to mortal eye. It is there to this day, that the oppositions in God are seen to be harmonies most simple and most worshipful. All parts of creation give us double views of God, simultaneous views of his seeming opposite perfections, just as on the Mount of Olives the eye may rest at will either on the Dead Sea or on the Holy City. But of no part of creation is this so true, or true in so high a sense, as of the Precious Blood. Redeeming grace tells the whole history of God, so far as it can be told, unfolds his character in all of its breadth which is comprehensible, and as it were recites and magnifies each separate perfection: and redeeming grace is the specialty of the Precious

Blood. Moreover, the Precious Blood dwelt also in the Mind of God as the type and model of all creation, whether fallen or unfallen. In its unity lay the germs of all created loveliness and of all created variety. Mary was its first shadow, its first reflection, the freshest copy of the original. No wonder then that it was an infinite delight to the Three Divine Persons. To them it was none the less real because it was not yet actually created; for to God the solidest created substance is but as shadow compared with the reality of his ideas. Thus from all eternity did the Precious Blood reign like a sovereign thing in the adorable complacency of God.

As it had lived an eternal life in the Mind of God before creation, so also did it live a life of visible effects and real jurisdiction from the beginning of the world, before it had become itself an actual created thing in the mystery of the Incarnation. It was the Precious Blood which hindered the fall of man from being as irretrievable as the fall of angels had been. It did real work in every single soul which was created in those four thousand years. It altered their position in the world. It made the eye of God look differently on them. It rained supernatural graces upon their hearts. It diminished temporal chastisements. Neither was it less influential in the counsels of God than in the souls of men. It caused his compassion to overspread the whole earth. It turned the chronicles of the world into a succession of types, and shadows, and predictions of itself. While it was itself preparing all things for its own coming and shedding, it so controlled all things that they rather seemed to be a preparation for itself. It sounded in every thing that God said. It impressed its character upon every thing that God did. It underlay all heathen life, and all Hebrew life. It was the significance of the most significant, and also of the most insignificant, events. It moulded all sanctity into an onlooking for itself. It beautified the hearts of men for God with supernatural desires. For all those forty ages it was the secret meaning and the hidden agent of the world. All that blossomed upon earth blossomed only because the Precious Blood watered the soil under ground. Who would not long to see it, as it would one day be, in the actual Human Heart which was to be its living

chalice? Even the patience of the long-waiting God might vouch-
safe to yearn for the actual creation of the Precious Blood. How
sweet then to him must have been that dear sanctity of Mary,
whose beautiful compulsion caused the Word to anticipate his
time!

But the hour arrived, and the Creator became a part of his
own Creation. The Precious Blood was actually created, and rose
and fell in pulses of true human life, and filled with joyous being
the Sanctuary of the Sacred Heart, and lived its life of Three-
and-Thirty Years among men. These Three-and-Thirty Years
formed in all true senses the longest and most important epoch
of the history of creation. They were filled with countless actions,
the value of each one of which was infinite. The vocations
stamped upon millions of souls came from those actions of God
made man. Their energies are vigorously ruling the world at
this hour. They have moulded age after age since then. All holiness has been but an infinitely diversified copy of them. Out of
their merits the attributes of God daily drink their fill, and yet
those merits still abound and overflow. Out of their merits the
Sacraments are drawing incalculable exuberances of grace all day
and night; and they are still full to the very brim, and capable of
saving unnumbered new creations. Out of the satisfactions of
those years the jurisdiction of the Church has drawn almost un-
limited indulgences; yet no visible impression has been made on
their abundance. Poetry and art go to those years as to a school of
heavenliest beauty; and all times and all minds find the lessons
fresh and new. Theology sits by them as by abysses of divine
wisdom, and one while is actively weaving her wondrous science
out of them, and another while, captivated by their beauty, for-
gets to weave, is rapt in contemplation, and becomes devotion. As
to devotion, those years are its very cloister and its garden. That
life is God made visible to his creatures as the rule of life. It lays
bare the very foundations of morals. It reveals the possibilities
of human actions, while it also paints as in a picture the indefinable operations of the Holy Ghost. It is a freshness and a joy to
think that, at this hour of the peaceful dawn, thousands of souls

are silent before God, caught in the sweet snares of the beauty of these earthly years of Jesus. Our Lord revealed to the Blessed Michael of Florence, the Camaldolese, how he longed that those who loved him should honor the Thirty-Three Years with affectionate minuteness. It has been the characteristic devotion of all the saints. The souls that have been most drawn to meditate upon the attributes of God have learned their science in that other science of the Three-and-Thirty Years. Sometimes this devotion takes special possession of a religious order for some length of time. Sometimes it fastens upon a single religious house, and develops itself with marvellous fertility. This appears to have been the case with the Carmelite convent at Dôle in the seventeenth century. To Sister Anne of the Cross, a lay-sister, it was the form and type of her whole life. It came natural to her to do even her ordinary actions in thirty-threes. Still more did her penances and devotions take that shape. When she was asked if she did not weary of such a reiterated devotion, she replied that, so far from it, it always came to her as new. The devotion of Mother Louisa of Jesus was even yet more remarkable. She could hardly occupy her soul with any thing but the Thirty-Three Years; and the abundant lights she received from God in prayer had chiefly reference to this devotion. The first years of the Sacred Infancy were "delicious" to her soul. She had an especial attraction to contemplate the first time our Lord bent his knees, and clasped his hands, in prayer to the Father. Her holiness seemed always to be a participation in some of the interior dispositions of Jesus upon earth; and the characteristics of her spiritual life, consequent upon this devotion, were persevering fervor and extreme joyousness. She imprinted this devotion upon the whole community, and also upon the externs who came across her.

We see remarkable traces of the same devotion in our Lord's answer to the prayers of Frances of the Mother of God, Carmelitess at Dieppe, distinguished for her devotion to the Precious Blood. When she was praying for the soul of Sister Catherine of the Angels, she asked our Lord after Communion to apply to Sister Catherine's soul one drop of his Precious Blood in order to achieve her deliverance. Our Lord answered, "I have given her one of my steps," thus showing the value of his least actions. At another time she made the same prayer for Sister Elizabeth of the Nativity, asking for one drop of the Precious Blood; and our Lord answered, "I will give her one of my tears, the efficacy of which is so great that it would turn hell into paradise, if it were applied there." These answers seem to imply a special devotion in Frances of the Mother of God to the Thirty-Three Years; and that saintly religious was one of the most remarkable among the holy persons of the seventeenth century.

We speak very truly when we divide the world into many worlds. We talk of the vegetable world, and the mineral world, and the animal world. We even subdivide these into lesser worlds. We go to the sidereal world to learn the immensities of space. Geology opens a world to us, which overshadows us with its distances of time. We call man a little world in himself; and the microscopic world, while it is so rife with new aspects of God, delights us with all that it insinuates of the possibilities and likelihoods of the invisible world of immaterial and angelic life. We call these by the name of worlds, because they seem like complete creations in themselves, and are each of them a distinct revelation of God, distinct from all other revelations of him, and yet harmonizing with them all. They are separate shadows of God. They are his wisdom and his beauty, his power and his love, seen from different points of view. He is many Creators in one Creator. We are very right in making his one world into many worlds. So it is with the Incarnation. The whole material universe is not so vast as that one world of the Incarnation, nor capable of so many or such magnificent subdivisions. Intellectually or spiritually, the Thirty-Three Years form a world far vaster than the world of stars. They can even bear to be subdivided into many other worlds, which are still spacious enough for the swift intelligences of angels, as well as the rapidity of glorified human minds, to traverse for eternity, finding fresh wonders evermore. The Precious Blood has one biography in Mary's Womb, where it issued from the lone sanctities of her immaculate heart. It has another in Bethlehem, and another in Egypt, and another in Nazareth, and another on the shores of Gennesareth, and another in Jerusalem, and another in Galilee. Each of these is a world beyond the measures of our science, a cloister for devotion, and yet a cloister in which eternity has ample room. God's vastness is a living vastness. It carries itself everywhere, and everywhere is entire and transcends the necessities of space. Each of these separate worlds of the life of Jesus upon earth is tied by some occult sympathy to some particular attribute, or group of attributes, in God. Thus we learn in the life of Mother Margaret of the Blessed Sacrament, Carmalitess at Dijon, that the souls which are called to a special devotion to our Lord's Resurrection have always a peculiar attraction to worship the divine sanctity. These are glimpses of that glad science of the Three-and-Thirty Years, which will be part of our unutterable bliss beyond the grave. Surely it makes the world seem wearier than ever, to think of the unsuspected grandeurs which the mysteries of our sweet Jesus are waiting to pour out into our souls, when he has received us into his kingdom.

It is plain, from what has been said, that our knowledge of the inward life of the Precious Blood during the Thirty-Three Years must be very superficial. Nevertheless, we must put it before ourselves as clearly as we can. Its first beginning was in the thrills of beatific joy. We shall see reasons afterward for carefully noting this. The beginning of the Human Life of Jesus was not gradual. It had no dawn. Its very union with the Divinity rendered this impossible. It broke out of nothingness into the blaze of conscious and blessed ecstasy. It saw God as not even Mary sees him now. It saw him, went out of sight of all creation toward comprehending him, enjoyed him as not all heaven after the Doom will enjoy him, and adored him as no fabulous number of possible worlds could ever have adored him. This was the first pulse of the Precious Blood. The very first throb had in it an incalculable immensity of gladness. Out of its first moment all worlds might be gladdened beyond their power of bearing gladness. Save the Uncreated Jubilee, the sweet Spirit of the Father and the Son, never was there jubilee like that of the Precious Blood in its beginning.

Yet from that hour the jubilee has never ceased; it has never lessened; it has never changed. Its pulses are not tides. They imply no vicissitudes. They betoken only an equable impetuosity of immutable delight. The gladness which flashed like lightning out of the eyes of the Infant into the heart of Mary was unabated when the same eyes drooped languidly toward her upon Calvary. The blessedness which broke forth like a creation of light in the glory of the Resurrection had never left the Sacred Heart even during the Way of the Cross. But, with the beatific joy, the Precious Blood had all other joys as well. That Human Life was a joy in itself, a joy in its divine union, independently of its vision of God. It was a joy in the love and possession of so sweet a Mother. It was a joy in the unearthly tranquillity of Joseph's deep, loving, adoring heart. It was a joy in the jubilee of the worshipping angels. It was a joy in the very bitterness of its redeeming woes, and it was a joy in the intensity of its own loves of God and men.

But it was a life also of colossal sorrows, even though they abated not the joy. Never did blood of man throb with such excesses of anguish as the Precious Blood of our most dear Redeemer. Its sorrows were lifelong. Their excesses exceeded all the tortures of the martyrs. There was never a moment which was not occupied with sorrow. The jubilee never commingled with the woe, nor tempered it, nor compensated for it. Nay, rather, all joys intensified the sorrows. Joy, surely, is in itself a diviner thing than sorrow; for there can be no sorrow in the Ever-blessed. But sorrow was more human; and therefore it was chosen as the instrument of man's redemption; and thus to us it becomes more divine, because it brings God to us and raises us up to God. Thus sorrow was more natural to the Precious Blood. It was a life more congenial to its nature. Moreover, it was its official life. For by sorrow it was to accomplish its redeeming work. Its shedding was to be not only the consummation of our Lord's suffering, but the chosen suffering, in which precisely the work of redemption was to lie. Jesus—thrice blessed be his most dear Name!—is all our own, neither can we spare any thing of him. Yet it was not precisely his Soul which was to redeem us, nor the Passion of his Body which was to be exactly our expiation. It was the shedding of his Blood which was to cleanse us from our sins. The remedy of the Fall was precisely in the Saviour's Blood. All the sorrows of his life grew up to the shedding of his Blood, and were crowned by it; and his shedding the last few drops of it after he was dead was significant of the work it had to do. The Soul, and the Body, and the Blood lay separate; and the sacrifice was thus complete.

The life of the Precious Blood was also a life of great secrecy. This is the invariable characteristic of all divine things. The more they have been the objects of God's eternal complacency in his ever-blessed Mind, the more instinctively do they affect secrecy. God is a God who hides himself, and who even manifests himself by means of new concealments. All holiness has the same love of secrecy imprinted on it as the seal of God. We should have imagined that the gladness of the Precious Blood would have made it prone to manifest itself, and to be forever manifesting itself out of its exuberant love of souls. We might have supposed that its intense desire to shed itself would have given it a character of publicity. Yet, as God is so secret that St. Austin ventured to name him "the most secret Being," and at the same time is also unspeakably communicative, so is it with the Precious Blood. It hid itself all through the Thirty-Three Years, and it hid itself most effectually at the moment it was being shed. It hid itself on the roots of the olive-trees of Gethsemane, only making the brown wood a little ruddier. It sank into the thirsty ground of Calvary. It hastened to mingle with the street-dust of Jerusalem. It clung to the soles of men's shoes, so that they might not notice it. In like manner it works behind a veil at this hour. It works in Sacraments, in invisible communications of grace, in viewless contacts of divine things with the soul. It is only when God opens the eyes of favored souls that it is seen working as truly the Blood of Jesus. Such a favored soul was Frances of the Mother of God, Carmelitess of Dieppe. When she held her chapters of faults, and the nuns accused themselves of their short-comings of observance, she saw Jesus by her side, touching those who accused themselves with simplicity and frankness with a drop of his Blood, and leaving untouched those who accused themselves unsimply and without any interior self-condemnation. On Palm Sunday, during a jubilee, she saw our Lord apply to the souls of the nuns at Communion the grace of the jubilee by means of his Blood; and he said to her, "To persons in the world I give my Blood by drops, but here I give it in profusion." One year, on the feast of the Circumcision, our Lord showed himself to her lying in the manger, bathed in blood and the blood dropping from him into a vessel. Her soul became "deliciously occupied" with the dignity and price of that adorable Blood, and she cried out, in a transport of rapture, "Ah, my Lord! that was enough to redeem the world, without so much suffering." He then vouchsafed to reveal to her that he had offered the Blood of the Circumcision to the Father for two objects especially. The first was to satisfy for the sins which had been committed since creation and before the Incarnation; and the second was to obtain for souls the grace of making a right use of his mysteries. Thus it has been in numberless revelations, that, when the realities of grace have been shown to favored souls, they have been shown as actual contacts of the Precious Blood, just as supernatural favors at Communion have so often taken the form of filling the mouths of the saints with blood, which had a sweetness beyond all known earthly tastes; and the way in which it veils its operations is but a continuance of the secrecy of the Three-and-Thirty Years.

The life of the Precious Blood on earth was also, and eminently, a life of love, or, as we may rather call it, a life of many loves. It was such a human love of God as immeasurably surpassed the collective love of Mary, angels, and men. It was a joyous and yet a reverential love of Mary, such as far outdid all the united devotion and enthusiastic affection of the angels and the saints for their mother and their queen. It was such a love of men, and particularly of men's souls, as the hearts of all mankind could not hold if it were divided among them and their hearts were enlarged to the magnificent capacities of apostles' hearts. Souls were its attraction, its passion. Its genius fastened upon them as its portion and its prey. Its choice, its work, its food, its rest, its joy—all were in human souls. The thought of it had won grace for souls before it was actually created. The figures of it cleansed souls. The shedding of it was the life of souls. It became almost omnipresent, that it might embrace all souls. It cast itself into Sacraments, that it might reach souls by a quicker road, in more diversified ways, with a more infallible operation, and with a more abundant success. Then, as if discontented even with the magnificence of the Sacraments, it threw itself into Indulgences and Jubilees. It made men after its own likeness, and called them Apostles. An apostolic call is a vocation of the Precious Blood. The mild judgments of moral theology are but the casuistry of the Precious Blood. Who can think unmoved of the tenderness and of the impetuosity of this soul-loving Blood? All sweet, eloquent patience in the Confessional is only the impassioned self-control of the Precious Blood. All true, simple, evangelical preaching is only the uplifted voice of the Precious Blood. Let me tell you again that old story of the Blessed Angela of Foligno. She saw our Lord in vision embracing some Franciscan Friars, and pressing them with a yearning fondness to his wounded side. He pressed them so closely to him that their lips were tinged with his Blood, some slightly, some very much; and some had their mouths all ruddy with it, so tightly had he pressed them against the wound. He told her that these were his preachers, and that the word of the Gospel only went with power to the soul when it passed over lips that were stained with his Precious Blood. Ah, we poor preachers! we have need to hang our heads at this tale; and yet it is one full of good cheer to our humility, if only our humility be generous and brave.

Finally, the life of the Precious Blood on earth was a life of incomparable sanctity. It was made up of the most gigantic operations of grace. We cannot approach to them even in thought. Let it suffice to say that they were multitudinous and manifold all day, and that sleep by night never interrupted them; and yet that the least of them transcended in spiritual beauty and dignity the gorgeous mystery of the Immaculate Conception. It was a life

made up also of interior dispositions of such vast heroism, of such
fiery love, of such majestic intensity, of such delicate complications, as have no parallel in any other created holiness. What can
we imagine of them, when it is sober to say of them that the least
and most transient of them surpassed all the dispositions of Mary's
Dolors? and, after the virtues of Jesus, are not those the most
colossal sanctities that were ever known on earth or ever crowned
in heaven? In all these operations of grace, in all these inward
dispositions, in all the glorious heroisms of the Sacred Humanity,
the Precious Blood was ever ministering, with most special intention, to those two kindred Attributes of God, his Dominion and
his Magnificence. Did I not speak truly when I said that the
Three-and-Thirty Years were an epoch of secular duration, a kind
of eternity of time?

The life of the Precious Blood upon earth after the Ascension
was, as we have seen, in one sense an actual life, and in another
sense not an actual life. We have lessons also to learn from this,
or, at least, fresh proofs of the character and disposition of the
Precious Blood. Its life upon earth may be divided into natural
and supernatural, or into direct and indirect, or into religious
and secular, according to the point of view from which we may
regard it. For our purpose no strict division is necessary. It is
enough for us to speak of it as it concerns the world and as it
concerns the Church. On the first head we need not say much,
as we have already seen in the second chapter what the world
would have been without the Precious Blood. Nevertheless, there
is still something to be said. There is not, and has not been since
Christianity was preached, a state or government which has not
been materially influenced by the Precious Blood. History shows
us that there is an obvious unity of life in states, of which they
themselves are scarcely ever conscious, or at least conscious only
during transient intervals. They do God's work without knowing
it. They serve the Church at the moment they think they are
thwarting it. After centuries of self-praise and pride they lose
their positions and sink into something narrower and smaller,
and find that they have all along been the unintelligent and un-

intentional servants of the Holy See. Sometimes individual states-
men make an impression on their age and country; and it is
curiously borne out by history that in this case the impression
is for the most part adverse to religion at the time, but turns
out to be for its advantage in the end. More often the state
makes the statesman, who follows rather than leads, while the
state itself is filled with a life it does not understand, and, like
a tree growing in a particular position, works out its instincts unconsciously. In both cases it is the interests of the Precious Blood
which are found at last to have presided over the revolutions of
states.

Civilizations and customs are also modified and controlled by
its genius, character, and influence. Its work in individual souls
is in the aggregate such an enormous power, that it cannot help
making itself felt in all social movements. To literature it has
contributed fresh forms and new ideas. In art it has been a fountain of beauty and inspiration far surpassing any other both in
the quantity and the excellence of its production. Philanthropy
owes more to it than it will acknowledge, and morality has hardly
any independent practical life without it. In what is called the
progress of humanity it has been at once a curb to restrain, and a
rudder to guide, a light to see by, and a compensation enabling
us to endure.

But, while we must never forget that the outer world is
always owing all that is good in it to the influence of the Precious Blood, we are rather concerned with its life in the Church.
We have already seen that the laboratories of its life are in the
wonderful Sacraments, which are the living present actions of
Christ, the actual going on of the Thirty-Three Years on earth.
We have seen that all processes of justification and of sanctification are in reality operations of the Precious Blood. We have
remembered its ubiquitous activity in those veiled triumphs of
death-bed graces, which will rank among the sweetest astonish-
ments of heaven. But its principal and most characteristic occupation upon earth is Conversion; and, as its energy in the Church is
so broad and so incessant that it is difficult to comprehend it in

one view without becoming vague, we may select this particular occupation to which it is so specially addicted, as a favorable illustration of its spirit and method, and as conveying to us by a single instance the most faithful idea of its life upon earth since the Ascension. But, while we put forward the phenomenon of Conversion as the best exponent of the normal life of the Precious Blood, we must not forget that it is only one out of many specimens of its fertility. Let us then think of what is implied in the Conversion of a soul, and what that agent must be like whose main and favorite occupation is Conversion.

It is not possible to exaggerate the importance of the Conversion of a single soul. As single souls, we feel lost in an overwhelming multitude. We are nobodies in the great grand world, and in the huge overmastering progress of human destinies. If we died, we might leave a temporary ache in some few hearts, and that would be all. But we are never lost, we are never nobodies, in the dear world of God's all-seeing love and all-loving providence. According to his standards, an empire is a less thing than a single soul. The empire will not last so long, nor can it effect so much. Even upon earth the divine importance of its history lies simply in the amount and kind of its influence upon single souls. In the next world, the truer world, it has no representative. It is as though it had never been, or at least it is a mere item in the sanctification of the saved. The fortunes of earth's most gorgeous empire cast no shadow upon heaven. God appears to make fewer arrangements for empires than for souls; and, when he occupies himself with nations, it is for the sake of souls. The degree and manner of divine interference are less for an empire than for a soul. Heaven's interest in an empire is less than its interest in a soul. The consequences of an empire are less than the consequences of a soul. This is the estimate which the Precious Blood takes of a single soul.

Now let us look at the machinery of Conversion. What is wanted, what is actually put forth, to convert a man in mortal sin? The Three Divine Persons work as one in all external works. Yet the Father represents in our imperfect views the power of the Godhead; and this power is wanted to convert a soul. Nothing short of omnipotence can do it. Mary's sceptre only reaches so far through the omnipotence of prayer. When I think of enormous power, I think of St. Michael; but he is too weak to convert a sinner: or of the choir of Thrones; but the magnificence of their repose cannot cleanse from sin, or infuse peace into a sinful soul. Secondly, it needs the wisdom of the Son. The Cherubim are very wise, and our dearest mother Mary is a very abyss of science. But they could not have invented the needful ingenuities for the Conversion of a sinner. Indeed, they are so far from being able to devise them, that they find it hard to understand them, and they are adoring them to this hour with unabated astonishment. Then, also, it needs the love of the Holy Ghost. The magnificent Seraphim live in the divine fires, and are themselves vast and huge abysses of burning love. Yet they are but sparks from the furnace of the Holy Ghost. His love is simply incomprehensible. They can but fall down and tremble before the unutterable conflagrations of his uncreated fires. Many things are hard to understand in God, but, most of all, the excesses of his love. Yet this power of the Father, this wisdom of the Son, and this love of the Holy Ghost, this threefold compassion of the Most Holy Trinity, have been engaged for the Conversion of souls through the exquisite pleadings and beautiful constraints of the Precious Blood.

It is part of the ordinance of our Blessed Lord that the prayers and dolors of his Mother should also go to the Conversion of a soul. But the power of those prayers and the merit of those dolors came from the Precious Blood. The whole of Mary, and all the benignity of her queendom, and all the glory of her exaltation, and all the splendor of her graces, and all the mystery of her motherhood, are because of the Precious Blood. No part of creation has been made so white by its redness as her unspotted heart. She is the creature of the Precious Blood, its daughter, its mother, its servant, and its queen. The angels of heaven must be stirred for the Conversion of a soul. Numberless ministries, each one of which is a heavenly wonder, are put forth by them. They plead in heaven. They visit earth. They do Mary's bidding. They conspire with the saints. They procure the Sacraments. They prepare. They co-operate. They confirm. They warn. They defend. They cross each other betwixt earth and heaven, like royal messengers on the highways in time of war. It is the Precious Blood which has merited these ministries for the soul. It is devotion to the Precious Blood which fills the angelic realms with jubilee when a sinner is converted. Our Lord loved to think of that jubilee, and spoke of it with pleased affirmation and tenderest delight.

The Conversion of a soul requires that a multitude of circumstances should be providentially ordered, and times, persons, and places made to fit each other in some one peculiar way. This harmony of circumstances is providence doing honor to the Precious Blood. There must be, ordinarily speaking, the knowledge of the Gospel; and the bringing of this to the neighborhood of each soul is a distinct act of love on the part of the Precious Blood. Much has to be merited for the soul by the good works of others; and no works merit except through the Precious Blood. The goodness of others has to influence the soul; and goodness only influences because the Precious Blood makes it so attractive. The moment of contrition is the moment of revolution in the soul; it was a moment foreseen and foreordained from all eternity in view of .the Precious Blood. It is part of God's eternal complacency in that redeeming Blood. The Sacraments, which are the resplendent instruments of Conversion, are the application of the Precious Blood to the soul in a manner which seems to intensify that which is already infinite. The actual shedding of the Blood on Calvary was the far-off preparation for this individual Conversion. The revival of old merits, and the restoration of forfeited rights to reward, are only instances of the energy of the Precious Blood, and of the completeness with which it does its work. This vitality of merits, this power of a resurrection in them when mortal sin has killed them, is only because it was the Precious Blood which made them merits at the first. Indulgences are the loving ministers of the Precious Blood, which understand its ways and enter into its spirit, and so go about picking up the fragments that remain after the Sacraments have had their fill.

The joy of God, of Mary, of the angels, of the saints, of the holy souls in purgatory, and of God's priests and servants upon earth, is only an emanation of that joy of which the Precious Blood is the universal and incessant fountain. Moreover, all through this process of Conversion there is a marvellous hiding, a divine extenuation, of sin's affront against God, which can only be because it is inundated by the Precious Blood, while at the same time there is such a revelation of the sinfulness of sin as can only be made by that same Blood, which is the beautiful reparation of God's sanctity.

By night and by day all over the earth is the Precious Blood engaged in this occupation of Conversion. It is going on in thousands of souls at once. In all of them is all this supernatural machinery at work, and at work all at once. In each case there is the same apparently exclusive concentration of divine love upon the single soul, which makes all God's dealings with us seem so inexpressibly tender. This has been going on for centuries. It will go on still for many centuries: for the end of the world does not yet seem near, unless its not seeming so be indeed a sign that it is so. Who can mistake the character and office of the Precious Blood, when he studies this work of Conversion which is its work of predilection? It is the one question of life and death with each one of us, whether this change has been wrought in us, either at our baptism or since. Who then can calculate the debt he owes to the Precious Blood? Is there a joy in life more invigorating than an overwhelming sense of our obligations to the Blood of Jesus? Who does not long to pay him back in love, and long all the more ardently the more he sees how the greatness of his debt makes the payment of it impossible? To be in debt to God is the lightheartedness of life. The grace he gives us is even sweeter to us as an obligation than as a gift. The weight of our obligations is the delightful pressure of his love; and the sweet feeling of it is in proportion to the weight.

This leads me to another matter, on which, for the sake of our dearest Lord, I would that I could speak with more than usual persuasion. We are considering the life of the Precious Blood in the Church. Its supernatural works of benignity are wrought in the Church and through the Church. The Church is in an especial manner, and in strict scriptural phraseology, the creation of the Precious Blood. It is its visible edifice, the house it has built for itself, the home where it hides itself, the bride it has espoused and then dowered with its Sacraments, the mother of its children, the monument it has erected and hung round with trophies of its victories. It is the living palace of the Precious Blood, built with the Blood itself as with cement, and beautified by it as by the brightness of very heaven. It is the life and love of the Precious Blood, made visible to men by an institution invented by God himself, and which copies upon earth the order and the hierarchies of heaven. Hence it follows that all true devotion to the Precious Blood must be accompanied by a hearty devotion to the Church. Heresies, which have done despite to the Precious Blood by narrowing its sphere or by limiting its prodigality, have also been distinguished by a want of loyalty to the Church. In all times we have seen that those who take a rigid view about the easiness of salvation also take a lax view about the exclusive privileges of communion with the Church; while, on the other hand, those who dwell more strongly on the doctrine of exclusive salvation in the true Church are also most given to magnify the abundance of redeeming grace within its pale. At first sight it seems a strange inconsistency, that those who make it hard to be saved in the Church should make it comparatively easy to be saved out of it. It is indeed curious that such men should regard what they must at the least admit to be one of God's chief means of grace, namely, the Church, as adding very little to the chances of a man's salvation. If two men, born in one country, the one in the Church with all the Sacraments, the other not in the Church at all, have, as some say, nearly the same chances of salvation, it must follow, either that God has one standard for the forgiveness of sin in the one case, and another in the other, which is surely an impiety, or that the Sacraments are of very little consequence or efficacy, which would be hardly a less impiety. That Jesus, God and Man, should be truly received in the Blessed Sacrament, and yet that this should not make simply an incalculable difference between the religious state of those who enjoy this privilege and of those who do not, is a supposition highly dishonorable to our Blessed Lord. Yet so it is that a light esteem of the overwhelming advantages of the Church, and a want of appreciation of the Sacraments, go along with the most rigid and harsh views regarding the easiness of salvation and the number of the saved; and these errors go together for want of a true and tender devotion to the Precious Blood. The doctrine of the Sacraments is the touchstone of all the theology of the day. He who constantly and devoutly adores the Precious Blood of Jesus will not think lightly of the Sacraments which are the vases to hold it and the channels to convey it. He who magnifies the glory of the Sacraments will make much of the Church whose especial possession and characteristic they are. It is thus, through the doctrine of the Sacrament, that the apparent contradiction of making salvation very difficult in the Church, and yet holding that the being out of the Church does not put a man at such a great disadvantage as regards salvation, comes from a want of devotion to the Precious Blood.

Hence it follows that all lovers of the Precious Blood should have a cordial devotion to the Church, and should immensely honor, revere, and prize the Sacraments. Scripture calls the Church the Body of Christ; and the chief of the Sacraments is precisely the Body of Christ; and St. Paul speaks wonderful things of the mysterious union between Christ and the Church. It is one of our greatest dangers of the present day to think lightly of the Church. Now that the world is overrun with heresy, and that in social life almost all distinctions between the faithful and others are obliterated, it is convenient to men's ease and acceptable to their cowardice to regard the faith as one of many saving opinions, and the Church as one of many saving institutions. Men will make light of the enormous privileges and of the exclusive rights of the Church, either out of human respect, or as an easy way of diminishing the difficulties of a problem which they are unable to solve and do not like to face. A disesteem of the Sacra-

ments follows upon this with a very speedy and disastrous logic.
The practical consequences soon work themselves out. Such men
destroy the souls of others by discouraging the frequentation of
the Sacraments, and they destroy their own by that laxity of
worldly, comfort-loving lives, which in almost all cases are found
in conjunction with very rigorous views. Such men either rest in
the very rigor of their view, as if its rigorousness were meritorious
enough of itself to save them, or they put feelings and sensible
devotions in the place of mortifications, and so make their whole
spirituality a delusion. They will be found restive and uneasy
under the praise of the great Sacraments; and this shows how far
they have drifted from the instincts of the Church. They will be
found to consider the chances of salvation for the poor as almost
less, even in the point of unworldliness, than those of the rich;
and this shows how far they have drifted from the mind of our
Lord, who blessed the poor precisely as entering the kingdom of
heaven more easily than the rich. A man who thinks lightly of the
really inestimable privileges of the Church lets go of every thing,
and must ultimately either end in active heresy or settle down
into a wearied irreligiousness. The Church is a kingdom, not a
literature—a life, not a congeries of doctrines; it is a rule and a
sovereignty, a royalty which belongs to the royalty of the Precious Blood.

Let us then cultivate with the most jealous care a fervent devotion to the Church. Love of the Church was part, and a great
part, of the Sacred Heart of Jesus. The Jansenists, who made so
light of the maternal authority of the Church, turned away with
instinctive displeasure from the devotion to the Sacred Heart.
We must look at the Church habitually as the sole ark in the
deluge of the world, the sole mistress of salvation. We do not
bind God further than he has been pleased to bind himself. We
do not limit the far-reaching excesses of his mercy. But we remember that his ordinary law is, that there is no salvation whatever outside the Roman Church. It is his ordinary institution that
no accurate beliefs, no right sympathies, no generous views, no
near approaches, no sensible devotions, no felt actual graces, will

make a man a living member of Jesus Christ, without communion with the Holy See. We must be jealous of the uncompromising simplicity of this old-fashioned doctrine. We must be suspicious of all the fine words, and specious theories, and ingenious abatements, which the spirit of the day would suggest. We must be misled by no circumstances of time or place, by no prevalence of heresy, by no arguments drawn from consequences, which are the affair of God's government of the world, not ours. The sins of men cannot change the truth of God. They are at his mercy, not he at theirs. In the days of Antichrist, when two-thirds even of the faithful shall fall away from the Church, their apostasy will not make it less the exclusive mistress of salvation.

We must be loyal to the Church in our least thoughts of it, nor even talk lightly of its majesty. We must put faith in it in all its contacts and concussions with the world, and in all its contradictions of the assumed grandeur of this nineteenth century, which is more than half spent, and has done nothing yet to justify its boasting. We must not measure the Church by unsupernatural standards, which it is the world's great object to persuade us to do. We must not be ashamed of it because it holds back when it seems grander to go forward. We must not be discontented with it when its action intersects some little favorite anticipations of our own. We must merge our own selves and our own views in its consciously or unconsciously Spirit-guided policy. When we are perplexed, we must stand still and believe. Silence makes us great-hearted, and judging makes us little-minded. We must do all we can to get ourselves infected with the instincts of the Church. We must like its ways, as well as obey its precepts and believe its doctrines. We must not theorize; for, if we once begin to theorize, we shall soon come to sneer. A mind not under authority always lies under a necessity of being pert. We must esteem all that the Church blesses, all that the Church affects. When the Church suffers, or souls suffer, we must not be content with the selfish consolation that, after all, the Church is eternal, and must conquer in the long run; but we must have an active sympathy with all its present vicissitudes, and an untiring zeal and an unquenchable thirst for souls; and the salvation of souls is a matter of the present; it cannot wait for a future, because men are dying daily.

We must even fear the Church with a filial reverence. If we are converts, we must never cease to dread the underground action of heretical habits of mind and heretical methods of controversy in ourselves. There is a leaven of inherent lawlessness in every man who has once been a heretic. We must be as afraid of these things as Scripture tells us to be afraid of forgiven sin. In some cases we should abstain from using all the liberty of speculation which the Church allows us, because we humbly distrust the strength or the genuineness of the principle of obedience within us, to stop us before we go too far. Neither must we allow ourselves to be discontented with the state of things anywhere or at any time. Discontent breeds in us the base and sour spirit of reformers. The chief discontent of the saints was with themselves. So should ours be. We read of saints being downcast and discontented about the sin that is in the world. We even read of their being discontented with political matters, when they concerned the free action and unhindered sovereignty of the Holy See. But I never read of any saint being discontented with the intellectual, or philosophical, or literary state of things in the Church. I doubt if such a discontent is compatible with true loyalty to the Church.

Our attitude must be always one of submission, not of criticism. He, who is disappointed with the Church, must be losing his faith, even though he does not know it. I hear of some foreign countries where the precepts of the Church are now thought lightly of, and a marked distinction made between them and other obligations; and I feel sure that the faith of those countries is failing, although there may be a show to the contrary. When I meet with new catholics careless about these same precepts, careless of the Masses and abstinences of obligation, I see in this, not so much a negligent spirit, as a downright want of faith.

A man's love of the Church is the surest test of his love of God. He knows that the whole Church is informed with the Holy Ghost. The divine life of the Paraclete, his counsels, his inspirations, his workings, his sympathies, his attraction, are in it everywhere. There is nothing in the Church or about it, however seemingly trivial, transient, or indirect, which is not more likely than not to contain some of the fire of the Holy Ghost; and this likelihood is the cause of a perpetual and universal reverence for the Church to the good catholic. The gift of infallibility is but a concentration, the culminating point, the solemn official outspeaking, of the indwelling of the Holy Ghost in the Church. While it calls, like revelation, for absolute submission of heart and soul, all the minor arrangements and ways and dispositions of the Church call for general submission, docility, and reverence, because of the whole Church being a shrine fulfilled with the life of the Holy Ghost. St. Philip Neri's special devotion to the Third Person of the Most Holy Trinity was part of that intense loyalty to the Church, which raised him to the rank and title of an apostle, and the apostle of the Holy City. In a word, our feeling toward the Church should be a devotion. A grandeur faded from the page of history, when the loyalty to the old monarchies went out; but even that loyalty was not enough for our feelings toward the Church. The Church is full of God, haunted by spiritual presences, informed with a supernatural life, instinct with Jesus. Our love of the Church is one form of our love of Jesus, the form on which the saints were moulded. It is our love of our Lord's love of us. It is the enthusiasm of our devotion to his Precious Blood. Surely it were a shame, if we did not love the Church more than the Jews of old loved their dear Jerusalem!

From this cultivation of a great devotion to the Church we should gain many of those graces of which we stand in especial need. It would bring with it the grace of simplicity, because it would be founded on the virtue of obedience, and because it would foster the gift of faith. In these days it is a huge evil to be inconsistent; and we are inconsistent as much from want of simplicity as want of courage. Simplicity makes a quiet spirit; and a quiet spirit is the true home of heavenly love. But times when we want simplicity are also times when we especially require prudence; and prudence is another grace which will come out of devotion to the Church. They, who have the habit of leaning upon authority, distrust themselves, and they distrust themselves, not timidly, but bravely. They are not precipitate. There is a maturity about their promptitude, and a security about their speed, and a vigorousness even in their delays, which are caught from the spirit and conduct of the Church itself. Moreover, devotion to the Church is a loyalty, and, further, it is a supernatural loyalty. But loyalty makes a man generous. It causes him to dare great things, to be forgetful of himself, to be disinterested, to love hard work, to delight in sacrifices, and always to be aspiring to something higher and more arduous. It makes a man genial; and it is only a genial mind which is creative, fertile, or successful. How many hearts are daily telling God that their want of wants is generosity! They will find it through devotion to the Church. Stability is another grace which the men of our day have need to covet. Multiplicity makes men vacillating. Those, who are always catching at things, grasp nothing. To be really earnest we must be constant. But the earnest man is the man who takes every thing in earnest. He is not merely the persistent man. True stability must be elastic while it is constant; or rather it will be constant precisely because it is elastic. This is an exact description of that changeful uniformity of which the whole history of the Church is an example. Lastly, a certain grace comes from secret union with the Church, just as unction comes from union with God. This grace of union with the Church gives us a winningness in the eyes of others, a sort of inward equable sweetness, which first fills our own souls with light and gladness, and then draws the souls of others into the light and gladness which are within ourselves. Each man knows how far he needs these things as helps to him in his spiritual life. To many of us in these days they are special needs.

There are still three lives of the Precious Blood remaining to be treated of; but we may in reality consider them as one. There is the actual life in heaven, which is contemporaneous with that life in the Church from the Ascension to the Doom, which we have just been contemplating. There is the life of the Precious Blood in the Blessed Sacrament, the heavenly life miraculously dowered with an earthly locality and with innumerous localities at once. There is, lastly, the eternal life of the Precious Blood in heaven after the Doom for all eternity, when Jesus has laid down his kingdom and changed the offices of his priesthood. These are certainly in many deep senses, and with regard to many curious yet edifying questions, different lives. Yet, for our present practical purpose, they may be regarded as one. The life of the glorified Blood is a life of beatitude. It is glad in itself, and ministers gladness to others, even to the boundless uncreated jubilee of God. The Precious Blood is the Human Life of the Word. Beatitude is the natural life of God; and so joy is the natural life of the Precious Blood. In truth, is not joy the nearest definition of life that we can have: for is it not God's first intention in the gift of life?

In heaven and in the Blessed Sacrament the Precious Blood dwells, incomparably glorified, in the veins of Jesus. Its beauty there is wonderful to see, wonderful to think of. The sight of it in our Lord's translucent Body is an immense gladness to the Blessed. Earth has no beauty to which we can compare it; yet earth is not therefore poorer than heaven; for it has this very beauty in the adorable Sacrament. But it is not only a joy to others. Its own life is an unbroken jubilee. As it goes and returns to and from the Sacred Heart it is filled with pulses of the most abounding gladness. It thrills with the exquisite delight of created life carried to its utmost ecstatic possibility. But, over and above this, there is the indefinable, unimaginable ecstasy of the Hypostatic Union, which is felt in every particle of that Precious Blood. It throbs with such pacific tumult of immortal love, as no created life could bear without some miraculous union with the Godhead. It thrills with sacred fear, with transports of intensest adoration, before the uncreated majesty of God. It is penetrated through and through with the excesses of this holy fear. That, which itself is worshipped by the hierarchies of heaven, trembles with a very jubilee of worship before the Throne of the Eternal. Possessed with such extremity of rapturous fear, how could the Precious Blood so tremble, and so exult, and yet live on, if it

were not that it rested for its dear support upon the uncreated
Person of the Word? It seems to stop the beating of one's heart
to think of this unutterable repose of that created nature, that
Sacred Humanity, that personless life, on the Person of the Eternal Word! The strange beauty of such a God-invented union, the
delight of the Divine Person in the touch of a created nature
which yet is no touch at all, for the Divine Person can suffer
none, the ecstasies of the Sacred Humanity as the unction of the
Word with soft sweet fire penetrates its secret sanctuaries of life,
the comprehension of that humble, affectionate, pathetic, material nature within the enfoldings of the Incomprehensible, which
embrace it with such forbearing gentleness of omnipotence, and
yet with such a riveted closeness of invincible union—to what
heart, sweetly smitten with love of Jesus, are not these things the
unfading joys of prayer, the unfailing wells of tears? What a life
is the life of that Precious Blood! Yet amid the untold magnificence of the Divine Union it feels its kindred to Mary, as a special
joy of its abounding life. Its orginal fountains are still flowing in
their sinless purity, beautified now with the gifts of glory, in the
Mother's Immaculate Heart; and the fountain in the Sacred
Heart beats in mysterious sympathy with the source from which
it came itself. Singular in all its wonderful prerogatives, it yet
intertwines the life of Mary with its own.

Look at the Precious Blood for a moment as it lies within the
Sacred Heart with a living peace, like the restless tranquillity of
ocean. It is itself the ocean of joy from which all other joys in
creation come. It is through it that the immensity of God's gladness pours itself into all the universe, and at the same time lets
itself also be mysteriously gladdened by the Precious Blood. All
the joys, and they are numberless, which are still left in the fallen
world, whether they be natural or supernatural, are in substance
Indulgences, Indulgences which are granted because of the Precious Blood. Sinners upon earth still have joys: they come from
the Precious Blood. Saints on earth are the gladdest of God's creatures. Their lives are all flight and song, like the hot-blooded lives
of the birds of the air. All this gladness is from the Precious

Blood. The saints in heaven are spirits overflowed with joy, spirits whose quietness is transport and whose soberness is ecstasy. It is the Precious Blood which flows over them forever. The wide, outspread vastness of angelic jubilee, the thing likest to immensity of all created things, created to mirror the immensity of God, is all an emanation from the Precious Blood. Nay, it is a changeful, changeless sea, with tides; for there are daily, hourly increases of new joys in the angels from the conversions of sinners; and these conversions are precisely the operations of the Precious Blood. Yet that ocean of angelic jubilee washes but the base of Mary's throne. Her joy is like the fringe of the blessedness of God. It is all the multitudinous joys of creatures made one joy by her Divine Maternity, and multiplied, as well as intensified, by being one. Yet the bliss of Mary is all from the Precious Blood, the nearest gladness to the gladness of the Sacred Humanity, the first heart filled from the Sacred Heart. But who shall tell the nameless, immeasurable joys with which the Precious Blood fills the Sacred Heart itself? It cannot contain its own jubilee. It multiplies itself in order to relieve its exultation. It has inundated heaven; but the vast shores of the empyrean confine it and restrain its floods. By the help of its omnipotence, behold! it escapes as if by miracle, sparkles in countless daily chalices upon earth, and within the cup of each chalice it peacefully outstretches itself, unhindered in its infinity, with its grandeur enfranchised, and its love set free from all material laws. But the jubilee of the Precious Blood lies onward still and onward, whither we cannot explore it. We listen to hear its breakers sounding on the misty shore. But there comes no sound. The shores are too far off; or are there shores at all? The Word delights eternally in his Human Blood. Its golden glow beautifies the fires of the Holy Ghost. Its ministries beget inexplicable joys in the Unbegotten Father.

I was upon the seashore; and my heart filled with love it knew not why. Its happiness went out over the wide waters and upon the unfettered wind, and swelled up into the free dome of blue sky until it filled it. The dawn lighted up the faces of the ivory cliffs, which the sun and sea had been blanching for centuries of God's unchanging love. The miles of noiseless sands seemed vast as if they were the floor of eternity. Somehow the daybreak was like eternity. The idea came over me of that feeling of acceptance, which so entrances the soul just judged and just admitted into heaven. *To be saved!* I said to myself, *To be saved!* Then the thoughts of all the things implied in salvation came in one thought upon me; and I said, This is the one grand joy of life; and I clapped my hands like a child, and spoke to God aloud. But then there came many thoughts all in one thought, about the nature and manner of our salvation. *To be saved with such a salvation!* This was a grander joy, the second grand joy of life: and I tried to say some lines of a hymn; but the words were choked in my throat. The ebb was sucking the sea down over the sand quite silently; and the cliffs were whiter, and more daylike. Then there came many more thoughts all in one thought; and I stood still without intending it. *To be saved by such a Saviour!* This was the grandest joy of all, the third grand joy of life; and it swallowed up the other joys; and after it there could be on earth no higher joy. I said nothing; but I looked at the sinking sea as it reddened in the morning. Its great heart was throbbing in the calm; and methought I saw the Precious Blood of Jesus in heaven, throbbing that hour with real human love of me.

CHAPTER V

THE PRODIGALITY OF THE PRECIOUS BLOOD

CHAPTER V

THE PRODIGALITY OF THE PRECIOUS BLOOD

LET us kneel down before the magnificence of God. It is out-stretched as an ocean of manifold Being and yet of indivisible, uncreated Life, intolerable in its splendor, uncircumscribed in its simplicity. His magnificence is the vastness of his beauty, the multitude of his perfections, the coruscations of his sanctity, the impetuosity of his communicativeness, the minuteness of his government, the strange celestial sweetness of his gifts, the prodigality of his tenderness, the abysses of his incredible condescensions, and the exuberance of his simplicity. These are many words; but the idea is one. Our thought of God's magnificence is as a sea. It changes not; but it changes us while we look upon it. We see the calm of eternity upon its waters, peaceful as an endless evening. Airs from a far country come quivering over its shining tracts, freighted with aromatic odors, which are diffused around and sensibly deepen the tranquillity. Then again the freshness of morning is upon its swaying fields; and a thousand waves crest themselves with foam, and fling up star-showers into the sunlight; and it booms upon the shore; and it makes us feel the gentleness of power which knows how to become terrible; and the visible unexerted omnipotence is an admonition to prayer. Then it clothes itself with the plumage of darkness, and murmurs in the midnight as if it were gone down to a great distance; in order that we may know how different it is when it is felt from what it is when it is seen. Another while it lies gray-green beneath a sunless sky, with snow-capped cliffs around, sovereign when all else is

189

subject, free when all else has lost its liberty, immutable when all else has suffered winter's change. It has also its tempests, more beautiful and more terrible than the glorious storms of earth. Its lightnings make the darkness round it palpable and solid. Its thunders command a universal silence. Its decrees rush after each other in mighty waves of orderly confusion, menacing the land like falling towers, and breaking in dull inarticulate shocks against the precipices of the divine justice. Yet ever more, in storm or calm, there lies upon the ocean the light of the Precious Blood of Jesus, restful as the golden red of evening, hopeful as the rosy flush of dawn. This is the figure of the magnificence of God.

There is nothing more glorious upon earth than magnificence, nothing which more delights the mind or expands the soul, while it gratifies the senses at the same time that it ennobles their pleasure. But, among creatures, magnificence is always a revelation of defects. Indeed, it not only discloses imperfections, but causes them. It is too great an effort. It calls for sacrifices which had better not be made. It is often obliged to be regardless of justice. It is made up of imprudences. There is for the most part a tyranny about it. Much suffering has generally to be contributed to it; and the suffering falls mostly on those who have not the glory of the magnificence. Moreover, it is debased by ostentation, and disfigured by pretence. Nevertheless it wins the applause of men, and even lives in history. The nations will pardon almost any thing to magnificence. It seems to satisfy a want of the soul which is rarely satisfied. It refreshes the littleness of the creature; and, even when it is the glory of one man, it is felt as if it were that one man's gift to all mankind. What then must be the beauty and the delight of magnificence when it is supremely holy? What must be its grandeur where it is natural? How great must be its splendor when it is the normal expression and the simple exercise of innumerable perfections! There is no effort in the magnificence of God, and no display. It is not a higher height rising above the lowlands. It is not a transient demonstration. It is the refulgence of his eternal quietude. It is the brightness of his infinite justice.

It is the unchanging aspect of his glorious sanctity. It is the inevitable light of the riches of the Godhead. It is the self-possessed enjoyment of his beatitude. To us all holiness is a form of restraint. We can hardly form to ourselves any other conception of it. If we try to do so, we shall be surprised to find how difficult it is. Think then what holiness must be, where it is a form of largeness, of prodigality, of boundless freedom! Yet this is the magnificence of God.

Roses grow on briers, say the wise men of the world, with that sententious morality which thinks to make virtue truthful by making it dismal. Yes! but, as the very different spirit of piety would say, it is a truer truth that briers bloom with roses. If roses have thorns, thorns also have roses. This is the rule of life. Yet everybody tells us one side of this truth, and nobody tells us the other. A kind-hearted man finds life full of joys, for he makes joys of things which else were not joys; and a simple-hearted man can be very joyous on a little joy; and to the pure-hearted man all things are joys. How can the world be an unhappy world, which has so magnificent a God? His magnificence is the fountain of all our joys; for it is the fountain of salvation. Here lies the secret of the inveterate happiness of the world. Even in its fall, it is so implicated in the blessedness of God that it has not a darkness anywhere without its light, nor a bitter without its sweet. God's simple presence is an overflowing of delight. His inanimate creatures have a changeless joy stamped upon their mute features. The multitudinous species of unreasoning creatures, whether they belong to the earth, to the air, or to the waters, plainly revel in life as a joy which fills their natures to the brim. We ourselves have a hundred happinesses, even when we fancy ourselves quite desolate. There is no real desolation except mortal sin. There is too much of God everywhere to allow either of permanent or general unhappiness. He, who can find his joy in God, is in heaven already; only it is a heaven which is not secured to him, unless he perseveres to the end. Yet is it hard to find our joy in God? Rather, is it not hard to find our joy in any thing else? The magnificence of God is the abounding joy of life. It is an immense joy to belong to God. It is an immense joy to have such a God belonging to us. Like the joys of heaven, it is a joy new every morning when we wake, as new as if we had never tasted it before. Like the joys of earth, it is a joy every evening resting and pacifying the soul. But it has a gift of its own besides. For its novelty grows fresher and more striking daily, and its repose more satisfying and more complete. The joy of God's magnificence more than counterbalances all mortal griefs. When I think of his magnificence, of all that his magnificence implies, of its intimate concernment with myself, and of the way in which I am always sinking more and more irretrievably into the abysses of his sovereignty, I often wonder how we can contain ourselves with joy at having such a God.

In treating of the prodigality of the Precious Blood it is necessary that we should have clear ideas of the magnificence of God: for the one is a part of the other. No one, of course, doubts the magnificence of God. Our loftiest conceptions must fall infinitely below the gorgeousness of the reality. No accumulation of beautiful ideals can reach the incredible glory of the truth. An immensity of omnipotent beauty is a thing which it bewilders us to think of. We should suppose that a single glimpse of the magnificence of God would annihilate us by its excess of impetuous light. Yet, notwithstanding all this, the character of God is never revealed to us more intimately or more clearly than when he is disclosed to us as the God who "orders all things in measure, in number, and weight."* He does every thing by measure. The Immeasurable decrees by measure, works by measure, rewards by measure, punishes by measure, delights in measure. The Eternal, of uncounted ages, of uncounted spaces, loves to count by numbers. He counts all things, and calls them by their names. He surrounds each unity with his whole Self, with his entire justice, with his complete love. He leaves out nothing. He overlooks nobody. It belongs to him as Creator to be accurate, to be methodical, to be infallible in his minuteness. The Illimitable weighs

---

*Wisdom xi. 21.

all things, as if their weight were an object even to his unsearchable riches. His magnificence delights in nothing more than in the strictness of proportions. His justice weighs out glory with the most unblemished accuracy. Even his measure that is pressed down, and shaken together, and running over, has all its merciful superfluity weighed out with minutest carefulness. The very orbs that roll in heaven keep up the universal harmony by the exceeding nicety and adjustment of their weights. So is it in the world of grace. So is it in the world of glory. Our God is an accurate God; and in nothing is he more adorable than in his accuracy.

Magnificence, in our idea of it, is above law. Now, to our eyes, the divinest of all God's propensities is his love of law. The grandeur of his liberty is, that it is an uncircumscribed law. Within his own infinite life all things are absolutely necessary, all things are, in the most transcendental sense of the word, laws. His knowledge of himself is not the Holy Ghost; but it is the Word. His love of himself is not the Word; but it is the Holy Ghost. Much more is this magnificent attribute of law-lovingness shown forth in his external works, wherein there is no necessity. He is himself a sufficient living law to his creation. Yet everywhere in the universe he is at once multiplying and simplifying laws. Every thing is done by law, the least no less than the greatest of things. He almost hides himself behind an impenetrable screen of laws. It is as if he wished to fetter his infinite freedom with an infinity of finite laws. He seems to make himself the captive of his own punctuality. Every time and place have their laws. There is not a corner of creation where there is not a whole code of laws. His omnipresence is an omnipresence of law. Every thing wears the chains of order, of sequence, of repetition. From this adorable love of law comes the unutterable tranquillity of all the divine operations in the world. It is this tranquillity which makes the earth so like a sanctuary, it is so manifestly the covering under which God hides himself. The silent calm of so much onward overwhelming power, the gentleness of such a gigantic pressure, the graceful, unsuspecting liberty amidst such a complication of restraints, the unhindered exuberance of such multitudinous and

seemingly eccentric life, the unending soundless conflict of op-
posing forces which ends in such unhindered amplitude of
repose and harmony—all these things are from that gracious
propensity to law which belongs to the sweet majesty of God. It
is his way to love uniformity; and the Creator's uniformity is the
creature's liberty. It is his uniformity and his slowness which at
once represent his eternity and yet hinder it from oppressing
time.

The magnificence of God, then, is no waste of splendor. It is no
lavish prodigality of glory. It is not a mere pageant of his royal
state. It is, if we may use the word, a necessity to God. He cannot
be otherwise. He is magnificent, simply because he is God. He
cannot lay down his grandeur, or be less grand, or be grander at
one time than at another. Magnificence is his divine life. It does
not cling to his perfections like a robe. It is inseparable from him.
It is the outward operation of his wonderful attributes. It is the
inward tranquillity of his incomprehensible life. His accuracy, his
punctuality, his love of law, his propensity to number, measure,
and weight, his fashion of uniformity, his ways of order and sequence—all these things are part of the magnificence of God;
and they are the ways by which his magnificence is imparted to
his creatures. This is very different from our human ideas of
magnificence, and must be borne in mind. The truth is, that God
is so high that we can only approach to truth in speaking of him
by speaking in superlatives. Thus we often speak of his love and
his compassion as if he did more for us than he need do, as if
less would be sufficient, as if he wasted grace with a kind of
spendthrift generosity, as if his magnificence were always in excess. All this expresses a most holy truth, so far as the inconceivable magnificence of his goodness toward us is concerned. Yet it
is not true, so far as regards the awful magnificence of God himself. In like manner we sometimes speak of the Incarnation and
of the Atonement, as if they had persuaded God to be less God
than he really is, as if they had given mercy some sort of advantage against justice, as if God would overlook now what he
would not overlook before, as if the terms of forgiveness of sin

had become easier because God's sanctity was content with less. This also expresses a kind of truth. I am not quarrelling with the language. Holy Scripture sometimes uses it, in order to make things plain to us. All language about God labors under the necessity of being inaccurate. It cannot even escape by being merely short of truth. But, when it becomes of importance to us to obtain a somewhat clearer view of any particular attribute of God, then we must do our best to correct this otherwise harmless error in our minds. It is necessary now, in order to understand what we popularly term the prodigality of the Precious Blood, to understand also that God's magnificence does not overwhelm, as with an inundation of glorious light, his love of law, repetition, order, and accuracy, or his methodical uniformity, or his punctual strictness, or his undistracted attention to details; but rather it brings out all these characteristics still more strongly, because it shows him to be magnificent precisely in these things, and because of them.

Thus the divine magnificence is a divine method of order and measure. So far from being above the restraints of law, its grandest developments of itself are by means of laws. So far from being oblivious of petty details, its infinity confounds the distinction between great and small, and makes all things equal in its sight. May I not even say that in some mysteries, and from some human points of view, there is even an appearance of parsimony in the magnificence of God? Is there not, to our ignorance, this semblance about the fall of the angels, and about the long delay of the Incarnation, and about the low tides of grace which are known to the experience of most men in their own lives? It is not so, but it seems so. God is never parsimonious; but he is sometimes sparing. He proportions graces to temptations in a way which disquiets us because it makes our risks plainer. His very liberality is adorably just. His gifts are given under laws. They are the administration of his laws. Thus it comes to pass that his magnificence partakes of the severity of his holiness. What looks to us like economy is in fact the operation of his exceeding sanctity.

Nevertheless, when all this order, and sequence, and law, and proportion, and number, and weight, and measure, and accuracy, are upon a scale which is infinite, when they are all clothed in immensity, when they are the vast sweeping circuits of everlasting decrees, when they hold a love which is inexhaustible and a compassion which is unwearied and a tenderness which has no likeness to itself outside of God, they have all that exuberance, lavishness, and prodigality, which are the characteristics of magnificence. Only they have these things without the corresponding imperfections which are inseparable from them in the case of creatures. Prodigality in this higher sense is a characteristic of all the divine works. Finite and limited as they are, nothingness and the children of nothingness, yet in that they are also the creations of God they wonderfully shadow forth the munificence of his immensity. We have already seen this in the number of the angels. We cannot meditate upon their countless multitudes without astonishment. So vast a populace, of such surpassing beauty, of such gigantic intelligence, of such diversified nature, is simply overwhelming to our most ambitious thoughts. A locust-swarm, and each locust an archangel, the myriads of points of life disclosed to us by the microscope, and each point a grand spirit, the sands of the seas and the waters of the ocean, and each grain and each drop a beautiful being the brightness of whose substance we could not see and live—this is but an approximation to the reality. So theologians teach us. Or, again, let us think of the multitudinousness of the starry skies. Astronomers tell us that our Milky Way is but one of hundreds, perhaps of thousands, of nebulae to which our instruments may hope to reach. Yet our one Milky Way, in which we ourselves are dwellers, is reported to contain thirty millions of suns; and we are but a little planet of one of the lesser suns. Moreover, it is probable that the depth in space in which our instruments can reach is but as the ankle-deep water on the shore, through which the fearless child can wade in sport, compared with the yet unfathomed depths of the mid-ocean. Figures are hardly a help to us in estimating the probable number of God's worlds. St. John speaks with rapture of the multitude of the saved, as of a number that no man can count. The same magnificence of numbers reigns in the laws and the lives of the material world; and who can doubt but that the spiritual far outstrips the material world in its prolific exuberance of graces and inspirations? We are speaking only of numbers; and yet see the magnificence of God! For the vastness of the numbers is but a lesser development of the boundless love from which creation springs. It is the royalty of his love which the blameless custom of the faithful has named his prodigality.

Now let us apply all this to the prodigality of the Precious Blood. In nothing was he more likely to be prodigal than in this work, which was especially to minister to his Dominion and his Magnificence. In nothing was he more likely to be prodigal than in that which represented in itself the whole series of his divine decrees. In nothing is it of so much importance to us that he should be magnificent as in the shedding of his Blood. It would be part of his Dominion, part of his Magnificence, to be accurately prodigal of that which made his Dominion more dear to him, and his Magnificence more magnificent. Yet I would fain keep before you what I hinted at in the Second Chapter—that the prodigality of the Precious Blood is simply necessary for our wretchedness, that we could not do with less of it, that, if so infinite a price were to be paid for our redemption, it must be infinitely paid. I said a while ago that magnificence was a kind of necessity to God. He could not help being magnificent, precisely because he is God. Now, I want to say that, in a sense which is full of devotional reality, the magnificence of the Creator is the creature's necessity. We could not do without it. We could not live, still less rejoice, if God were less magnificent. It is true we cannot comprehend God. But we can possess him, we can enjoy him; nay, we must possess him, we must enjoy him, in his whole Self. We must do so, or fall into the abyss of eternal death. Unless his infinity thus supports, sustains, fulfils, our finiteness, we are but ruin and desolation. It is his infinity thus compassionately and delightedly acting upon our finiteness, which we call his magnificence. It is an attribute which ought to be most dear to us, and which we should honor with a special devotion. If the tranquillity of holiness comes of our loving to be overwhelmed by the sovereignty of God, we come to love his sovereignty by delighting in his magnificence.

What we have said amounts to this. The magnificence of God was nowhere more needed than in the Precious Blood; and, as a matter of fact, it has been nowhere more shown. It was of surpassing importance to us that it should be so. Moreover, we have seen all along that the magnificence of God is the attribute to which the Precious Blood is very specially addicted, and that the attribute of dominion is never separated from that of magnificence. The Precious Blood conquered creation back for the Creator, and reconquered the lordship of creation for the Sacred Humanity of Jesus. It is a magnificent price for sin, because it is infinite; and sin is only infinite by a figure of speech or an invention of mind. We did not therefore require an infinite redemption: though on the side of God's sanctity there may have been a propriety, looking to us like a necessity, for an infinite expiation. Furthermore, one drop of the Precious Blood would suffice to redeem all possible worlds; so we did not require more than our share of that drop. We did not require of absolute necessity that it should be so often shed; or that it should be shed under such a variety of pathetic circumstances, every one of which is a beautiful allurement of love; or that it should be all shed, shed even by a miracle of jealous prodigality after death. In all this, the magnificence of God goes beyond our necessities, and envelops us in its own immensity. But those other wonders of his magnificence, that we should have unrestricted, repeated, incessant access to the Precious Blood, that it should be to us more copious, more prompt, more at hand, more abundant, than the water of our wells and streams, that at every turn of life it should be conveyed to our souls by glorious aqueducts of divine invention, namely, the Sacraments, that it should be as common and as convenient to the life of our souls as the air is to the life of our bodies—all these wonders are simply necessities to a wretchedness and a feebleness so utter and prostrate as ours. The sinfulness of sin causes us to require nothing short of this. Thus there are two prodigalities of the Precious Blood, both belonging to the adorable magnificence of God; but one of which is a simple necessity to us, while the other is a liberality of his magnificence, befitting his love, in keeping with his perfections, but not a necessity to us.

I have laid some stress upon this, for the following reason. There is often a good deal of exaggeration in devotional books, and it is for the most part practically harmless. Yet there are cases in which it may come at last to be mischievous; and these are generally cases where the exaggeration in question tends to give an erroneous idea of God, and especially of his strictness and sanctity. Thus, writers, as I have said before, sometimes speak of the Incarnation as if God were less strict and jealous in consequence of it; and this leads men not to think sufficiently of mortification and good works. So, if we dwell one-sidedly upon the goodness of God in giving us such abundant access to the Precious Blood, we may easily fall into an unreality. Of course, it would have been a wonderful disclosure of God's magnificence, if he had justified us once for all in Baptism through the Precious Blood. It would have been worthy to have sustained the wonder of the angels through eternity. What then are we to say to the bewildering varieties, facilities, repetitions, and exuberances of the Precious Blood? Plainly, no language that we can use can really exaggerate the magnificence of God's goodness in this respect. But we may come to think that we wanted less than God has given us, that his magnificence was not a necessity to us, but that the very meaning of his magnificence is excess, is his doing more than we require. Thus, we become less careful about corresponding to grace and about fidelity to inspirations. We imagine ourselves in a great wasteful sea of grace, which we may move about in, as a fish moves about in the waters of the ocean, drinking when it will, but not requiring for its whole life more than a few sips of the unfathomable depths. Whereas the truth is, that not a single grace comes to earth which does not come addressed to some individual soul, and is not noted by God, and has not to be given account for at the last. There is not one least grace, not one most transient inspiration, which is not part of God's accurate and orderly providence over each one of us for the salvation of our souls. Consequently there is not one which can safely be neglected. We have no more grace than we require. St. Teresa tells us that, even where the grace of perfection is given, it is often necessary for mere salvation. As a theological speculation, we could be saved with less; but in practice we should be lost if we had less.

Thus, while, on the one hand, the masters of the spiritual life warn us not to attempt to go beyond our grace, they teach us still more emphatically that we must be faithful to the grace we have. We read that one Communion is enough to make a saint. So it is in itself; and it is important that we should know this, as it brings home to us the value of Communion. Yet, in fact, hundreds of Communions may in our case be practically necessary, not to make us saints but just to save our souls. The grand practical mischief to men's souls is the neglect of the Sacraments. The grand practical mistake of pious people is the neglect of fidelity to grace. I believe that unintentionally spiritual writers are somewhat to blame for both these unfortunate delusions. They cannot magnify too much the magnificence of God. They cannot magnify too much the redeeming grace of our Blessed Lord. But they may magnify both one and the other without making proper distinctions. What I have wanted to dwell upon, and experience has shown me the utility of it, is that, while God's magnificence gives us a superabundance of grace, that superabundance is not in reality a superfluity. We have not a grace which we can afford to spare. Our frequent absolutions are not too frequent for us; nor our many Communions, if under obedience, too many. One grace may be enough in itself to save a soul; but it will not save it if it was not precisely meant to do so. It does not derogate from God's magnificence, that we should stand absolutely in need of its grand largeness. But the knowledge of this necessity gives us a truer view of our wretchedness, and fosters our humility. So also God's magnificence is not a perfection which rough-rides his exactness, his accuracy, his punctuality, his methodical minuteness, his jealousy of law, and his scrupulous distributions and proportions. Yet we often speak as if it did do so; and hence we come to think, not to put into words, but practically to think, that God in Jesus Christ is God with one half of his ever-blessed perfections dispensing themselves from the other half. This lowers our standard of his sanctity; and whatever lowers that lowers also our estimate of the sinfulness of sin, and our carefulness in avoiding little sins. May I consider that I have proved that God's magnificence is sometimes a necessity to us, and that it is not on that account less magnificent?

There are then two prodigalities of the Precious Blood, both belonging to the magnificence of God; and one of the two belonging also to our necessities. We must examine both of them. As I said before, the very choice of the Precious Blood as the instrument of our redemption is part of God's magnificence. There were merit and satisfaction enough in a single tear of the Infant Jesus to have redeemed us all. Nothing in the external works of God is necessary; and therefore the Precious Blood is not necessary. God was free to have chosen some other expiation, or he was free to have pardoned us without any expiation at all. Yet nothing is merely gratuitous with God; nothing is unnecessary, even though it be not necessary. There was doubtless on the side of the divine perfections such a propriety and fitness in the choice of an infinite sacrifice for sin, that it was in one sense necessary to have one. There were doubtless, in the depths of the same perfections, reasons and fitnesses for the Precious Blood of the Incarnate Word being chosen for that sacrifice, which may form part of the blessed science of another life. Divine love, divine justice, and divine sanctity, have necessities of their own, which do not interfere with their freedom. All this, then, belongs to the magnificence of God without belonging to our necessity; and may be considered truly as a prodigality of the divine compassion. But I will illustrate what I may now venture, without fear of being misunderstood, to call the unnecessary prodigality of the Precious Blood by the manner and circumstances in and under which it was shed during the Three-and-Thirty Years; and we shall be most closely following the mind of the Church, if we select, as our examples, the Seven Bloodsheddings, which are put before us as the objects of indulgenced devotions.

There has been some variety in the enumeration of the Seven Bloodsheddings by different holy persons, though the difference has been little more than one of division. The enumeration which we shall follow is the one approved and indulgenced by Pius the Seventh. The Seven are the Circumcision, the Agony, the Scourging, the Crowning with Thorns, the Way of the Cross, the Crucifixion, and the piercing of the Sacred Heart. There is no doubt a divine intention in these particular seven mysteries. We shall find that they illustrate in a most complete and touching manner the spirit of the Precious Blood. While they are like each other, they are also different. They have that mixture of likeness and of difference, which so often makes up the beauty of divine works. One of them belongs to the Infancy, and the other six to the Passion. Six of them were sufferings of Jesus, and one was that mute preaching of his love which took place after he was dead. The first and the last had nothing to do with the redemption of the world; the first because it had no connection with his death, and the last because it only took place after he was already dead. Of some of the others also, but less certainly, we may say that they did not belong to our redemption. At all of them our Blessed Lady was present, in spirit, if not in body, and all of them were sorrows to her immaculate heart. In the number of times that the Blood was shed, in the quantity shed, and in the mysterious manners of its shedding, it is the magnificence of God which is revealing the excesses of his love. Each Bloodshedding has its own way of touching our hearts, and its own attraction for our devotion. The whole Seven together have also a distinctive unity, and form a complete picture and a definite spirit in our souls.

The first Bloodshedding was the Circumcision. To the Heart of Jesus, already enamored of sorrow and suffering, seven days were enough for the tranquil joys of Bethlehem, joys over whose tranquillity the shadow of Calvary was already cast. The stainless Mother had only one short octave of the Precious Blood for her own delight. She knew its mission and its mystery. She saw it in the almost transparent vase of the Infant Body. She saw the pulses of its life beat with all the natural rapidity of childhood. Through the veil of snowy skin she saw its purple streams. From time to time she saw it mantle in his Face, and flush his little cheek. She saw its coral upon those tiny lips, over which were to flow the words of everlasting life, and also the awful judgments of uncounted millions of human souls. In the still night she heard its throbbing, and adored the mysteries of that busy sleep, the secrets of that silent Heart. When she clasped him to her breast, she felt the beatings of the Precious Blood, and knew that it was the harmless force of the vast omnipotence, which had with such sweet craft imprisoned itself in the frailty and the littleness of a new-born Babe. She knew it was that Blood, which the justice of the Father sought after. She knew how lovingly and how severely his sanctity thirsted for its shedding. She was awe-struck with the thoughts which crowded upon her; and yet, those amazing thoughts! how full of joyousness they were! She knew the temper of that dear Blood, and bore with its impatience, an impatience which love might have deemed unreasonable; only that the love of Jesus is the adoration of him also. He had hastened the time of his coming, because of the loveliness of Mary. He had been impatient even in heaven. Now he had come into her arms. He had looked in her eyes but seven short days. How much the two silences of the Mother and the Son had to say to each other! Could he not rest a while? Need he begin redeeming all at once? Nay, he cannot redeem yet. There are Three-and-Thirty Years to be spent before that, crowded with the fulfilment of numerous eternal purposes. No! he cannot rest. He could not rest in his Father's Bosom. He cannot rest in his Mother's arms. His rest is in the shedding of his Blood. Let the Child shed his Blood, and then he will be content to rest: and so he shed it in the Circumcision, being yet but eight days old.

Strange thought! but there were seven days during which our Blessed Lord was nameless. How did Joseph name him? if indeed, in the fulness of his joy, that peaceful saint needed to speak at all. Now with the Blood comes the sweet Name of Jesus, as if he had no right to it, until he shed his Blood. Impatient Blood! Yet its first act is to put itself beneath the law! It will begin by obeying, though it is in no wise bound to such obedience. It will let itself be taken captive by a ritual, as soon as it is born. See how full it is, from the first, of the law-loving instincts of God's magnificence. But of what use were those first drops of that Precious Blood? They had no redeeming power in them, because they were disconnected from his Death. They were not a part of the Blood shed for the sins of the world. Doubtless they had special purposes and did secret wonders, as we have already seen in the revelation to Frances of the Mother of God.* All the things of God are pregnant with undisclosed mysteries, are endowed with unsuspected powers, and have eternally-foreseen destinations. For us it is enough to see in this dear impatience, in this sweet child-like waste, if we may dare thus to speak, most touching revelations of our Saviour's love. The days of type and figure had not yet gone by; and he gave us this mystery as a type and figure of his future life and work. He taught us doctrine by it also, the doctrine that, now that man had fallen, he had only assumed his Blood in order that he might shed it. It was so completely for us, that it was more ours than his. By needing redemption, we made his Blood more utterly and more intimately ours, than if we had never sinned. All things turn to love, all things turn to our profit, when they belong to Jesus. Perhaps, too, this mystery was also very specially for St. Joseph. It was his Calvary. He saw no more of the Passion, except that it was shown him mystically, and that, after the fashion of the saints, he was perhaps made partaker of its mysteries and inward stigmata. Otherwise he saw the Precious Blood no more, until the morning of Easter. Joseph counted for much in the plans of God. He shared all, or most, of those Mary-haunting years at Nazareth, when the whole wide world without had but a three years' Ministry bestowed upon it. Doubtless many mysteries of the early years of Jesus were meant singularly for St. Joseph. This Circumcision

---

*See pages 167, 168.

was his one mystery of the Precious Blood. It begins each year for us. It is our new year's day. It braids upon the front of every coming year of life the Name of Jesus, our life's dear Lord, and it braids it in those red snow-drops of his Infancy, the first blossoms of his Precious Blood.

But who shall tell the share of Mary in this mystery? It was an exceeding joy to her; for to what holy heart would not the sight of the Precious Blood be a jubilee? It had been a wondrous joy to her, after her months of expectation, to see the Face of Jesus in the cave of Bethlehem. It was a beauty, the thought of which had fed her desires, but the reality of which was bliss unspeakable. So now it was a joy, in which was mingled perhaps still more of wonder, to see the Precious Blood, which had purchased her own Immaculate Conception, and the redemption of all mankind. It was a joy to her also to read in our Lord's translucent Heart the inward dispositions in which he first shed his Blood. His abounding gladness, his inexpressible adoration of God, his intense love of souls, the unsearchable riches which his own Blood was to himself, as enabling him to satisfy so many loves and so many worships—all these things she saw, and rejoicing she adored. Doubtless also many hidden meanings of the mystery were visible to the clear eye of her sinless soul. At the same time it was a bitter grief as well. It was a public beginning of sorrows, as the marriage at Cana was the public beginning of miracles. As her dolors at the foot of the Cross made her one of his executioners, so his little Passion now was her own ministry. If, as some think, and it seems by far the truest thought, it was her own hand which shed the Blood, who does not see how fitting it was that she first should shed that Blood which, before all others and above all others, was to be shed for her?

Long years have passed since that cruel New Year's Day of the guiltless Babe of Bethlehem; and now another scene opens to our view. It is the Agony in the Garden. The spot looks tranquil, innocent, and unconscious now, when the crisp foliage of the olives turns its silver lining to the wind, and, within the latticed fence of the Franciscan friars, the tall sceptres of the golden-rod rise up from among the trailing gourds, and the roses bloom among the yellow flowers, and all is gay and garden-like. But it was once the scene of a fearful mystery, the mystery of the second Bloodshedding. Jesus kneels there. He is now a grown-up man. Three-and-thirty years have passed over him. They have been the longest, because the fullest, years that earth has ever known. His weary Ministry of three years has drawn to its close. He has often been weary. He was weary when he sat by Jacob's well and asked the Samaritan woman for an alms of the cold fresh water he himself had created. He has been weary on the mountain-sides, when he prayed instead of sleeping, while the moon shone tremulously on the limestone rocks, as if it hardly dared to light up the furtive figure of its Creator keeping watch among the crags. But his love of souls has never yet been tired. His weariness has never reached the yearnings of his Sacred Heart. This Thursday night amidst the olives we find him still unchanged. We ventured to charge his dear love with impatience three-and-thirty years ago. We charge it with impatience now. Why will not the Precious Blood keep back until its time? Can it not wait now some twelve or fifteen hours more for Calvary? It is the way of human desire to grow more impatient, as it draws nearer to its object. See what a true human heart this Heart of Jesus is! We dare to love it more when it looks so very human. Tomorrow men will crucify his blessed Body, and pour out his Blood like water. But tomorrow is not soon enough. Tonight his adorable Soul, that King among creatures, that royallest of all the works of God, will itself crucify his Body. He will suffer a martyrdom tonight even more mysterious than that martyrdom on Calvary. What impatience! What precipitation! He began his ministry by an act of precipitation, by working a miracle before his time, because his Mother asked him. He ends it with another act of precipitation: he anticipates his Passion. But what is it about him which is so impatient? It is his Blood. It is burning to be shed. It longs to leave its sanctuary in the Sacred Heart, as if it were wearied with so much waiting. He himself had waited four thousand years before he came. There was delay enough then. Now all things are quickened, are even anticipated. It is the pulses of the Precious Blood which are hurrying all things forward. See now what that Soul is doing. It gathers round it all the sins of men, manifold, multitudinous, ponderous. Over its beautiful sanctity it puts on all this hideous apparel, which burns like poison and like fire. It clothes itself thus with the most awful human shudderings. He only preserves his life by an energetic miracle. Never on earth was there such mortal heaviness, such aching sadness, such a drying up of life's fountains, such a tormenting languor, such an exceeding sickening of soul. Then it lifts up its hands, that mighty Soul, as if with more than Samson's strength it were about to pull down the big heavens upon itself; and it draws down upon itself the huge storm of God's eternal justice and overwhelming wrath, and then lies crushed beneath it, a plaintive Human Life almost extinguished, and only not extinguished because it is a Divine Life as well. Such Manhood! Such Godhead! Who is equal to so terrible a mystery? Ah, Jesus! how dreadful is this solitude, which is even deepened by the presence of that one trembling angel whom thy cries have drawn from heaven! The Sacred Heart can bear no more. It gives out its red life, as in a wine-press. Drop by drop, unnaturally, through the burning pores of the skin, the beads of Blood ooze out. They stand upon his brow, and then roll down his face. They clog his hair. They blind his eyes. They fill his mouth, otherwise than as the chalice of his Blood filled it three hours ago. They mat his beard. They wet his hands. They suffuse every limb as in a universal Sweat of Blood. They stain his garments. They ruddy the olive-roots. They spot the white dust with black. Truly, if ever suffering was beautiful—and how little suffering there has been on earth that was not beautiful!—it was the woe which the paschal moon beheld beneath the olive-trees that night.

Who can tell the mysteries of this Second Bloodshedding? Yet here again we have the same feature of prodigality. This Blood shed itself through the desire of redeeming the world; yet it did not itself redeem it, because it was not the Blood of his death. It was his own act, not the appointed sacrificial act of others. But what a vast significancy of love there was in this miraculous portent of the Bloody Sweat! He was straitened, it was his own word, with eagerness for his Passion. He had desired with desire, it is his own expletive, to drink his own Blood with his disciples. So had he desired with desire to shed it, and thus he had anticipated noonday at midnight, and had made a Calvary of Olivet. Mary was present in the garden, though she was also in the house of John. All men were asleep. Alas! even the three Apostles close at hand were sleeping. Only Judas was awake, and the handful of the servitors of tyranny that were with him. Yet even for them Jesus would not wait. His Blood so burned with love of souls that it could not contain any longer its impetuous instinct to be shed. He could get no man to wound him in that lonely garden, which had been to him so often a sweet haunt for prayer. So he let his heart wound him from within. Observe also that the very pressure of his Passion in thought could only translate itself into the language of a Bloodshedding. When the vehement, ponderous justice of God crushed him to the earth, the mark that it left upon the earth, as afterward on the napkin of Veronica, was an impression traced in Blood. The sin he had assumed was within him; it had sunk into him; the anger of the Father was upon him. Thus the inward and the outward of his Passion met, and they were one—in Blood.

The sun in the heavens and the shadows in the streets mark it to be about nine of the morning in Jerusalem. It is the hour of the Third Bloodshedding, the Scourging. This is the most intolerable of all the mysteries of our Blessed Saviour's Passion. It is the one which is the hardest to contemplate in the quietness of prayer. There is something revolting in the anguish of sheer bodily pain. There is something degrading in the intentional infliction of shame. Yet these two horrors are combined in the mystery of the Scourging. Our Lord is left in the hands of the vilest satellites of criminal justice. There is neither the pomp of a court, nor the pageant of an execution. He is at the mercy of the vilest and most abhorred of men. The punishment is one, in his case, without check, without measure, and without order.

When we think of the contact of their loathsome hands, and their
abominable sacrilege in stripping his Sacred Body, a shudder
of anguish passes all through us, as though some secret sanctuary
of God were being violated. The shame of it seems to gather
round ourselves, and we are hardly able to hold up our heads.
We pray about it with our eyes shut as if by instinct. The shape,
the gaze, the variety, of the instruments of torture are alike hor-
rible. The muscular violence and brutal gestures of the executioners offend our very thought. Then the sounds! the dull
sounds of the scourges as they fall upon the living Holy of Holies,
monotonous yet various, changing as the whips are changed, and
then the wet sound as the thongs become soaked with Blood—
who can bear them? The echoes from the houses in the place,
and the spiritual echoes from out the indignant meek heart of
the outraged Mother — are they not fearful also? The sound,
hardly perceptible till the ear becomes unnaturally quickened by
excitement, as of light-falling rain, which we know to be the
Precious Blood, mingles with that still fainter sound, as of the
almost inaudible bleating of a dying lamb, which we know to be
the Voice of God, complaining with that inextinguishable human
tenderness. Though our eyes are closed, we see the staring looks,
the compressed lips, the ferocious countenances, the knotted arms,
the rude swarthy chests, of the myrmidons of cruelty, denaturalized
by the brutality of their task. We see them sprinkled with Precious Blood, which mixes with their sweat and rolls down their
limbs with discolored stains. Him we do not see, even with the
eyes of our souls; for we have thrown ourselves on the pavement
in his Blood, and are holding his feet and are devouring them
with kisses. It is an intolerable mystery; yet, if we love him, we
must endure it. We must not be fastidious. He was not. We sent
him to this. It was suffered for us. We must not turn away. It is
an intolerable mystery; but it has a sweet gift. There is no mystery
of the Passion which so uncovers his Divinity to us. It is almost
like a vision of the Godhead. There is no mystery which fills our
souls so full of so deep an adoration.

But in this third Bloodshedding there is the same character of prodigality. It was shed in an excess of pain and an excess of shame; and it was shed in an excess of wasteful copiousness. It was as if it foresaw how on the Cross it would have but five local vents, five wells distilling salvation for the world, and it could not bear to be thus restricted. So now it presents the whole surface of the Body, that it may be able to gush forth in unrestrained abundance, as from one vast wound. A thousand channels, all gifted with exquisite sensation, and now burning with insufferable fire, are torn up and lacerated with the scourges. Streams of Precious Blood, infinite in price, each of them laden with the magnificence of God, broke forth in hundreds of places. Yet the Blood of the Column was not the Blood shed upon the Cross. It did not redeem the world, nor was it necessary to its redemption. It was simply one of the mysterious magnificences of the Precious Blood. Moreover the Blood of the Scourging was sprinkled as it were at random over careless multitudes, as if it were in type or prophecy of its future sacramental prodigality. Our blessed Lord himself appeared in strange symbolical guise in this Third Bloodshedding. In the Agony he had been seen by the Father clad in all the darkness of human sin. No human eye saw him in the shadowy moonlight, nor could have discerned his fearful transfiguration, even if it could have seen him. But now he was an open symbol to the city and the people. He was bathed in his own Blood. He was clad in a living robe of royal purple. He, the Redeemer, put on the image of the redeemed. As his Church was always to be, so was he then, all red with Precious Blood. As he was in the open place of Jerusalem, so are we in our Father's eyes at this hour, so shall we be in our happiness through all eternity, red, and red all over, with the glorious dye, better than that old imperial dye of Tyre, of his most Precious Blood. As he was in his shame and misery, so shall we be in our glory and our joy, all beautified with Blood, that self-same Blood wherewith they clothed him when they had stripped him of his garments.

But now the Precious Blood has swiftly formed a habit of being shed; and who shall stay it? It was with no bitterness, but with truthfullest love, that Jesus named that Friday the Day of his Espousals. But we read that his Jewish mother crowned him with a diadem in the day of his espousals. Whose heart does not leap up at the thought of such a mystery—the Coronation of the Creator by his creatures? Crowned as is each man's life with a beautiful coronal wreathed for him by divine love out of all God's perfections, what grateful crown shall they set upon his Head who has set them free by reigning over them as King? Alas! it is another Bloodshedding, the Fourth Bloodshedding, the Crowning of Thorns. It is his dear dominion which is distasteful to their hearts. They cannot bear that he should call himself a King. They would fain deride his kingship; but they feel and fear it all the while. If he had never been a King before, had he not become one now through the very royalty of his gentleness under the ignominies of the past night and the outrages of that morning? Only a king's face could look so venerable through such disfigurement. But his sweetness embittered them. It sank them in their own estimation. It taunted them by the mildness of its silence. There was something so worshipful in his woe that it uncrowned their vulgar bravery. His look humbled them, because it was so beautiful. So in the blindness of their malice they wrought a divine mystery. They crowned him King. The oppressed are given to be oppressors, and the violent to be brutal. If there be no other use of the Eternal God for Roman soldiers, at least he shall relieve the tedium of a Syrian guard-room. They have trouble enough with these Jewish criminals; they shall have sport out of them also. Sun and rain had come alternately on the green briers, which the unsuspecting earth had grown for the Creator. They had trailed over the sward. They had tangled themselves with many a juicy shoot. They had grown up into matted bushes, and the sun of autumn had hardened their soft spikes into strong, tough barbs. Perhaps the honey-bees had come to their flowers to extract sweetness, and the restless butterflies had been attracted for a moment by their aromatic fragrance, or the birds had rifled their golden berries with their beaks. But who would have dreamed that they were yet to be gilded with the Blood of their Creator? Protecting their hard-skinned hands with their leathern gauntlets, the soldiers weave a crown of these sharp and obstinate thorns. What matter if it be not exactly round? What matter if it be not made to fit the head of their mock Cæsar? With jest, and gibe, and heathen oath, the rough work is speedily accomplished. Then they rise and come near their King. It is not as we draw near to the Blessed Sacrament, or the angels to the Throne. Jesus is sitting on a bench. We hardly dare to look at him, he is so God-like in his abjection. How love constrains our hearts to worship, and then how worship encourages our hearts to love! How patiently he sits, blood-stained, dishonored, wan and pale, yet strangely pleasant to look on, and exceeding gracious! They come nigh to the Eternal. They are reeking with sin, and swaggering in their recklessness. The guard-room is silently filling with the splendor of his Godhead. Do they not see it? No! Fearless and peremptory and loud, they lay hands on his long hair. If they only waited a moment, they might feel the pulses of that blessed life beating in his Head. They swear by their gods, and make vulgar pleasantries in their Roman tongue, as if before a foreigner. But they see by the Hebrew's face that he knows Latin. It is but an amusement the more. They thrust the crown upon his Head with rude vehemence. It is not round. It will not fit. They force the spikes into his skin; and the Blood comes, blackly and slowly, and with excruciating pain. The Jews cheer these Romans in their barbarity; and one of them, not without loud jocose applause, takes a heavy reed and beats the crown into the Sufferer's Head. Long spikes go under the skin of the forehead, and come out above the eyes. Others pierce his ears. Others fret against the nerves of his neck. Others penetrate the skull, and burn like prickles of fire. He trembles from head to foot with the intolerable agony. His beautiful eyes are clouded with pain. His lips are bloodless with the extremity of endurance. But the face of a sleeping child is not more sweet than his, nor its heart more calm. He has grown more beautiful, now that he is crowned. O Precious Blood! Lover of God's Dominion! Thou hast thirsted for thy kingdom long; but with what strange and startling ritual hast thou ordained thy Coronation!

In this Fourth Bloodshedding there was not much Blood. Yet it was not without its note of prodigality. If it was little, it was very precious; for it was the Blood of his Head. It was the Blood which had just been feeding his brain, the Blood by the help of which he had been thinking unutterable thoughts. Each of those thoughts had been broader and deeper than an angel's science. They had been sweeter and gentler than a mother's love. They had all been tinctured with that passionate love of souls which was the spirit of the Precious Blood. The Blood shed was little: but why was it shed at all? Our Lord's Head had envied his Body. His whole Body had been ploughed and seamed by the scourges. Each limb had made its offering of Blood. But they were not to slay him; and so they had not scourged his Head, though doubtless in their careless fury chance bruises were made upon it. Now the Head will take its turn. It will have a whole Bloodshedding to itself. Indeed, it will do more than take its turn. If the Heart loves, is it not the Head which rules? Moreover, is not the Precious Blood in a special way the minister of his royalty and of his headship? It then must shed its Blood, and shed it in a mystery apart.

Sweet Blood of Jesus! longing to be shed and loving to be shed, impatient and yet so patient too, prodigal yet counting itself out drop by drop with a kind of avaricious pleasure, thou, like all other loves, wert driven to be inconsistent in order to preserve consistency! But a while ago it was hurrying on and would brook no delay. It was anticipating time, and precipitating mysteries. Now it is all for delay. Now, in the Fifth Bloodshedding, it enters upon a mystery of slowness. But there are still the same instincts, still the same ends. It contrives to be prodigal by being tardy. This Bloodshedding is the Way of the Cross, that singular mystery of the Passion in which the Hearts of Mother and Son, hitherto to outward eye divided, meet in one current, and flow together till the end. The two victims of the Scourging, the Son's Body and the Mother's Soul, come forth into the streets. The King and the queen both wear their Crowns of Thorns, the King wears his upon his Head, while the queen wears hers upon her heart; for the queendom of Mary is in her heart. We spoke in the last chapter, of the procession of the Precious Blood, out of an unbeginning eternity, over long epochs and ages, until it re-enters the portals of its second eternity. This Fifth Bloodshedding is a veritable procession of the Precious Blood. Slowly winding and unwinding itself out of the streets of Salem up the ascent of Calvary, it had not far to go; but it was long in slowness, long in suffering, long in the manifold mysteries which were densely compressed within it. Every wound was bleeding. The drops from the Crown trickled slowly down, or gathered and curdled upon the Face of Jesus. The hundred fontinels of the Scourging oozed out into his garments, as the wet rocks on the mountains ooze through their robes of moss. The wounds of the night's arrest, and of the indignities before the High-Priests, and in the yard of Herod, flow silently with Blood. The weight of the Cross opens the wounds wider still, and increases the Bloodshedding. It also disturbs the Crown, and keeps it freshly bleeding; while it makes another wound of its own upon the shoulder, and is the cause of new wounds in the knees through the cruel falls which it occasions. The sight of Mary's face quickens the beating of his Heart, and makes the Blood flow more freely. He leaves his footprints in the way; and they are of Blood. He imprints the likeness of his features on the napkin of Veronica; and the impression is in Blood. They that brush against him are stained with Blood. They that walk after him dye their sandals in his Blood. His march to Calvary is a perfect triumph of the Precious Blood. It covers every thing. It clings to the meanest objects. It seems to multiply itself. Its old fountains in Mary's heart break up in sympathy with it; and she sheds tears of blood. The Way of the Cross is a mystery of many objects, of constant movement, a transition from one mystery to another. What is its unity? It is in its prodigality, in its endless, manifold Bloodshedding. It seems a time, an interval, a journey, contrived for the very purpose of letting the Blood flow, and flow in the most indiscriminate way, and in the most promiscuous places. For the most part it flowed from old wounds. It was the going on of the Scourging and the Crowning. It was as if when those mysteries ceased the Blood loved still to flow, and therefore took a mystery to itself, which was to be engrossed simply with its flowing.

But there are also other peculiarities in this Fifth Bloodshedding which should not be overlooked. It was a mystery of unions, of meetings, of harmonies. We have already seen that it was the mystery of the Passion in which the Mother and Son came together again. In the Agony, and the Scourging, and the Crowning, they had been visibly separate, though closely and miraculously united in a mystical way. She had seen in spirit, and suffered in soul, all that he had endured. Her body also had mysteriously sympathized with each changing state of his. But now they come visibly together again, and are not disunited until the tomb is closed. Then also the Cross and the Precious Blood are now for the first time united. Hitherto the saving Blood has flowed apart from the saving Cross. It is the union of the two in which the secret virtue of redeeming grace resides. Now the weight of the Cross, as we have seen, opens old wounds and causes new ones. The Blood and the Cross are together now. This is the Betrothing; and the Marriage will be on Calvary. Here is the actual prelude of redemption. Moreover, the Way of the Cross is a great mystery of prophecy and figure. It is a prophecy of the history of the Church; it is a prefiguring of the fortunes of the Holy See; it is a type of our Lord's own life in the Church through all the ages of unjudged time—a Blood-dropping life, wearily up to the Doom. This is the meaning of its indiscriminate profusion. Good and evil alike are stained with it. It flows to save souls; but it will flow over souls who will not let it save them. It has but one law: it must flow. Anywhere, everywhere, always, it must flow. It is the one mission of the Precious Blood—to be shed. Then see how the Way of the Cross ends! It finishes in another shame, another stripping, another tearing open of the wounds of the Scourging. It looks as if, to the Precious Blood, the Scourging were its mystery of predilection. It returns to it again now, and, as nearly as possible, repeats it over again. The Bloodshedding of the Scourging was the most exuberant, the most vehement, the most penal, the most universal. Thus it coincides most with the genius of its love. Hence it will have it reiterated, so far at least as Bloodshedding is concerned, at the foot of the Cross. Now that it is going to begin the strictly needful work of our redemption, it seems to hanker after the freedom of its unnecessary sheddings. There is a great deal to think of here. In this Fifth Bloodshedding the Precious Blood begins to be unlike itself, in order that it may be more like itself than ever. A while ago it was impatiently looking onward; now it is looking half regretfully backward; yet it is the same spirit which rules it in both these dispositions—its love of being shed.

Men can lie for hours, and look upon a running stream. It seems to afford them at once occupation and repose. Its uninterrupted sameness fills them with tranquillity, while its unintermitting lapse gratifies their sense of life. They feel that they are thinking; yet they are hardly conscious of their thoughts. Their eye is fixed with a sort of fascination on the noiseless gliding waters, and they are soothed, rested, and engaged. This is a faint picture of what often happens to us in our prayers, especially with regard to certain mysteries, such as the Crucifixion, which is the Sixth Bloodshedding. It is so familiar to us that, like the river, we understand it all at sight. We cannot reason about it. It is too much part of our daily lives for that. We do not need to elicit the right affections; for they come unbidden, and flow in an order of their own. The significance of the mystery is at once too deep and too plain for words. It is so vast an object of faith, that simply to gaze upon it seems to be the broadest study of it. Moreover, like all large objects, it is one of those mysteries which are best seen at some distance. We see the whole of it then. We comprehend its size, its shape, its fashion, and the disposition of the groups round about it. Who does not know the strange, vivid, palpable peace which distance gives to sunlit vistas in a forest? There is something of this kind about meditation on the Crucifixion. How almost visionary looks the bone-strewn sward and the tufted grass of that green hill-top, with its crosses standing against the dark sky, and a kind of wan sunshine creeping up the mound, as if it came rather from the white roofs of the city than from the sun in heaven! The Precious Blood has been out in the vast calms and ocean-solitudes of the mind of God. It has voyaged through the beautiful tranquillities of the creations of spirit, matter, and men. Its lanterns have gleamed like red beacons in the unspeakable tempests of the divine anger, in falls of angels and of men, in floods and fires, in judgments and captivities, in discordant panics of Babel and bituminous upheavings of Gomorrah. It has kept its course over thousands of years of the uneasy currents of human history; and lo! that hill-top was all the while its haven! The Cross was its predestinated anchor, holding it to earth. How marvellous a harbor! How like one of those plans of God, which are so little like any plan of ours!

The Precious Blood has found at last a home, which is seemingly dearer to it than the Sacred Heart. It is the wood of the Cross. It has been so impetuous, that it has shed most of itself before it reached the Cross. It flows very slowly now. Those wounds in the Hands and Feet are too parsimonious; and, besides that, they are almost obstructed by the nails themselves. But the discomfort of the Cross makes the Sacred Body hang downward and outward, and so reopens the almost exhausted wounds of the previous Bloodsheddings. The Blood flows very slowly. In some places it still trickles over the pale limbs. In others it only blackens round the wounds. Here we may see just a visible oozing, while there it barely keeps itself red and blood-like. It flows very slowly, as if it would prolong its delight in flowing. It looks as if it were conscious of the grandeur of its work. This is redemption; this is the world-saving flow; this is the crown of all its flowings; this is the enduring and omnipotent shedding of itself, the end of the battle it has won for God, the final and total accomplishment of that array of eternal decrees which all along have clothed it like royal robes. How slowly it flows, with a fascinating slowness, and so silently! Yet the scarcely-moving streams blend with each other in many places, and steal down upon the Feet. The Cross is wetted by it, and the wood is darkened. Mary's hands are red. The dear Magdalen has an unconscious consciousness that the Blood of her Love is upon her hair; and the innermost wells of the Sacred Heart drop and drop as if with pulses upon the disciple, who had pillowed himself upon that Heart the night before. Here and there a blade of grass is ruddy. There are spots on the skulls of the dead; for the dead also have their interest in the Precious Blood. The torturers and soldiers have gone down the hill with their garments and their accoutrements discolored; for the Precious Blood shrinks not from the vilest resting-places. How slowly it flows, as if the very grandeur of redemption made it cautious, or caused some difficulty! The slowness fascinates us more and more. But it is a relief to have the silence broken. There is no look of life but in the Blood. Nothing is moving but the Blood. Blood is life. It was within him. Now it is almost all outside him. Those seven words are the voices of his Blood. With what a clear ringing sweetness they come forth, and the darkness round the mount murmurs with them as if it were tingling with delight! How beautiful are his thoughts upon the Cross, beautiful like the beauty of God! How beautiful are the seven words, with their revelations of the beauty of God! Each word is a ravishing melody, in which the Eternal Word utters himself with human utterance. Then what a perfect abyss of rest is the interval between each word, silences like the silences which the angels keep in heaven! The soul flutters over them as over hollow seas, and wellnigh faints with love. But in the silence the Blood creeps slowly, outward, onward, earthward. Still it flows, but so industriously, so carefully, so methodically, and yet so secretly, so noiselessly, so mysteriously. It not only evades the ear by its soundless footfalls: but now it almost evades the eye. Its movement is scarcely visible over the pale Form, like the hands of a timepiece. It seems as if we should never see that dear impetuous Blood precipitate again. But do not old habits come back at last in all created things, and youth rise again to imprint its character on death? The Precious Blood has come within reach of its end, so near it as to be impatient. It abandons the slowness of its oozing, it will be precipitate once more; and, as if to show that all shedding of itself, all surrendering of its precious life, was voluntary, it bids one cell of the Heart to keep what it contains, dislodges all the rest of itself with a loud cry of miraculous strength, and leaps forth at once from every cavern of the Body; and death accomplishes itself, so far as it was a natural death, by the shedding of the Blood.

Is there to be more Bloodshedding still? Why, like a miser on his death-bed, had the Precious Blood hidden that little treasure? Why did it die, hoarding itself? It was that the Dead Body might shed Blood. It was to deride death, to survive death, to proclaim love's victory over death, to show that its own propensity to shed itself had not been killed by death. Hence the Seventh Bloodshedding, the Piercing of the Sacred Heart. We often know men best by what they do when they come to die. So it is with the Precious Blood; or rather we know it best by what it did when it was dead. It was so liquefied by love that death could not curdle it; and still it flowed, as if flowing were the unchangeable feature of its character. Death contents men. Hearts ask no further proof of love. Monarchs consider it the extremity of loyalty. Death contents God. He asks no more than martyrdom; and he cherishes the martyrdoms of his Saints as the inestimable rubies of his creation. But death does not content the Precious Blood. That Sixth Bloodshedding was necessary. In many ways it was prodigal; but it was also necessary. Redemption was a needful task, a task of love, but still a task. The Precious Blood, as I have said, hankered after the days of its unnecessary sheddings, the days when its love wantoned in the pure prodigality of its royal riches. As it shed itself before the work of redeeming the world, and without redeeming it, so will it shed itself again now that the work of redemption is accomplished. Once more it will reveal its character in that wastefulness which is a secret of divine economy. O Divine Love! there is no more inveterate prodigal than thou!

Moreover, the work must be a complete work. All the Blood must be separated from the Body, and enjoy, by itself and in its separation, its union with the Person of the Word. It must be a total outpouring. Divine things are never done by halves; and

mercies above all insist upon completeness. The Heart had been
bidden to keep some of the Blood within itself, and had obeyed.
It was undecided whether to obey reluctantly or gladly. On the
one hand it was the home of the Precious Blood, and loved it
with the fondest love. To be untenanted by the Precious Blood
would be its uttermost desolation. Yet, on the other hand, that
Heart had learned the instincts of its inhabitant. Mothers have
sent forth their own sons to martyrdom with a strange covetous
love, which had more of heaven in it than of earth. So would
the Sacred Heart fain send forth that lingering Blood to the cruel
glory of its shedding. As the Head in the Crowning had been
jealous of the Body in the Scourging, and so had claimed the joy
and dignity of a Bloodshedding to itself, so now the Heart was
jealous of the Hands and Feet. It envied them their dripping
wells of life. It grudged them the beauty of their eternal stigmata. Even when dead the Sacred Heart has irresistible attractions. The Soul of Jesus beneath the earth felt the dear familiar
constraints of that grand Heart; and so the Heart wooed the
lance of the centurion, and the hidden Blood sprang forth, baptized as if in gratitude its heathen liberator with all the cleansing
graces of conversion, and stole gently down the Side of Jesus,
kissing the Flesh which it had animated so long.

The time was to come when the Body was to resume the
Blood. While the Sacred Humanity had been as it were unloosed
and dispersed for the salvation of mankind, the Soul busied in
brightening limbus, the Body reposing in the borrowed grave of
the Arimathean, and the Blood scattered with a sort of wasteful
ubiquity all over the vicinage of Jerusalem, the Hypostatic Union
of the Divine and Human Natures had never been broken, nor
even impaired, for one moment. The separate Soul was to be
worshipped with divine worship still. The Body lay peacefully
among the rocks, always and absolutely to be adored. The Blood,
vagrant, outlying, parcelled, indistinct, apparently commingled
with or adhering to other substances, was also in each drop, in
each stain, in each colored impression, in each voluntary burial-
place of its own, to be adored with absolute adoration, in virtue

of its unbroken and unstrained union with the Godhead in the Divine Person of the Word. But these worshipful Three, the Soul, the Body, and the Blood, were to come together again in one of the holiest of all mysteries, the Resurrection. It was to be the grandeur of this mystery that it should as it were open to us the magnificent abysses of the Hypostatic Union, and show us the glorious strength and the invincible bond of the Incarnation, while it should also seem to be like a new Incarnation in itself. But even amidst the repairing and beautifying force of the Resurrection, it was the will of our dearest Lord, one of the most affectionate and characteristic of all his wills, that some marks at least of the old Bloodsheddings should be retained. Ten thousand times a day should his whole Blood be poured forth from heaven into the Chalices of the Mass. But this was not enough. He clung to the memory of those old Bloodsheddings. He would have us cling to the memory of them also. It should be a new joy to the angels forever to see his stigmata. They should fill the souls of his elect with fresh jubilee for all eternity, and keep their angelic glory tempered with the human tenderness he loves so dearly. So he bade the glory of the Resurrection, as it beautified him by its immortalizing fires, not only to respect and to retain the Five Wounds of his Sacred Body, but to beautify them with a tenfold beauty. They were to be roseate luminous suns to gladden the palaces of the Heavenly Jerusalem, which the cruel artificers of earth's Jerusalem had wrought upon him with such unintending skill. He keeps his stigmata for the love of us. He keeps his stigmata for the love of his Precious Blood. Many single mysteries seem to tell me the whole of Jesus; yet I find I cannot spare the rest; for each has its needful revelation of his sweetness. But, if I were compelled to choose one thing only as being all memorials of my Saviour in one, I would choose this keeping of his stigmata. It signifies so many things, and it signifies them all so tenderly. When one we love does something more than usually like himself, our love leaps up with joy; and when he does it unexpectedly, our hearts burn hotter for being taken unawares. Jesus has described his whole Self, as in a concise Gospel, in this one act of keeping the stigmata of his blessed Wounds. I seem to know him better, and to be more sure I know him rightly, because of this dear pathos which abides unconsumed amidst the burnings of that Easter-glory, this lingering of the Passion among the splendors of the Resurrection.

Let us now turn from all this prodigality of the Precious Blood, which was unnecessary for us, but necessarily befitting the magnificence of God; and let us turn to that other prodigality which is so needful for us that we could not afford to spare one out of the numberless reiterations of its exuberance. What an incredible history it is! and yet of such daily occurrence, of such commonplace appearance, of such matter-of-fact practice, that it is difficult to steady our minds to the right understanding of it. We grow confused with numbers, or teased with the childishness of imaginary calculations, when we come to think of the sacramental applications of the Precious Blood, which the souls of the living and the dead are receiving daily. The bounty of redeeming grace, state it as soberly as we please, has all the unnatural unpersuasive dazzle of an Arabian tale. It is all gold and precious stones in impossible profusion. It seems like a fairy-land vision rather than a human reality. The ungenuineness of devotional exaggerations makes us angry and incredulous. But divine love has a marvellous sobriety; and under its restraints let us speak of this matter more coldly than we feel.

If we go round the world, there can hardly ever be an hour in which some children are not being baptized. Baptism is the application of the Precious Blood to their souls. No act in life can surpass it in importance. It effects a most complete spiritual revolution even in the unconscious child. It effects it in a most wonderful way, and by means of mysterious infusions, and in consequence of a mysterious Incarnation, and through the virtue of mysterious Bloodsheddings; and these things take their effect through the pouring of water simultaneously with the pronunciation of the grand Names of the Divine Persons, accompanied by an intention on the part of the person baptizing, priest or lay, man or woman, or even child. Theology composes volumes in order to elucidate scientifically the group of mysteries which lie compressed in the Sacrament of Baptism. It is enough for us to remember that it is the difference between heaven and hell. Each Baptism is a greater, a diviner, a more magnificent work than the creation of the material world. Yet, in sober truth, the waters of Baptism are flowing perennially, so that if they could run together they would form a flowing rivulet, undried throughout the year. The creation of a new star every second of time would be but a little thing by the side of this. Even in heathen lands this amazing stream is flowing. Amid the dense populations of China it moves visibly to God's eye like a sweet silver brooklet. It has made the national atrocity of child-murder the channel in which its beautifying love might ingeniously run. Children in fair France, and in green England, and in German towns, and over the Atlantic, contribute to keep up this strangely-characteristic work of Christianity. European and American children send their baptismal missionaries to take up the exposed and dying children from the fields and from the dung-heaps, and to baptize them, in thank-offering to God for the grace of Baptism to which they themselves have reached. European and American mothers send to purchase of Chinese parents the children they would slay, or at least to purchase permission to baptize the doomed innocents, in thank-offering for their own children having attained to the grace of Baptism. If we put all this continuity of Baptism into numbers, and remember meanwhile the spiritual magnificence of Baptism, we shall be able to form some idea of the prodigality of the Precious Blood hidden in those waters of salvation.

What is Absolution? It is the authentic dripping of the Precious Blood upon the head of the repentant sinner. It is God's patience grown so patient as to be magnificent. It is, almost but not quite, the limit of the outstretching of the eternal arms of mercy. In it human acts reach to one of their highest heights. They are lifted up to merit salvation by the merits of the Precious Blood. Human sorrow is consecrated and made divine by the touch and the anointing of the sorrow of Jesus; and that unction was only to reach us with the flowing of his Blood from his gracious Wounds. Without shedding of Blood there was to be no remission. Millions of souls are at large in heaven this day, who without Absolution would have been in hell. Yet it were better a whole solar system should be shattered to pieces than a single soul lost. If there is something very divine in the facility of Baptism, reminding us of creation when the word was spoken and forthwith the work was done, there is also something very divine in the difficulty and effort of Absolution, reminding us of redemption which was only accomplished by a Passion and with Blood. Hearts have to be softened, habits weakened, dispositions changed, occasions deserted, new tastes infused, entanglements untied. The Precious Blood has to put forth more of its strength here than in Baptism; because it has to overcome more inveteracy and resistance. It has also to venture its sacred riches more prodigally here than in other Sacraments. In all Sacraments it runs two generous risks, the risk of invalidity, and the risk of sacrilege. Both these risks are more especially run in the Sacrament of Penance. Yet what numberless confessions are daily heard! What hundreds, or thousands, of Absolutions are daily given, the greater portion of which I am undoubtingly certain, from the character of God and the experience of the confessional, are valid! How many Absolutions have we ourselves received in our lives, and hope still to receive! Surely, if we could see as God sees, and as perchance the angels are allowed to see, we should behold innumerable streams of Blood intersecting the crowded souls of men, as a vast river-system shows like a net-work on a map; and this would be a vision of the prodigality of Absolution.

How beautiful are the graces of the Sacrament of Marriage! Full of human tenderness, yet so softly insinuating the sovereign love of God; teeming with habitual self-sacrifice, yet filling the sacrifice with such sweetness that it becomes, not painless only, but a joy; breeding in young hearts such a gravity of new heavenly duties, and yet flinging over life the lustre of an additional light; hardening the changeful heart with a supernatural preparation of perseverance, and yet softening every harshness and making every sensitiveness more exquisitely keen; fortifying the soul with boldness to do right, at the very moment it is gracing it with all the bashful timidities of love; elevating affection into devotedness, and giving therewith a beautifulness of purity which is akin to the white innocence of virginity: these are the graces of the Sacrament of Marriage; and they are all creations of the Precious Blood. They are all of them working daily in millions of hearts, hearts in sorrow and hearts in joy; and their life is in the throbbing and pulsation of the Precious Blood. This time it is not a stream of Blood we see, but a wide-stretching inundation.

Of all the Sacraments, Ordination is the most like marriage. It weds hearts to Jesus. It makes those hearts his homes. The priesthood is his domestic life in the Church. It is replete with images of Mary and of Joseph. It repeats Nazareth. But what a complication of graces is implied in Ordination, and then also what a magnificence of powers! Moreover, it is a manifold Sacrament. Its unity is a threefold unity in Bishops, Priests, and Deacons, a shadow of unutterable divine grandeurs. Furthermore, it is as it were the sacred vessel in which the other six Sacraments are kept, and out of which they radiate their glory and their life. This grand Sacrament is the earthly heart of the Precious Blood. It is to it on earth what the Sacred Heart is to it in heaven. It gives the movement to its life. It takes it back and gives it forth. It regulates its energy, and makes its beatings equable as well as forcible. It concentrates the Precious Blood in itself, and then vehemently diffuses it all over the earth through every remotest vent of missionary fervor. The graces of this Sacrament are like the graces of angels; and yet they are of all graces the most human; for they impart the likeness of the Sacred Humanity as no other graces can impart it. Each grace of Ordination is a characteristic of Jesus. Its gift is to make the clear heart of the priest a mirror into which the Saviour is for ever looking down, and his Countenance is marvellously glassed therein. Yet, for all this, men must be partially changed into angels by the operation of these intensely human graces. In truth, Ordination is specially a Sacrament of the Precious Blood. Jesus became a priest by the shedding of his Blood, by the offering of his Bloody Sacrifice. His Blood is the virtue of his priesthood. Yet when it lay separate from the Soul and from the Body, it was angels who kept it, and not men. This is the figure of the strange mixture of the human and angelic in the graces of the priesthood. But how many are the anointed of the Lord, how multiplied are their works, how manifold their vocations, how vast their missions, how continuous their recruits! All this implies so much prodigality of the Precious Blood.

Jesus once looked into a young man's face, and loved him. He has perpetuated this incident in his Church. It is perpetuated in the Sacrament of Confirmation. When Jesus went, and the Holy Ghost came to take his place and to administer the Church, he also was forever looking into the faces of the young; and his look was a gift, a magnificent substantial love, an imparting of that fortitude which youth so much requires, and the want of which made the young man of the Gospel turn away in the cowardice of an earthly sorrow. But the seven gifts of the Holy Ghost were only purchased for us by the Precious Blood. The very title, which the Gospel gives to the times before the sacrificial shedding of our Redeemer's Blood, was "the times when the Holy Ghost was not yet given." Now look at the multitude of Christian youth. If there is much to sadden, how much also is there to cheer! How much generous piety do we behold, how many early breakings with the world, how many works of mercy, how many edifying confraternities, how many levites in the seminaries, how many beautiful vocations in the cloisters! What is all this but Confirmation's gift of fortitude, made fertile by the Precious Blood?

We have seen that the Precious Blood shed itself chiefly round about the death of Jesus; and that his Death was in reality a death by bleeding. Hence the hour of death is the chosen hour of the Precious Blood. It is the favorite season of its ingenuities. Thus it makes a Sacrament for itself at that precise time, the Sacrament of Extreme Unction, the last of its anointings, the anointing reserved for the supreme contest of the soul, the last of its sacramental visitations to the elect. This wonderful Sacrament shrouds its graces in mystery, a mystery congenial to the darkness which belongs to its dread hour. But the very fact of its being a

Sacrament at all, and the season of its administration, sufficiently testify to the grandeur of the graces which it must convey. God is eminently a God of time and place, as we have seen; and his places and times are the measures of his gifts. Extreme Unction, like the oil of the Grecian wrestlers, anoints us for our mortal struggle. Whatever relics of sin there may be in us, the powers of darkness will fasten upon them. But the grace of this Sacrament searches them out with a mysterious penetration, and puts them to a supernatural death. The best name for its grace is the grace of health; and so, if God does not will that it should impart health to our bodies, it turns its exotic medicinal virtues upon the soul. Other Sacraments liken our lives to the life of Jesus. This likens our deaths to the death of Jesus. It diffuses itself over our souls, strewn with the work of a whole life, and gathers up the fragments which other Sacraments have left untouched. It cleanses them with a last cleansing. It arranges them with neatness and order for the coming of our Lord. It puts them in their right posture and attitude for being most safely judged. Must not its graces be very peculiar, and yet also very magnificent? Throughout the world there is a whole population dying daily. A section of the world is always on its death-bed and in its agony. How prodigal then must the Precious Blood be of its magnificent peculiarities in this pathetic Sacrament!

But what shall we say of that twofold wonder, the Sacrifice of the Mass and the Sacrament of Communion? There the Precious Blood puts on the vesture of omnipresence, and it becomes it well. Multiplied by how many hundreds of thousands of times is it not dwelling, whole, living, and glorified, in the Hosts reserved within the tabernacles of the world? Into how many thousand human hearts does it not descend daily, whole, living, and glorified, in the glory of the dread reality of Communion? Into how many thousand chalices does it not empty itself from out the Sacred Heart in heaven every day? The very whirling of the earth, as it makes day and night by turning to or from the sun, ministers to the longings of the Precious Blood. It is bewildering to think of the countless graces of expiation which flow daily from the Sacrifice, or the countless graces of union which flow daily from the Sacrament. This is the great laboratory in which the Precious Blood makes holiness. In the heart of the Andes, vast, interwoven, and mutually enfolding mountains cover themselves with gigantic forests. The condor, as he wheels above, looks down upon an ocean of impenetrable foliage, without a rent, or break, or insight into the green abyss. So does the Precious Blood, in Mass and Communion, mantle the whole Church with tropical exuberances of grace, as they appear, hiding the natural features of the ground with the ample folds of their verdant overgrowth. The tinklings of the mass-bell, like new-creative words, change the whole aspect of the unconscious world. Unknown and unsuspected temporal calamities are daily driven away, like clouds before the wind, by the oblations of the Precious Blood. Nay, through the crust of the earth the superincumbent weight of that Blood presses its way, and reaches to the sinless caves of Purgatory. Consolations of all shapes and patterns come there, and are the cooling rains of the Precious Blood. Who can class them? They are like the monotonous diversities of crystals, beautiful for their variety, and beautiful also for their sameness. The angels, who had the Precious Blood in their keeping during the Triduo of the Passion, have also the administration of it in Purgatory, and are well pleased with this labor of congenial love. But the arithmetic of all this prodigality of the Precious Blood, is it not impossible to the imagination and distracting to the heart? It disquiets our love. Let us leave off the calculation, and contemplate in quietude the ocean of painstaking graces, of vast satisfactions, and of kingly expiations, into which the daily Masses of the Church outpour themselves, lighting the patient darkness under ground, flashing up to the skies as so much additional light and song, and beautifying the poor exiled earth in the eye of the all-holy heavens.

In closest propinquity with the Sacraments we should make mention of the Holy See, wherein dwells the paternity of all the Sacraments, and in which resides with incredible plentitude the jurisdiction of the Precious Blood, the regalia of the kingdom of the Sacred Humanity of Jesus. At no point of history can we look at the Sovereign Pontiff without seeing as it were before us, in most vivid type, the Fourth Bloodshedding, the Crowning of Thorns. The pontifical monarchs of the Middle Ages, no less than the marytr-pontiffs who haunted the Catacombs, or the modern popes who toil, like patient heroes, through the pusillanimous hostilities of diplomacy, equally bear upon them this peculiar image of our Lord. They administrate his Headship. They are his Head made visible to us. The tiara is the most veritable crown of thorns, and the pontificate the most literal of martyrdoms. It is the Head ever bleeding, bleeding slowly. There is the old suffering patience in its majesty. It is a true royalty; but men mock it because its kingly mantle is soiled with all earth's poverty. It is a hidden kingliness, like the kingship of the guardroom at Jerusalem. It is a sort of sacrament of the Sacraments, the sacrament of the royalty of the Precious Blood. The papacy is the Fourth Bloodshedding continued till the Doom.

This is one department of the prodigality of the Precious Blood, its sacramental prodigality. But, besides this, there is a whole world of extra-sacramental prodigality. At least we may for distinction's sake call it so. But in reality all holiness is tied to the Sacraments by innumerable, indirect, and hidden fastenings. Good works come out of the Sacraments, or come out of other works which have done so, or they go into the Sacraments, or are the accidents and superfluities of Sacraments, or minister to the Sacraments, or are, we know not why, contemporaneous with them. Even the grandeur of perfect contrition is tied to the Sacraments by desire. The martyrdom of the catechumen is riveted to Baptism by secret desire, desire which may even be unconscious as well as secret, yet must infallibly be there. The whole system of redemption is interpenetrated with Sacraments. The sacramental tendency in it is ineradicable. It coheres by Sacraments. Sacraments are the tissue of its life; and its life is the Precious Blood. Therefore when we come to consider the daily penances and supernatural actions which are consecrated by the Precious Blood in the Church, although we may fairly call them extra-sacramental, we must at the same time bear in mind, that there is probably not one which has not some relation, open or occult, with a Sacrament, and that the genius of them all is an affinity to the Sacraments and an instinctive sympathy with them. They dart into the Sacraments, and blend with them, and lose themselves in them, with a swiftness and a volatility which remind us of things in chemistry.

If we are devout to the Church, if we have keen sympathies with the Holy See, and if we are interested in missionary enterprise, we can rapidly make for ourselves a geographical picture of the Church. We know what countries belong to her, and where her missions are growing, and where they are receding. We can pass in swift thoughts from one pole to the equator, and from the equator to the other pole. We know how much life goes on in a little space—especially spiritual life. The religious actions, inward and outward, of one rural parish are multitudinous and rapid, a dense world of thoughts, motives, words, and works. How innumerable then must be the daily supernatural actions of the wide Church! Yet wherever grace is, there is the Precious Blood. Whatever may merit can only merit by coming in spiritual contact with the Precious Blood. In all this seething mass of actions, it is the Precious Blood which is causing all the movement and all the fermentation. Wheresoever nature is raised above itself and lifted into the supernatural, there we discern infallibly the agency of the Precious Blood. But what a ubiquitous life, what a universal energy, what rapidity and what persistence of operation! Then look at the other side of the question. Who could number the sins in the world at any one given moment? Is not evil always like the sea which is with difficulty banked out from low-lying lands? It is bursting the banks, tearing away the gates, flooding the sluices perpetually. The thought of the number of sins at any given time is at once distracting and oppressive. Yet I believe that always, in some way or other, proximately or remotely, the Precious Blood is trying to hinder each one of these sins. The number of sins makes us wonder how the Precious Blood can divide itself into such numberless activities, while the gravity of the sins shows us how prodigal it is, not only of its presence, but of its strength. The life of the Precious Blood in the religious houses of the Church is amazing. The crowds of daily heroic actions which are sustained by it, each of which seems to draw it up from its choicest depths, and then the plentiful harvest of more ordinary merits, the quantity of sanctified suffering, the amount of supernatural obedience—how immense is all this! and yet it is but one department of the sleepless business of the Precious Blood! Another and a vaster world is to be found in its favorite sphere of death-beds. All that activity, all those inventions, all that concentration of converting love, all that precipitate accumulation of sanctifying grace, all that lightning-like formation of habits which are to be eternal, all those strange heroisms of death, those resurrections of old selves, those creations of new selves, those almost overwhelming embraces of nature by grace, must all go to the account and enter into the calculation. Nay, look at the multitudes who wander outside the Church; even those desolate tracts of the world, those unwatered regions, are yet beautified in some degree by the overflowings of the Church, the prodigal outgoings of the Precious Blood.

All this prodigality of the Precious Blood, whether in the Sacraments or alongside of them, I call necessary, as distinguished from the prodigality of the Thirty-Three Years, which was not necessary to us, but belongs to the magnificence of God's love. The other prodigality is necessary to us, because without it we should not be saved. Our corruption is so active, our weakness is so lamentable, our vileness is so great, our dangers are so terrible, our carelessness is so incredible, that we could not for the most part work out our salvation with any access to the Precious Blood less free, less easy, less common, less abundant, than that which God's magnificence has opened to us. Still, if we consider the grandeur of the Sacraments in themselves, or the immense capabilities of grace, or the intrinsic glory of the mysteries so reiterated, and if we look at all these things from a theological rather than a practical point of view, we must acknowledge that they betoken an amazing prodigality on the part of God, even though our necessities be so hungry that they consume it all. We must be continually replenishing the shallowness of our finite lives, and we can only replenish them out of the Divine infinity. We cannot satisfy our thirst at any fountain less magnificent. It is another joy which God's love added to his beatitude, that we should drink of those wells for evermore, and drink of them with liberty and gladness.

Now let us come out under the starry sky, and think of this prodigality of the Precious Blood. The great tent of heaven above us seems to waver, and the stars to swing like lamps from its purple roof. But the desert could not be more silent than this outspread scene. If the uninstructed man looks at the starry skies, he either feels no mystery in them, or feels that it is a mystery which he cannot understand. Some feeling, which if it is not poetry is akin to poetry, and which if it is not religion is akin to religion, would surely be awakened within him. But all would be vague, restless, and uncertain, and therefore would soon weary him, and so be transient, and speedily forgotten. The astronomer would look on the loveliness of this spangled night with far other eyes. His knowledge would disentangle the constellations for his eyes. The orbs would be individuals to him, with names, known points, and some peculiarities. The purple concave would at once inscribe itself for him with glittering lines and orbits, better than the grooved spheres of Ptolemy. It would be a joy to him to inform so much seeming confusion with so much real order. He might think little of the beauty of night, and still less of the beauty of the God of night. But the scene would speak in grand sonorous language to his understanding. Then let us bring a poet to the place. He might know as little of the mechanism of the heavens as the uninstructed man. But he would understand the scene by feeling it. He would feel that the starry heavens outside corresponded marvellously with the starry heavens within him. Behold him. His soul is taken captive with the beauty of night. He looks. He grows calm with a sweet calmness. Chafings cease. Breathings as of far-off music rise up from some deep sanctuary within his soul. The beauty melts him; the glory masters him; and he sings the infinity of God. Both the astronomer and the poet have their truth. But the poet's truth is a truer truth than that of the astronomer.

So it is in looking at the world redeemed. The uninstructed man sees nothing in it but puzzle and contradiction. His faith is vague; and where faith is not clear there is seldom earnestness. There is truly a look of God about the world, and a wandering fragrance of Jesus. But it breeds little more in him than a kind of incredulous superstition. To the instructed believer, who is without the poetry of religion, whose head errs because his heart does not help it, whose thoughts go wrong because they are speculations instead of prayers—to him the aspect of redemption is what the starry skies are to the astronomer. He admires; he is amazed; he praises. Yet adoration is so little to his taste, and worship so uncongenial to his disposition, that the demand for it at once awakens a kind of skepticism even in his faith. He doubts whether so much be done, because he sees so little come of it. He judges by what he sees with the eye. He does not know how to divine with his heart. He does not perceive that the world he sees is nearly as far beyond his understanding as the God who is invisible. Sight does not help us to understand men. Their actions are not their hearts. Still less does it help us to understand grace, which, when it supernaturalizes nature, lies undermost, not uppermost. To understand God and God's world, we must look at him and it from the Precious Blood point of view. The saints of the Church are the poets of redemption. It is from this point of view that they always see the world. It was thus that Mary saw the world at all times, a vision most awful, yet most touching and most dear. It is the way in which God sees at this instant. All things to him, good or evil, are tinged with the Precious Blood. He beholds them all in his own repetition of Josue's miracle, in that unsinking crimson sunset of the Precious Blood, which he has bidden to hang in all its beauty on the horizon of creation forever.

CHAPTER VI

THE DEVOTION TO THE PRECIOUS BLOOD

CHAPTER VI

THE DEVOTION TO THE PRECIOUS BLOOD

Most men live in an imaginary world; and yet their imaginary world is a real one. They make a beauty for themselves, and throw their heart into it. Some men live among the stars, either as observers or as astronomers. It becomes the passion of their lives to do so. The movements of the heavenly bodies are to them as the activities of practical life. To watch, to discover, to verify, up in the heavens, is their vocation. It is the way in which they will enjoy themselves, and the way also in which they will benefit their kind. Others spend their lives with equal devotion among the strata of the earth and the long interesting epochs of geology. Others give themselves up to dwell with patient vigilance among the secret laboratories of matter, where its separations, combinations, and transmutations are discovered, and whose mysteries are yearly spreading themselves more and more over daily life in the shape of most important practical utilities. Another becomes the companion of animals, and reigns like a natural king, as he is, among his beasts and birds and fishes and reptiles. Another is the doctor and prophet of plants, and another of minerals. Men can make fascinating scientific worlds for themselves out of the flooring of the sea, out of the stormy circles of the air, out of the rushing thread-like arteries of electric force, and out of many other subprefectures of nature. These worlds are imaginary, and yet real: real because of the substantial truth and practical utility of them; imaginary because of the exclusive enthusiasm with which they are dwelt upon, and the breadth of responsible life which is consumed in them. The world is not only or altogether a celestial globe, or a geological map, or an arithmetic of chemistry, or a hierarchy of animal life.

Neither again, indeed much less, is the length and breadth of human life contained in the straits of politics, the shallows of diplomacy, the quaking mosses of balances of power, or the frail clockwork of constitutions. I can understand better than most of these idolatries a passionate occupation of the mind with statistics, out of which time will evolve revelations of the nature of man and of the laws and storms and methodical fluctuations of human actions, which cannot fail to illuminate in some wonderful way and with unexpected light the adorable character of God. But statistics are not commensurable with life. Men may easily live in an epic of metaphysics and psychology, and neglect all else; but they can establish no right to such a concentration of themselves, any more than the physiologist with the patient slowness of his singularly attractive pursuit. Life is broader than any science of life; for it is a law, a duty, a responsibility, an affection, a religion. Yet all natures have their poetries. Most men must have their ideal, or one of these imaginary real worlds which subserve all the better purposes of an ideal. These are the devotions of the intellect, which absorb within themselves the interests of the heart. We are placed in creation as kings; and, often quite unconsciously, our kingly instincts work in our souls; and we take creation to pieces, and choose the provinces over which we intend to rule. But we are quarrelsome kings. We do not like neighboring rulers. The proverbial jealousies of scientific men are like the peevish diplomacies of fretful politicians.

Now, what astronomy, and geology, and chemistry, and other cognate sciences, and what politics, statistics, metaphysics, and their congenial sciences, are to many men, and to most men, the Church is to us. It is our devotion, our pursuit, our passion. It is our favorite science, our chosen study, our life's enthusiasm. As a matter of taste no one can blame us; for tastes are facts, and facts which are mostly inculpable, and hardly admit of criticism. One man has as much right to be immensely interested in a Sacrament, as another in a curious dip of strata, or the varying magnitude of a perplexing star, or in some new property of a metalloid, or in the dethroning of an old element by dividing it. If one man may without blame make all other sciences, literatures, and pursuits, subordinate to his one science, literature, and pursuit, another may make all sciences, literatures, and pursuits, subordinate to his exclusive devotion to the Church. This is putting devotion to the Church upon its lowest ground. It is well sometimes to remember lowest grounds for things. Important rights are often founded in them. Not unfrequently the essences of things lie hidden in them. They ought not therefore to be abandoned or despised. To me, then, the Church is what the starry skies are to the astronomer. I know there are other things in creation besides the Church; but I am only very partially interested in them. Practically to me the world means the Church. For the only interest I can take in the world outside the Church arises from the fact that the Church must be affected by its movements. I delight in all progresses of science, because they are an addition to the science of theology. I sympathize ardently with all social progresses, because they are at once, whether as difficulties or as facilities, questions of soul-saving. The revelations of statistics form a sort of hand-book for catholic charity. Psychology illustrates the Sacraments. Political changes interest me; for they all act upon the wonderful fortunes of the Holy See, and are mostly for its ultimate advancement. All real widening of men's minds by education, or literature, or art, is an effacing of prejudices against the Church, and facilitates conversion. In almost every department of knowledge the world, as it advances, keeps answering its own objections to religion; and this is both grateful and interesting. All that is wide, deep, forward, active, trustful, is most congenial with the spirit of the Church. Even the grand old science of history has taken to discovery; and its discoveries, one after the other, are so many reparations to the Church. The Church is my centre. I look at all things as revolving round it; and my interest in them is proportioned to their action upon it. The Church is my science, my taste, my interest, and my attraction. I do not sneer at the devotion of the astronomer, and he must not sneer at mine. I tolerate the metaphysician, and he must tolerate me. I have neither fears, suspicions, nor jealousies of his philosophy; he must have none of my theology.

But, in reality, devotion to the Church may rest upon higher grounds than these. In my own mind it rests upon this—and I say it with all reverence—that it is God's own devotion. It is God's creation within his own creation, a creation called into being with a specialty of love, created with the miraculous toil and human Bloodshedding of the Omnipotent. It is his own life, his own created life, in creation. Its history is his biography upon earth. Its form is the abiding of his Incarnation among men. It is thus forever repeating his Three-and-Thirty Years. It is not that he does not love the whole world, and the most out-lying souls in the world, with a strange surpassing love. On the contrary, it is for the very sake of the world that he loves the Church with a better love. If his almighty wisdom saw fit to overwhelm our liberty with its constraints, its first act would be to turn the whole world into the Church, making the Church and the world one and the same thing. The world is his creation as Creator; and our wretchedness did not find its prodigality of love sufficient. The Church is his creation as Redeemer; and it lies in furnaces of divine love heated seven times hotter than the furnaces of creation. Thus the Church is his devotion, his complacency. He loves it with a special, an electing love. This is the true ground of our devotion to the Church. It is God's own devotion. It is his choicest way of loving us. It is our choicest way of loving him.

But let us think of this, both more in detail and more at large. As a place the Church is a creation within creation, the royal residence of the Creator-King. To its privileged jurisdiction is granted the full royalty of the whole world. Its laws are holiness. Its atmosphere is grace. Its forms are copies of divine things. Its nature is transfigured with supernatural energies. Its solemnities are celestial mysteries. It is a life, and a giving of life. But it is not only a divine copy of divine things. It contains divine things, and lives by them. In peculiar ways of its own, it contains the Divine Persons. Thus, its life is not a mere likeness of God, though it is a likeness of him. But, when faith looks upon his likeness, it sees a further vision. The tabernacles of the Church blossom as with light; the lineaments of the Church fade as in a glorious conflagration, obliterated by the intensity of splendor; and, behold! it is Jesus himself, God and Man, within whose life we have been living; and the glory had been so gentle that we perished not! The mystery of the Blessed Sacrament is the truth of the life of the Church. We can see and revere the magnificence of the Church. But we shall know the Church better, and appreciate it more truly, when we have seen God. We shall perceive then, that the Church was even more full of divine mysteries than we supposed it was. This is the case with all created things. We must see the Creator, in order to understand the plenitude of their beauty. But it will be more especially so with the Church, because of its special dignity in creation. We see the mountains mirrored in the lake with exquisite distinctness. But when we have looked up to the mountains themselves, and learned them in themselves, the images in the lake are more charming, more distinct, more evidently like, more fascinatingly like, than they seemed to be before. To the eye of God the Church must look most wonderful. It is the work of art on which all the adorable incredibilities of redemption have been expended. Every attribute has tried its handicraft upon it. It expresses the secrets of the Incomprehensible, the yearnings of the Ever-blessed, the desires of the Eternal. It is draped with the golden magnificence of everlasting decrees. The beauty of the Divine Mind is suffused around it like an impalpable atmosphere of loveliness. Once he saw the woods, and the mountains, and the lakes, and the foaming rivers, and the flowery plains, which he had made, and he remained outside them, and gave them his paternal benediction. But when he had created the Church, not of earth and of his word, but of his Blood and Breath, its fair beauty so won upon him that he came into it, and multiplied himself, and hid himself, in her tabernacles, as the birds hide themselves within the mighty woods.

This is the simple account of the Church, the chief thing to

be said of it, but not the only thing. It mirrors the hierarchies of
the angels as well as the magnificence of God. It not only imitates
their orders and operations, but it supplies them with new ministries, and is every day enlivening them with fresh joys. Its life
is bound up with theirs, and its children mingle with them and
become members of their choirs. As to men, it initiates them into
a divine citizenship. It explains their destinies. It ennobles their
disabilities. It anticipates their glory. It gives a value to their sorrows and a significance to their joys. It emancipates them from
their own littleness, and it conveys to them God's forgiveness of
their sins. It puts them to dwell in the suburbs of heaven even
while they are still being tried on earth. As a power, the Church
has been the most unearthly, the most remarkable, the most successful upon earth. It has no parallel and no analogy. It is a problem which neither historical nor political nor philosophical
solutions satisfy. It has a history of peculiar interest and of the
most extraordinary variety. In duration its chronicles surpass
those of the most ancient monarchy. The records of revolutions
are less various, while the history of a single town is less consistent.
In the romance of vicissitudes and in dramatic changes no history
is to be compared to it. In our own times it is leading a very
peculiar life under entirely novel circumstances; and in the midst
of universal fluctuation and distrust it is a monument of self-
confident tranquillity. It is certain of ultimate conquest, and
equally certain of present suffering. Its power and its spirit are
felt in the most retired sanctuaries of the private life of a hundred
bloods and nations. Yet all this is without sound and without
effort. While it is as solid as adamant, it is as pervasive as the air.
Who ever saw any thing earthly like it? Moreover, it is the only
institution of time which will be prolonged into eternity. The
grandest monarchies of earth will cast no shadow in heaven.
Dumbness and oblivion will pass upon all philosophies. Not a
single literature has any eternal meaning. The most magnificent
civilization represents nothing on the other side of the grave.
The most glorious revolutions have only a temporal significance.
The fortunes of the whole earth will leave no impression, will

transfer no lines, upon eternity, further than as they may have helped or hindered the salvation of this or that individual soul; whereas the grandeur of the Church on earth is but a prelude to its grandeur up in heaven.

It is no wonder, then, that the Church should lay such a singular grasp on our affections and our loyalty. On the lowest grounds it may rank with astronomy, or psychology, or politics, as the devotion of a life; only that the exclusiveness of the devotion, which in the case of those sectional sciences is a narrowness and a defect, is here a devotedness rather than an exclusiveness, because that which is universal cannot be exclusive. Devotion to the Church combines all interests. It takes in every duty. It provides for every responsibility. It intensifies every love. It embraces all social life, and ennobles it by its embrace. It penetrates all private life, and sanctifies it by its penetration. It is the unity of all knowledge and the harmony of all philosophy. It is interested in all diplomacies, and it survives them all. Its minuteness allows nothing to be overlooked, while its comprehensiveness includes every thing within its influence. In a word, the Church is that part of every thing, that side of every thing, that view of every thing, that interference with every thing, which represents the double sovereignty and jurisdiction of the Creator and the Redeemer.

All this, as we shall see shortly, is part of the devotion to the Precious Blood. But we must pass on at present to look at the Church from one particular point of view—its life of devotions. In nothing is the beauty of the Church more ravishing, or its disclosures more intimately divine. Full of divine instincts, its worship grows with all the exuberance of a tropical forest, covering itself with verdure and with blossoms. It puts forth its devotions with all the freedom of a tree which has liberty to spread on all sides. Everywhere it is free of the sun and air. There is nothing to hinder its development, nothing to hamper its genius, nothing to disfigure its natural forms and amplitudes of beauty. The diversity of its blossoms is astonishing. It makes devotions out of joys, out of sorrows, and out of glories. It has a treasury of innumerable mysteries, and out of every mystery it can unfold many devotions. Ages roll on. None of the old blossoms wither or fall off. Yet new varieties are added. Its colors grow more beautiful than ever, and its fragrances are multiplied. This is the way in which the age of the Church is forever clothing itself with the loveliness of a new youth. It is more beautiful now than it was three centuries ago; and three centuries hence we shall almost envy out of our calm in heaven the fortune of those who come after us, and are sanctified by the novelties of glory in the Church. Taken with all its array of manifold devotions, the Church worships the Holy Trinity with such magnificently expansive freedom and such large variety that we can hardly, even in our imagination, embrace it in one view. Yet there is a deep-seated unity in this diversity of worship. When we see a tree in a favorable soil and position as it were wantoning in its robust vigor, flinging out its year's growth on this side and on that, here filling itself in with close pendant foliage in curves which might have been drawn with instruments, there presenting an indented outline with inlets of blue sky among its branches, it seems hard to believe that there is a law under all this irregular exuberance; and yet so it is. In like manner dogmatic theology is the hidden law, the infallible unity of all this multiform devotion of the Church. It is a law, whose control is unerring and never relaxed, and yet whose pressure in no way checks exuberance. Indeed, it would be more true to say that the very law itself is the prolific fountain of these varieties. The science of theology is forever passing into love, and, as love receives it, it transmutes it into devotion. These devotions of the Church are the giving forth of its private affections and secret inner life. By them we know the Church better than by any thing else. They are the action of the Holy Ghost upon her heart, made visible by this perennial springtide of heavenly flowers. We may say that we come to know that Ever-blessed Spirit better by these devotions than by any thing else. They are a revelation of himself.

If we examine this seemingly confused multitude of devotions, we shall find that they may be parted off into two spheres, forming indeed but one world, and the one sphere for the most part lying within the other. Nevertheless, we shall attain clearness by so regarding it; and in fact the division is a real one. One sphere of devotions is based upon the Incarnation. It glasses the Thirty-Three Years, and continually lives them over again in devotions. The Soul of Jesus, his Body, his Blood, and the Divinity, as united to the Sacred Humanity, are abysses which seem to give forth devotions inexhaustibly. In reading the lives of saints and holy persons we are constantly coming across devotions which we never heard of before. The seventeenth century alone gave birth to some hundreds. Among the Carmelites they have gone on blooming as in a garden ever since the days of St. Teresa. Sometimes a holy man has looked at the Incarnation under a new aspect, due partly to the peculiarity of his own genius and partly to the characteristics of his times—not of course without God impressing a direction upon these things—and then his influence or his writings have given birth to manifold devotions. This is the case with Cardinal Berulle, with Father Condren, Father Eudes, and also with Olier, in France. The same may be said of Maria Tommasi, Isabella Farnese, Domenica del Paradiso, St. Mary Magdalene of Pazzi, and Cherubina dell' Agnus Dei, among the Italians. St. Gertrude, St. Mechtildis, and Elizabeth of Schaunberg have done the same in Germany; and Marina d'Escobar, Mary of Agreda, Mary of Antigua, and Isabella of Beniganim, for the Spanish peninsula. While one set of devotions have followed the division of the Soul, the Body, the Blood, and the Divinity of Jesus, another set have gone by times and places. Bethlehem, Egypt, Nazareth, Galilee, and Jerusalem have each their constellations of devotion proper to them. Then again, devotions follow the different lives of our Blessed Lord—his Life in the Womb, his Infant Life, his Hidden Life, his Public Life, his Suffering Life, his Risen Life, his Ascended Life, and his Sacramental Life. Or they follow his offices, or his Names, or his joys, or his sorrows, or his glories, or his journeys, or his words, or his apostles, or classes of his actions. Again, his Mother is a perfect world of devotions, with her various mysteries and ministries and offices and graces and endurances and identifications with himself. For eighteen hundred years Catholic devotions have come forth from the Incarnation, as from an inward world of spiritual beauty, in magnificent procession. There is no sign of their ending. Each new devotion seems to make more devotions possible. They multiply by the very outpouring of them. Each devotion becomes the head of a family of devotions. It seizes upon some saint or upon some religious congregation, and perpetuates itself, and multiplies itself, and is a fresh visible adornment to the Church. Nothing gives us such a vivid idea of the inexhaustible treasures of the Thirty-Three Years as this multiplicity of devotions. We see how the eternal contemplation of the Blessed may feed itself upon those years, and they shall yet remain unfathomed and, by created intellect, unfathomable.

These devotions are like particular revelations. They are constantly telling us either what we did not know before about our dearest Lord, or what had never struck us before. It is the Holy Ghost adding to our knowledge of Jesus, or bringing to our minds his sayings, his doings, and his ways. The theology of these devotions, and the way in which they are started and propagated by the private revelations of the saints, by visions, voices, and apparitions, make them to be a sort of complement to the Four Gospels. This, then, is one view which the Church presents to us in her devotions. If we could see her in her whole extent, we should see this Bride of Christ living over again, in all its breadth, if not in all its depth, the earthly life of Jesus: or, to speak more accurately, he is living it endlessly over again in her. There are a thousand Bethlehems, a thousand Nazareths, and a thousand Calvaries, scattered through the Church. There are visible similitudes of his outward actions. There are ascetical reiterations of his inward dispositions. There are mystical continuances of his various lives. The whole earth has come to be a Holy Land. Palestine has swelled out into a world. Every Christian family is a Bethlehem. Every catholic village is a Nazareth, every city a Jerusalem. All shrines of human sorrow are Gethsemanes. There are Calvaries everywhere. There are countless cloisters, nay, countless single hearts, which are in themselves Bethlehem, Nazareth, and Calvary at once. Look over the Church with this light upon it; and then look upward to the Face of Jesus bending over it in tenderness and joyous love, and think how holy and how zealous and how ardent must be our devotion to the Church, if it is to resemble his complacency.

The other sphere of the devotions of the Church is based upon the Attributes of God. What the various mysteries of Jesus are in one sphere of devotions, the various Attributes of God are in the other. The Church receives from heaven upon its placid bosom the image of Jesus; it receives also the image of the Un-created. We can worship God in his simplicity. We can also have a special devotion to his simplicity. But in this latter case we are regarding his simplicity as one of his Attributes. We cannot have a devotion to God as God. We simply worship the Majesty of the Godhead with trembling adoration. The feeling and the act are distinct from devotion. But we can be said to have a devotion to the various Attributes into which we divide his simplicity and by which we conceive his perfection. In strict truth, as I have warned you before, he is all his Attributes, and all his Attributes are him-self. But, in our language and in our conceptions, his Attributes are not himself: they are less than himself; they are parts, for so our ignorance necessitates us to depict them, of him who is indi-visible. Thus they stand in the same relation to God that the mysteries of the Incarnation stand in to our Lord. When we have a devotion to one of our Lord's joys, we know that there is some-thing which it does not include, either other joys, or his sorrows, or his glories. So when we have a devotion to God's justice, we know that we are for the present leaving out of direct view his mercy. The finite may worship the Infinite as infinite, and in his unity. It can only *study* the Infinite in detail; and these details are the creations and conveniences of its own limited mind, not substantive external truths. Thus there is no such *thing* as omnip-otence: but there is a *Being* who is omnipotent, or (if the idiom of our language would have permitted me so to express myself) who is omnipotence. There is no such *thing* as omnipresence:

but there is a *Being* who is omnipresent. I say this for the sake of accuracy, and to anticipate misunderstanding. But the devotion to the Attributes of God is practically a very simple matter to the most ordinarily pious believer.

Among the children of the Church, chiefly but not exclusively those who are aiming at perfection, there exists this devotion to the Attributes of God. It is less universal, as a special devotion, than devotions to the Incarnation; and it has also this peculiarity, that, whereas devotion to the mysteries of the Sacred Humanity can exist without any special or pronounced devotion to the Attributes of God, this last devotion is always accompanied by some special devotions founded on the Incarnation. It is one of the common marks of a spiritual delusion, when men are without some special devotion to the mysteries of Jesus, and affect to meditate or contemplate the divine perfections instead. Some holy persons have a peculiar devotion to the Attributes of God in general, and in their prayers change from one to another; and this change is very often influenced by the feasts and seasons of the year, in consequence of the connection and sympathy which appear to exist between particular Attributes of God and particular mysteries of the Incarnation. Others, again, devote themselves to honor some one Attribute, and to make it the main, if not the sole, subject of their meditations. There are examples of this devotion, which carry with them great authority. Some have always had this attraction to the Attributes of God; and it has even given a peculiar shape to their devotion to the mysteries of Jesus, especially the Passion. Some have arrived at it through long meditation on the Sacred Humanity, as if they had been raised by the contemplation of the Sacred Humanity to that of the Divinity. But even in this case the devotion to the Sacred Humanity is rather heightened than abandoned. These positive devotions to the Divine Attributes arise very often from the characteristics of the mind and disposition, not of course without the concurrence of grace, and even some special leadings of the Holy Ghost. Sometimes the attraction seems to be entirely supernatural, and not unfrequently distinct and sudden like a vocation.

But these attractions to the Divine Attributes, like those of the mysteries of the Incarnation, do not always rest in devotion. They assign vocations and pursuits. They cast a man's external actions into some peculiar mould. The whole life becomes shaped on the Attribute to which the soul is specially devoted. This is more particularly the case with the two Attributes of justice and sanctity. Some saintly persons, devoted to these Attributes, have been bidden to lead lives of marvellous expiations or reparations. The instincts of the Holy Ghost have urged them into terrible novelties of penance, or strange depths of inward self-abasement. Their lives have been admirable rather than imitable. Instances of this might be given from the Chronicles of Religious Orders, especially those of Carmel and the Visitation, and also from the lives of many of those who have had the stigmata. If devotion to the Attributes of God proceeds to the extremity of moulding the outward life, much more may we expect to find it shaping inward holiness, and stamping a peculiar character upon our spirituality. Even the eternity of God, seemingly the least likely of his Attributes for such a purpose, has been made to be the form of the holiness of some very interior and elevated souls.*

I believe the agency of the Attributes of God in the spiritual life to be much more extensive than is commonly supposed. In other words, the Church is a truer image of the invisible majesty of God than our faith is ordinarily allowed to perceive. His perfections impress themselves upon his creatures, very deeply, even when invisibly. There are certain phenomena in the spiritual life, very delicate and very volatile, which lead to the supposition that the action of some one Attribute lies at the bottom of each man's vocation, as well as of each devotion in the Church. If this be so, and if we consider it in connection with the affinity between nature and grace, we shall sometimes wonder whether each soul that is created is not created in the special likeness of some one Attribute of God, ranged as it were under the banners of that

---

*See the instance of Anne Seraphine Boulier quoted in Chapter I.

one Attribute, and called by a very sweet vocation to form its life upon it.

But these are speculations. Certain it is, that the Church worships God in all his breadth, so far as creatures can do so, and produces a unity of worship through this multiplicity of devotions to his perfections. One soul, one saint, one order, cannot do the whole work by itself; but the whole work is done, and it is done by the harmony and conjunction of them all. It is the affectionate conspiracy of all created beauty to make a worthy offering to the Uncreated Loveliness. It is difficult to make pictures of spiritual things. But it brings wonderful thoughts into our minds, and vast indescribable images, if we try to picture the Church to ourselves as thus outstretching itself to enclose all the Attributes of the Most High, one while rising to each of them, like the arms of the great sea flung upward to the moon, and offering to each the incense of a peculiar devotion—and then another while lying passive while they descend upon it, and leave upon it nameless signs of their mysterious contact. The depths of the Church, like the depths of ocean, are fields of wild flowery loveliness, strangely lighted by the sun through the translucent waters; and thither the glory of God descends, at twilight as he came to Adam, or at midnight as he came to Mary, or in the morning as he came to Israel in the wilderness, to pasture the beautiful flock of his perfections. The Church—it is the fairest of her splendors—is the mother of her Maker's glory.

It is natural, almost necessary, when we are speaking of the devotions of the Church, to speak also, and once again, of devotion to the Church; but it is still more necessary to do so, when we have to speak of the devotion to the Precious Blood. The Church, as we have already said, is the creation of the Precious Blood, the institution which it has founded, and wherein its virtue continues to reside. It is impossible to study the grandeurs of the Precious Blood without being led at almost every step into the magnificences of the Sacraments; and then again the Sacraments are the structure of the Church. The theology of the Sacraments and the theology of the Church are but one. We cannot separate them without making both of them unintelligible. With these theologies, the theology of the Precious Blood is also inextricably intertwined. This will strike any thoughful student of theology. Moreover, as we have seen, the Precious Blood ministers especially to the dominion and magnificence of God; and the Church is the living vicegerent of God's dominion, and the Sacraments are a peculiar and unparalleled emanation of his magnificence; and thus from another point of view the Precious Blood is bound up with the Church and the Sacraments. The instincts of the saints have united the two devotions. Those, whose lives strike us because of the active interest they took in the outward politics and destinies of the Church, an interest often at seeming variance with their manifest call to contemplation, are almost always found to have had a peculiar devotion to the Precious Blood. The Precious Blood magnifies the Church, and the Church magnifies the Precious Blood. There was once a narrowminded heresy which denied that the Precious Blood was shed for all, maintaining that it was shed only for a chosen few. Like all heresies which depreciate the grandeurs of Jesus, it was an especially soul-destroying heresy; and, like all soul-destroying heresies, it clothed itself in the garb of harshness, as if the pomp of rigor was to give it the venerable dignity of holiness. We shall avoid falling into cognate errors about the Church, if we remember its connection with the Precious Blood. The object of the Church, like the object of the Precious Blood, is universality. It is not a snare of God to overwhelm poor souls with the insupportable responsibilities of terrible privileges. It is an institution for the express purpose of making salvation easier, shorter, safer, more various, and more universal. Its exclusiveness is concentration rather than exclusiveness. It is its surest and its swiftest road to being universal. If the responsibilities of grace were actually difficulties in the way of salvation, it is plain that heathenism would be the best religion, because it would be the least perilous. If the prodigality of God's love be only a burden made the more crushing by its beautiful excess, then God's gifts are snares to entrap his creatures, for the future purpose of justifying his vengeance.

If men are less likely to be saved because they have more to answer for, it is cruel to preach the Gospel, barbarous to invite them into the Church, treacherous to allure them to the Sacraments. On this theory, the Church is part of the machinery of God's vindictive justice; and it is not life, as the Bible calls it, but a greater likelihood of death, "to know God and Jesus Christ whom he has sent." This unfilial depreciation of the Church is also a depreciation of the grandeurs of Jesus, similar to that of Jansenism, though coming by a different road and from an opposite quarter. It will be found to be accompanied with the same disesteem of the Sacraments, and to delight in the same parade of rigor. But it is a theory which cannot consist with a life of prayer, and which will wither before a growing devotion to the Precious Blood. We must learn the theology of the Church and of the Sacraments in its union with the theology of the Precious Blood. Theology will make our devotion more devout; and devotion will make our theology more true.

In treating of the devotion to the Precious Blood we naturally begin with its history. In one sense, and a very notable sense, the whole history of the Church is a history of the devotion to the Precious Blood; for it is a history of the preaching of the Gospel, and of the administration of the Sacraments. It is the prominent devotion of dogmatic theology; for it is that upon which the doctrine of redemption lays the greatest stress. But we are speaking of it rather as a special and separate devotion. It certainly seems to have existed as such in the mind and heart of St. Paul, if we may judge from the evident fondness with which he dwells upon it in his epistles, with reiterations made on purpose, as if they were grateful to his love. We may call him the doctor of the Precious Blood, and the author of the special devotion to it. It was in this devotion that the strength of his apostolic instinct lay. It was the natural fruit of the peculiar magnificence of his conversion and vocation. Among the Fathers we have St. Chrysostom in the East and St. Austin in the West, who may be regarded as striking examples of a special devotion to the Precious Blood. The zeal for souls, which burned in St. Chrysostom, and the en-

thusiasm for the liberalities of redeeming grace, which was quite a
passion with St. Austin, explain the prominence of this devotion
in their writings. Among the saints, St. Gertrude's revelations are
full of the sweetest and deepest things about the Precious Blood.
But the devotion seems to take its modern form and consistence
chiefly in St. Catherine of Siena, whom we may justly term the
Prophetess of the Precious Blood.* She has singled out this devotion with a more obvious predilection; and she has singled it out
as a remedy needful for her times, and one upon which, in her
judgment, sufficient stress had not been laid. We read of Osanna
of Mantua, that, so vehement was her devotion to the Precious
Blood, she could never see any human blood without at once
going into an ecstasy. Coupled with her singular devotion to the
Person of the Eternal Word, St. Mary Magdalene of Pazzi had
also a special devotion to the Precious Blood.

The lives of the saints are of course replete with instances of
devotion to the Precious Blood; and it would be impossible to
enumerate them all. Let it suffice to give some specimens. The
Venerable Maria Francesca of the Five Wounds, an Alcantarine
nun at Naples, was communicated by St. Raphael out of the
chalice, the priest missing it at the time of mass, and observing a
diminution in the Sacred Blood. We can hardly doubt that this
grace was an answer to an intense desire, and a reward for a special devotion to the Precious Blood.† In that amazing and delightful repertory of spiritual science, the Chronicles of the French
Carmelites, we read of Frances of the Mother of God, that one
day before Communion those words of the Apocalypse were
deeply imprinted on her mind: He hath loved us and washed
away our sins in his Blood. Presently our Lord said to her in-
teriorly, I have shed my Blood for your sins, and now I come in
Holy Communion to wash away the stains which remain. When she

---

*It should be remembered now that it once pleased God to save Italy by means
of St. Catherine of Siena, and to restore the Pope to Rome. By an increased devotion to the great Dominicaness may we not help the Holy See, and the poor land
which does not know its own blessedness in possessing the Chair of Peter and the
Holy City?

†Vita, p. 155.

had received our Lord, she saw her soul all covered with Blood.* In the life of the Venerable Anne of Jesus, the companion of St. Teresa, we read that once in communicating she had her mouth sensibly filled with very sweet Blood, which flowed from the Host; and another time she had a vision of the joy which an infinite number of blessed souls have in that Blood in heaven.† Marcello Benci often when he served St. Philip's mass, saw after consecration the chalice full of Blood.‡ Margaret of Beaune, the Carmelitess, is well known in the Church for the new devotions to the Infant Jesus with which she enriched it. Patrignani, in his life of her, tells us that she so habitually saw the Blood of Jesus in the souls of men, and saw them so beautified by it, that she could not bear to hear any one blamed, however justly; because of the reverence she felt for wicked souls through the Blood of Jesus which she beheld in them.** When Margaret of the Passion, Carmelitess at Rouen, was on her death-bed, she said that the Blood of Jesus had been applied to her, and that it had caused her a light and brief pain, while it had filled her soul with God, and infused into her a profound peace, and had pardoned all her sins.†† But it is useless to multiply instances.

Another development of the devotion to the Precious Blood has arisen from the possession of relics, whether of what was once Precious Blood or of miraculous Blood. These have been the object, not only of a local worship, but of devout pilgrimages, which have often led to signal conversions of sinners. Beyrout, Bruges, Saintes, Mantua, the imperial monastery of Weingarten, which claimed to possess the portion of the Blood of Mantua which had been given to the Emperor Henry the Third, and the English monasteries of Ashridge and Hailes, may be quoted as instances of this kind of devotion.‡‡

---

*Chroniques, ii. 595-596.
†Vie, pp. 512-513.
‡Bacci, Vita di Filippo Neri, p. 82.
**Vita, p. 99
††Chroniques, ii. 417.
‡‡See Haag Sanguis Christi in terra vindicatus, 1758.

There is no surer sign of the growth of a special devotion in the Church than the erection of a Confraternity, representing and embodying it. There was an ancient confraternity of the Precious Blood at Ravenna. Another was erected in Rome in the Pontificate of Gregory XIII which was confirmed by Sixtus V. It was afterward merged in the confraternity of the Gonfalone. Its members were priests, and took upon themselves the obligation of preaching missions. But the pontificate of Pius VII was the great epoch in the history of this devotion. An archconfraternity of the Precious Blood was set up at Rome in the Church of San Nicola in Carcere by Albertini, Bishop of Terracina, Bonanni, Bishop of Norcia, and Gaspare del Bufalo, Canon of San Marco. The pope enriched this confraternity, and also the devotion independently of the confraternity, with great indulgences. He also granted indulgences to the Passionists and to the Missionaries of the Precious Blood, in favor of this devotion. The Congregation of the Missioners of the Precious Blood was founded in the same pontificate by Gaspare del Bufalo, who was likewise the founder of a congregation of religious women devoted to the worship of the Precious Blood. He died at Rome in the odor of sanctity on the 28th of December, 1837. It was in the church of his Missionaries of the Precious Blood at Rimini, that the miraculous appearances took place a few years ago, in connection with a picture of our Lady; and this fact is probably not without some supernatural significance regarding the devotion to the Precious Blood.

I have not been able to trace satisfactorily the rise of confraternities of the Precious Blood. But their existence in Spain seems to betoken some special devotion to the Precious Blood in that country, which has been the nursery of so many grandeurs of the faith, and which the supernatural has so often chosen with a kind of predilection as the theatre of its manifestations, as if it were a kind of Western Palestine shutting up the end of the Mediterranean, to pass the faith across the broad Atlantic. In the life of Anne of St. Augustine, the Carmelitess, it is said that she always received with hospitality those who went about collecting alms for the confraternities of the Precious Blood, which are spoken of as having been "erected in many places." She died in 1624.* In the life of Brother Francis of the Infant Jesus, a Carmelite lay-brother, mention is made of a confraternity of the Precious Blood in the street of St. Vincent at Valentia in 1601.† But I have not been able to find any account of these confraternities. These scattered notices suffice to show that it was a popular Spanish devotion.

Among the reforms of the Cistercianesses, there arose a Congregation of Divine Providence, with which St. Francis of Sales had to do, as it was founded with his assistance, and by the Mother de Ballon, a near relation of his. Out of this Congregation, and under the auspices of the Mother de Ponçonas, sprang another Congregation, entitled Bernardines of the Precious Blood, which reached its full development in Paris in 1654. The strife between the Mothers de Ballon and de Ponçonas occupies perhaps the least edifying chapter of monastic history, and it is only alluded to here because of its connection with the history of the devotion to the Precious Blood. At the beginning of the seventeenth century, Vincent of Gonzaga, Duke of Mantua, founded a military order of Redemptorists of the Precious Blood, in order to guard the relic of the Precious Blood in the cathedral of St. Andrew at Mantua. Our own England was not without its place in the history of this devotion. Richard of Cornwall, brother of Henry the Third, brought from Germany a large relic of the Precious Blood, and founded a Congregation entitled the Congregation of Good-Men (Bonhommes), in order to keep, to watch, and to honor this relic. He placed two-thirds of it in a monastery which he built at Ashridge near Berkhampstead, in Buckinghamshire and the other third in a similar monastery at Hailes, in Gloucestershire. The Bonhommes had the reputation of being great mystics. They lived under the rule of St. Augustin.‡‡

---

*Vita, p. 146.

†Vita, p. 326.

‡‡See Helyot, Hist. des Ordres Rélig. under the words Divine Providence, Précieux Sang, and Rédempteurs: Morigia, Istoria di tutte le Religioni, lib. 1, cap. lx.:

Leo XII enriched this devotion with indulgences. But the present pontificate of Pius IX has been another grand epoch in the history of this devotion, similar to that of Pius VII. In this pontificate the red scapular of the Vincentians has been instituted, in consequence, it is said, of some private revelation; and it has been indulgenced by the Sovereign Pontiff. The confraternity of the Precious Blood has been enriched with still further indulgences; and similar confraternities have been multiplied. One—it is believed the first in England since those of Richard of Cornwall in the middle of the thirteenth century—was established in the Church of St. Wilfrid among the Staffordshire hills in 1847, with the approval of the bishop, and had a great success. It was afterward transferred to the church of the London Oratory, and was re-erected by a papal rescript, August 12, 1850. In this confraternity more than thirty-eight thousand members have been enrolled, and one hundred and four religious communities; and the numbers are increasing daily. Besides this, there are several other local confraternities affiliated with it; and others which have been independently erected at a subsequent date, both in England and Ireland.

There was already a commemorative feast of the Precious Blood in Lent. But when Pius IX returned to the Holy City from his exile at Gaeta, he issued a decree to the whole world, instituting a new feast of the Precious Blood on the first Sunday of July. There is surely a great significance in this decree. The Holy See has taken the lead in this special devotion, and has thereby immensely increased its popularity, the usual result of authority. Moreover, the selection of the devotion is of still greater significance. The latest new devotion of the Church was the devotion to the Sacred Heart. The choice has fallen next upon

---

and Dugdale's Monasticon, under Ashridge. Morigia gives the date of Richard of Cornwall's foundation as 1257; Tanner dates it in 1283; Mr. Todd, who wrote the privately-printed history of Ashridge for Lord Bridgewater, dates Richard, the first rector, from 1276. Thomas Waterhouse, the last rector, surrendered the house to Henry the Eighth. The seal represented the Agnus Dei with the Earl of Cornwall's lion beneath it.

the Precious Blood, which is as it were a development of the devotion to the Sacred Heart. So that there is a sort of historical or chronological fitness in it. It seems part of catholic piety to believe that, while these things are by no means supposed to lie within the gift of infallibility, there is a peculiar guidance of the Holy Spirit in them. It is he who as it were writes the history of the Church. It is to his instincts that we reverently refer all movements which have to do with the spiritual life and devotion of the faithful, and also the choice of the times at which these movements are made. Such movements are parts of a whole, steps toward an end; but the whole and the end only become visible to us when they have grown a portion of past history. They mean much more than we see, or than can be comprehended by one generation. The circumstances, under which this decree of a new feast of the Precious Blood was issued, stamp upon the feast the same character of thanksgiving which belongs to the feast of the Help of Christians. It is an historical monument of a vicissitude of the Holy See, a perpetual Te Deum for a deliverance of the Vicar of Christ.

All devotions have their characteristics; all of them have their own theological meanings. We must say something, therefore, upon the characteristics of the devotion to the Precious Blood. In reality the whole Treatise has more or less illustrated this matter. But something still remains to be said, and something will bear to be repeated. We will take the last first. Devotion to the Precious Blood is the devotional expression of the prominent and characteristic teaching of St. Paul. St. Paul is the apostle of redeeming grace. A devout study of his epistles would be our deliverance from most of the errors of the day. He is truly the apostle of all ages. To each age doubtless he seems to have a special mission. Certainly his mission to ours is very special. The very air we breathe is Pelagian. Our heresies are only novel shapes of an old Pelagianism. The spirit of the world is eminently Pelagian. Hence it comes to pass that wrong theories among us are always constructed round a nucleus of Pelagianism; and Pelagianism is just the heresy which is least able to breathe in the atmosphere of St. Paul. It is the age of the natural as opposed to the supernatural, of the acquired as opposed to the infused, of the active as opposed to the passive. This is what I said in an earlier chapter, and here repeat. Now, this exclusive fondness for the natural is on the whole very captivating. It takes with the young, because it saves thought. It does not explain difficulties; but it lessens the number of difficulties to be explained. It takes with the idle; for it dispenses from slowness and research. It takes with the unimaginative, because it withdraws just the very element in religion which teases them. It takes with the worldly, because it subtracts the enthusiasm from piety and the sacrifice from spirituality. It takes with the controversial, because it is a short road and a shallow ford. It forms a school of thought which, while it admits that we have abundance of grace, intimates that we are not much the better for it. It merges privileges in responsibilities, and makes the sovereignty of God odious by representing it as insidious. All this whole spirit, with all its ramifications, perishes in the sweet fires of devotion to the Precious Blood.

The time is also one of libertinage; and a time of libertinage is always, with a kind of practical logic, one of infidelity. Whatever brings out God's side in creation, and magnifies his incessant supernatural operation in it, is the controversy which infidelity can least withstand. Now, the devotion to the Precious Blood does this in a very remarkable way. It shows that the true significance of every thing is to be found in the scheme of redemption, apart from which it is useless to discuss the problems of creation. It is a revelation to us of the character of God as well as of the work of Jesus. By bringing out the wonders of the Church and the energies of the Sacraments, it insinuates into our hearts the love of the sovereignty of God, together with a sense of perfect freedom and enlargement. By drawing out into strong lights the most intimate human realities of the Incarnation, it meets the false spirituality, which sometimes runs into heresy, about the Sacred Humanity. More especially does it war against that dangerous fastidiousness which even believers sometimes feel, through want of reverential discipline of mind, about the physical mysteries of Jesus, especially those of his Passion. This fastidiousness is a deep source of widely-spreading evil. It makes us ungenuine and profane. Reverence contemplates divine things, and does not divert its thoughts from the physical horrors in which, because of our sins, those divine things have deigned to manifest themselves. Magdalen holds Jesus by his feet, while the Gerasens entreat him to depart from their vicinity. We lose much which we cannot afford to lose, by any thing which makes our devotion to the Passion less faithful and less real.

Another characteristic of the devotion to the Precious Blood is the way in which it brings out and keeps before us the principle of sacrifice. Sacrifice is peculiarly the Christian element of holiness; and it is precisely the element which corrupt nature dislikes and resists. There is no end to the delusions which our self-love is fertile enough to bring forth in order to evade the obligation of sacrifice, or to narrow its practical application. If it were enough to have correct views, or high feelings, or devout aspirations, it would be easy to be spiritual. The touchstone is mortification. Worldly amusements, domestic comforts, nice food, and a daily doing our own will in the lesser details of life, are all incompatible with sanctity, when they are habitual and form the ordinary normal current of our lives. Pain is necessary to holiness. Suffering is essential to the killing of self-love. Habits of virtue cannot by any possibility be formed without voluntary mortification. Sorrow is needful for the fertility of grace. If a man is not making constant sacrifices, he is deceiving himself, and is not advancing in spirituality. If a man is not denying himself daily, he is not carrying the cross. These are axioms which at all times offend our weakness and self-indulgence. But they are of peculiar importance in times like these, when comforts and even luxuries are almost universal. It is comfort which is the ruin of holiness. Gayety, fashion, ostentation, expensiveness, dissipation, frivolity, and the other things which make up a London season, are undoubtedly not the component parts of sanctity. But in my estimation they are far less worldly, have far less of the poison of worldliness in them, than the daily worship of comfort which distinguishes the great bulk of quiet people in these days. Many are not attracted by balls, parties, and similar fashions of amusement, and therefore have no merit in keeping away from them. But these same persons may set a great value upon the uninterrupted course of their daily comforts. They rise when they will, and gather every convenience round their rising. Their meals must be elegant, and pleasant, and faultless. Their servant-machinery must go smoothly, anticipating wants and keeping out of sight annoyances. Their time must be for the most part at their own disposal. They must have the pastime of amusing conversation and of social intercourse; and they must be able to satisfy their restlessness, when they please, by change of air and scene and company. There is generally a far greater intensity of worldliness in all this than in the pleasure-hunting riot of a London season. Thus we often find, in connection with this last, great graces, generous sacrifices, unexpected mortifications, and unkilled heavenly longings. But these are hardly ever found in the quiet unobtrusive worship of domestic comfort. Yearly out of the dissipations of the great world come grand vocations. Every London season inscribes against its will some few glorious conversions in the annals of grace, conversions whose peculiar glory is the frankness of their generosity. Nothing grand ever comes out of the daily round of comfort. The heroic things of Christian attainment have less chance in quiet gardens and by pleasant riversides than in the ballroom or the court. There is a smoothness in the mere lapse of a comfortable life which is fatal to holiness. Now, all the forms, and images, and associations, and pictures, and ideas, of the devotion to the Precious Blood breathe sacrifice. Their fragrance is the odor of sacrifice. Their beauty is the austerity of sacrifice. They tease the soul with a constant sense of dissatisfaction and distrust with whatsoever is not sacrifice; and this teasing is the solicitation of grace. In time they infect us with a love of sacrifice; and to gain this love of sacrifice is to have surmounted the first ascent of holiness, and to be breathing the pure air and yet treading the more level road of the upper tableland of the mountains of perfection. It is the very mission of the devotion to the Precious Blood to preach a crusade against quiet sinless comforts. The Mass is the compendium of the Gospel. It is a heresy in doctrine to acknowledge the Sacrament and to deny the Sacrifice. Worldliness is guilty of a similar practical heresy with regard to holiness. It admits the claims of all its obligations but one; and that is the obligation of sacrifice.

It is another characteristic of the devotion to the Precious Blood that it does not usurp the place of other devotions, but by its own growth makes more room for them. We cannot have an equal devotion for all the things to which we ought to be devout. We have not breadth enough for it. We are obliged to take things in detail. Calvary on the whole turns our thoughts from Bethlehem, and Bethlehem on the whole turns our thoughts from Calvary. One mystery comes in the way of another. Devotions stand in each other's light. There is no harm in this. It is a blameless imperfection. But it is a peculiarity of the devotion to the Precious Blood that it does not interfere with other devotions. On the contrary, it rather fosters them. For it is not only a devotion by itself, separate from other devotions, and with a spirit of its own, but it is also a part of other devotions, a particular form of other devotions, a shape which many other devotions may assume. It mingles in the most natural way with devotion to our Blessed Lady. It is an additional splendor to every one of her mysteries. It throws light upon them. It brings her into the mysteries of Jesus. It has, as we shall see afterward, a peculiar connection with the Immaculate Conception. It forms in itself a separate devotion to our dearest Mother, as the fountain of the Precious Blood, a devotion of the most inexpressible tenderness, a devotion to her immaculate heart and sinless blood.

It is also a variety of devotion to the Passion. It furnishes a point of view from which we may regard each separate mystery, while it is also a mould in which we can fuse all the mysteries of the Passion into one. It is thus a unity of the devotion to the Passion as well as a variety of it, besides being in itself an additional devotion to the Passion. When we wish to range the whole

Passion into one view, we find that simply to look upon it as the single mystery of the Passion, it is too large for us, and becomes vague. Now, vagueness is precisely what we must try to avoid in devotion to the Passion. Its virtue resides in its vividness. Unless it be vivid, it will not be true; and unless it be true, it will not be reverent. Thus we have various devices by which we make the Passion into one mystery and yet preserve its details. We take the five trials of our Lord, or the seven journeys, or the seven words, or the five wounds. All these are excellent contrivances of love. But the Precious Blood supplies us with a more natural unity and also with a more vivid detail.

We may say the same of devotion to Jesus Risen. It is a devotion which we cultivate by separate meditation on the beautiful apparitions of those Forty Days. It is a devotion out of which we draw bright thoughts of God, the sunniest views of his adorable sovereignty, heavenly yearnings, a more reverential and amazed devotion to our Lady, an increased zeal for souls, and all that ministers to the alacrity of holiness. Alacrity is the characteristic of this devotion. But, when we desire to make a unity of this devotion to Jesus Risen, we find it either in devotion to the Soul of our Blessed Saviour, or to his Precious Blood.

Devotion to the Precious Blood also supplies us with an additional form of devotion to the Blessed Sacrament. The devotion to the Precious Blood in the chalice may be considered not merely as an additional form of devotion, but as an additional devotion, to the Blessed Sacrament; while the special adoration of the Precious Blood, when we are kneeling before the tabernacle, is a form of devotion bringing much doctrine before us, and enabling us better to comprehend the august realities of that tremendous Sacrament.

But the closest alliance of the devotion to the Precious Blood is with the devotion to the Sacred Heart. The Precious Blood is the wealth of the Sacred Heart. The Sacred Heart is the symbol of the Precious Blood; yet not its symbol only, but its palace, its home, its fountain. It is to the Sacred Heart that it owes the joy of its restlessness and the glory of its impetuosity. It is to the

Sacred Heart that it returns with momentary swiftness, and assails it, as a child assails his mother for fresh powers, for new vigor, and for the continuance of its unwearied impulses. The devotion to the Precious Blood is the devotion which unveils the physical realities of the Sacred Heart. The devotion to the Sacred Heart is the figurative expression of the qualities, dispositions, and genius of the Precious Blood—only that the figure is itself a living and adorable reality. The Sacred Heart is the Heart of our Redeemer: yet it was not the Sacred Heart which redeemed us. It was precisely the Precious Blood, and nothing but the Precious Blood, which was the chosen instrument of our redemption. It is this singular reality, this unmated office, this unshared privilege, in which the grandeur of the Precious Blood resides, a grandeur which is also communicated to the devotion. If it were not for this, the devotion to the Precious Blood and the devotion to the Sacred Heart would be but one devotion, two aspects of the same devotion. The one would honor the actual workings of the Human Nature of our dearest Lord, while the other would magnify its inward dispositions, its hidden sweetness, its tender characteristics, its profuse liberalities, and its magnificent affections. One would have to do with operations, the other with significances. One would be occupied with processes, the other with consequences. The one would be the meaning of the other, and a commentary upon the other. So close is their alliance. But the mysterious fact that the Blood, and only the Blood, of Jesus, was the chosen price of man's redemption, and that it was only the Blood, and the Blood shed to death, which did actually redeem us, confers a distinctive majesty upon the Precious Blood, in which our Lord's Body and his Soul only participate concomitantly. Hence, while we commonly see that a devotion to the Precious Blood and a devotion to the Sacred Heart go together, we also see occasionally, and it is an exception to the rule given above, that the one does stand in way of the other, as if it were only a different aspect of the other, more congenial to the spiritual taste of the worshipper. But in reality this seeming opposition is only an evidence of the closeness of their alliance.

In connection with this harmony of the devotion to the Precious Blood with other devotions, we should mention another of its characteristics, which is of much interest in a devotional point of view. This is the way in which it links all the lives of Jesus into one. It does in devotion what it does also in reality. As it pervades the whole Body of our Lord and is its life, so does it mould into one all those lives, into which we are accustomed to divide our Lord's most blessed life, for the purposes of devotion. Every thing about our dearest Lord is so adorable, and at the same time so full of manifold attractions, that love is compelled to feed itself upon all the details which it can understand. Thus the divisions, and subdivisions, and the divisions of the subdivisions, which give the theology of devotion so technical an appearance, are in reality so far from being evidences of dryness that they are the very work of the assiduity and faithfulness of love. Jesus in the Womb, and an Infant, and a Boy, Jesus in his Ministry, in his Passion, and his Risen Life, and in his Ascended Life, and Jesus in his Sacramental Concealment, are all different lives, and yet the same. His Nine Months in the Womb are an epoch of the most amazing mysteries, the pleasant food of deep and contemplative worship. His Infancy is not his Boyhood, nor his Boyhood his Infancy. The Preacher in the green fields is not the Sufferer upon Calvary—is not, and yet also is. The Risen Jesus haunting the seclusions of his dear Galilee is not the Ascended Jesus whom the angels are welcoming with triumphal pomp in heaven upon his Session at the Father's Right Hand. He is not the same, and yet he is the same. Jesus in the miraculous coverts of the deep-enfolding Sacrament, hiding in the profound recesses of the light thinness of the Host, is another Jesus from any of the other seven; and yet it is the same dear Lord, so wondrously like himself in all the transmutations of his love. What interminable regions of delight are there not to traverse in these eight lives of our Blessed Lord! His sacred Humanity seems to grow to the dimensions of his divine immensity. Any one of these lives is too big a world for the mightiest scholar to fill with his intelligence. What could St. Michael himself do with the very shortest of them?

Even Mary does not fully comprehend the beauty of her Son, nor has she ever come to the last depth of his sweetness. Yet we shall understand nothing of these lives separately, unless we also realize them as one. This is the secret charm of the Rosary. It simplifies while it divides. It is a unity, while it is a variety as well. It parts our Lord in the Joys, the Sorrows, and the Glories of his Mother, and five times subdivides each of those three divisions; and yet it is all the one Jesus as Mary saw him, Mary's Jesus, Mary's view of him, love of him, and worship of him, which the complete Rosary brings before us. The devotion to the Precious Blood performs the same office differently to those eight lives; and in this function lies that affinity to the Rosary which those who practise it are not slow to discover. The Precious Blood runs through all those lives, and is the one human life of all of them. Yet it is not a mere fanciful string upon which our devotion may hang them for convenience' sake, as if they were so many beads. It is a living unity. It runs them into one, and gives a special meaning and imparts a special light to each. It is the one devotion to the Precious Blood eight times multiplied by the thoughtfulness of love.

Its use as a power of intercession is another characteristic of the devotion to the Precious Blood. It is a special office of our Saviour's Blood to plead. Its very existence is the mightiest of prayers. Its presence in heaven is a power which nothing but omnipotence exceeds. It was the power by which God redeemed man. It is the power by which man prevails with God. It was the oblation which, when actually offered, reconciled the offended Creator to his sinful creatures. It was the oblation the mere foresight of which made God overflow the world with mercies, and the imitation of which, in the blood of animals, was once the acceptable religion of the earth. It is the oblation, in spiritual union with which all Christian oblations are efficacious now. It is the oblation, the real repetition of which upon the altar is the continuance of the world's right to its Maker's forbearance. In this respect, also, the devotion to the Precious Blood has a more lively and intimate reality than other devotions. We shall speak hereafter of the spirit of this devotion, which we shall see to be a spirit of intercession. We are speaking of it here as a power, or instrument, of intercession. Many revelations from the other world testify to the peculiar devotion of the Dead to the Precious Blood. Souls in Purgatory have been allowed to appear and to tell how, in their patient land of woe, it is Blood, and only Blood, the Blood of the Adorable Mass, which can quench the flames. The pictures, which represent the angels holding chalices to the Wounded Side of Jesus, while Mary prays beneath, and then pouring those chalices into the fires of Purgatory, simply represent this catholic truth as it exists in the sense of the faithful. Prayers for the conversion of sinners naturally seek their efficacy in the oblation of the Precious Blood. The Precious Blood shed itself for their conversion. Conversion is its principal occupation upon earth. It is its own work more than it is ours. Used for this purpose, it is something more than intercession: it is the doing of the work, at once the prayer and the answer to the prayer. Prayer for the exaltation of the Church spontaneously flies to the Precious Blood; for the Church is the peculiar creation of that Blood. Its own devotion is devotion to the Church. It hastens therefore with promptitude to overwhelm our petitions with an unexpected magnificence of fulfilment. If we pray for the extirpation of heresies, it is the glory of the Church which we are seeking. If we pray against schisms, it is for the peace of the Church that we are pleading. If we pray for Christian kings, it is the freedom of the Church for which we are interceding. If we pray for the missions, it is the fertility of the Church upon which we ask a blessing. If we pray for the intentions of the Sovereign Pontiff, it is the sweet Spirit-guided will of the Church which we are assisting to its accomplishment. In all these things we are exercising devotion to the Church, in which devotion the Precious Blood only waits our invitation in order to join us with impatient love. Hence we may name the devotion to the Precious Blood the Apostolic Devotion.

There is yet another characteristic, which the history of this devotion suggests to us, but which by no means depends only upon the circumstances of its history—its peculiar alliance with the Immaculate Conception. It is curious that both these devotions have received great contemporary developments during the present pontificate. After centuries of growth, first in popular piety and then in the schools of theology, the Immaculate Conception has received its crown in the glorious definition of the dogma. This is the grandest event of the nineteenth century. The devotion to the Precious Blood has also had its indulgences and privileges augmented, and a new memorial feast instituted in its honor. The Pope's exile at Gaeta was sweetened by his Encyclical in favor of the Immaculate Conception. His return to Rome was celebrated by the institution of the new feast of the Precious Blood. The chief function of both these mysteries is to illustrate redeeming grace. They both preach redemption. The Precious Blood was the very instrument which redeemed the world. The Immaculate Conception was the first, as it is the grandest, victory of redemption. Thus the Immaculate Conception is the highest and the eldest work of the Precious Blood. But there is more than this in the matter. There is a sweet circle of cause and effect; now the cause is effect, and now the effect is cause. For in the Immaculate Conception, which was its choicest work, the Precious Blood first took its rise. The Immaculate Conception was for the sake of the Precious Blood. It was for the insuring of its purity and the protecting of its honor. The Precious Blood raised up the mountains of the Immaculate Conception by the subterraneous heavings of its fiery love, and then flowed down from the summits as a sweet fountain for the gladdening of the nations. The Immaculate Conception is therefore actually part of the devotion to the Precious Blood. It is creation's richest offering, made by the queen of creatures, who thus in the jubilee of her sinless dawn crowned the Precious Blood by being crowned herself with its choicest crown.

It is no wonder, then, that we find in the two devotions, the devotion to the Precious Blood and the devotion to the Immaculate Conception, a similarity of spirit, a similarity of gifts, a similarity of graces. But what is the unshared distinction of the devotion to the Precious Blood? Has it no solitary grandeur of its own?

It has one, which is not solitary, but which it shares only with devotion to the Blessed Sacrament. The distinctive privilege of the devotion to the Precious Blood is that it has the peculiar union of adoration and devotion which is the spirituality of heaven. But let us look more minutely into the spirit of this devotion, as witnessed by the fruits which it produces in the soul.

First of all, it breeds in us an unexhausted loving wonder of the common things of the faith. The supernatural is not necessarily the same thing as the wonderful. A love of the supernatural is a higher thing than an appetite for the wonderful. It is a great grace, a mother-grace containing many graces. There are few graces more to be coveted; for many reasons, but for this reason especially, that it gives such fertility to the three theological virtues. People are attracted by miracles, by prophecies, by apparitions, by visions, and by strange heroisms of an inimitable Sanctity. We ought to be attracted by them. God puts them out as attractions. He meant them to attract us. But, to the thoughtful and to the loving, the common things of the faith are a hundred times more attractive; and for the most part they are in themselves more wonderful. Graces and inspirations, services and functions, beads and scapulars, jubilees and indulgences, the common marvels of prayer, and the commonplace blessings of the Church—these are what we ought most to wonder at, most to prize, and most to love. What is shared by the greatest number of the faithful ought to be more dear to us than what is shared by few or is singular to ourselves. Surely it is a higher thing to be a priest and to participate in the grand universal priesthood of the Church, than to be a canon of a chapter which may wear a bishop's mitre or a cardinal's red. In religion what is common is better than what is uncommon, because the common is universal; and it is his highest gifts which God gives to all men, and his peculiar gifts which he gives to the few. This is one of God's ways, to be observed and made much of—his choicest things are the most universal. Now, the Precious Blood is the commonest of all supernatural things, the most accessible, and the most universal. It enters into all the commonest things of religion with an unfastidious ubiquity; and the devotion to it partakes of the universality which belongs to itself. In spirituality, wise men value more and more each passing year this esteem and love of the common things of faith.

Here is another fruit of the spirit of this devotion to the Precious Blood. It is easier to love God than to trust in him. In human things it is not easy to doubt and yet to love; but in divine things it is not uncommon. The greatest defect in our worship of God is want of confidence in him. Confidence is the genuineness of worship, and the tranquil plenitude of love. What can give us more confidence in God than the study of the Precious Blood? Who can doubt Jesus, when he bleeds? Whether we look at the grandeurs of the Precious Blood, or its liberalities, or its tendernesses, or its peculiarities, the result of our contemplations is a steadfast childlike confidence in God. Out of this comes generosity with God, that other of our great wants, which we are always mourning over and never taking the pains to supply. It is more easy to be generous when we have come thoroughly to trust the object of our love. Moreover, we catch generosity, by a kind of infection, from the prodigality of the Precious Blood. We can hardly live in fire, and not grow hot ourselves. The excess of love betrays itself in unconscious imitation. We shall do great things for God, if we are conversant all day with the great things which God has done for us.

Another gift of this devotion is a vehement and intelligent hatred of sin. It is useless for the hatred to be intelligent unless it be also vehement, and worse than useless for it to be vehement unless it be intelligent as well. In these days what our loyalty to God most needs is sternness to the disloyal. This should be shown first and foremost to ourselves. Whom do we know to be so disloyal as ourselves? What resistance to grace, what contempt of warnings, what neglect of inspirations, what slovenliness of performance, make up our lives! If we hated sin, as we ought to hate it, purely, keenly, manfully, we should do more penance, we should inflict more self-punishment, we should sorrow for our sins more abidingly. Then, again the crowning disloyalty to God is heresy. It is the sin of sins, the very loathsomest of things which God looks down upon in this malignant world. Yet how little do we understand of its excessive hatefulness! It is the polluting of God's truth, which is the worst of all impurities. Yet how light we make of it! We look at it, and are calm. We touch it, and do not shudder. We mix with it, and have no fear. We see it touch holy things, and we have no sense of sacrilege. We breathe its odor, and show no signs of detestation or disgust. Some of us affect its friendship; and some even extenuate its guilt. We do not love God enough to be angry for his glory. We do not love men enough to be charitably truthful for their souls. Having lost the touch, the taste, the sight, and all the sense of heavenly-mindedness, we can dwell amidst this odious plague, in imperturbable tranquillity, reconciled to its foulness, not without some boastful professions of liberal admiration, perhaps even with a solicitous show of tolerant sympathies. Why are we so far below the old saints, and even the modern apostles of these latter times, in the abundance of our conversions? Because we have not the antique sternness. We want the old Church-spirit, the old ecclesiastical genius. Our charity is untruthful, because it is not severe; and it is unpersuasive, because it is untruthful. We lack devotion to truth as truth, as God's truth. Our zeal for souls is puny, because we have no zeal for God's honor. We act as if God were complimented by conversions, instead of trembling souls rescued by a stretch of mercy. We tell men half the truth, the half that best suits our own pusillanimity and their conceit; and then we wonder that so few are converted, and that of those few so many apostatize. We are so weak as to be surprised that our half-truth has not succeeded as well as God's whole-truth. Where there is no hatred of heresy, there is no holiness. A man, who might be an apostle, becomes a fester in the Church for the want of this righteous abomination. We need St. Michael to put new hearts into us in these days of universal heresy. But devotion to the Precious Blood, with its hymning of the Church and its blazoning of the Sacraments, will give us Michael's heart and the craft to use Michael's sword. Who ever drew his sword with nobler haste, or used his victory more tenderly, than that brave archangel, whose war-cry was, All for God?

The Precious Blood is His Blood, who is especially Uncreated Truth. It is His Blood who came with his truth to redeem souls. Hence, love of souls is another grace, which comes from the spirit of this devotion. I wish "the love of souls" were words that were not so shortly said. They mean so much that we should linger over them, in order to imbibe their sweetness, perhaps also their medicinal bitterness as well. A volume would hardly say all that wants saying upon this matter. In all ages of the Church a zeal for souls is a most necessary grace; and this is hardly an age in which it is less necessary than usual. Alas! it is a rare gift, incredibly rare, rare even among us priests, and a gift unfortunately dishonored more than most gifts by base counterfeits and discreditable impostures. Of all things that can be named, the love of souls is perhaps the most distinctively catholic. It seems to be a supernatural sense, belonging only to the Church. There are several classes of saints, classes divided from each other by wide discrepancies of grace, and a dissimilitude, almost an incompatibility, of gifts. Yet the love of souls is an instinct common to all saints of whatever class. It is a grace which implies the accompaniment of the greatest number of graces and the exercise of the greatest number of virtues. It is the grace which irreligious people most dislike; for even sin has its instinct of self-preservation; and it is a grace which is peculiarly obnoxious to the worldly. It is a gift, also, which requires an unusually fine spiritual discernment; for it is always and everywhere the harmony of enthusiasm and discretion. Natural activity, vulgar emulation, the bustle of benevolence, the love of praise, the habit of meddling, the overestimate of our own abilities, the hot-headedness of unripe fervor, the obstinacy of peculiar views, the endless foolishness of indocile originality—all these things prepare so many delusions for the soul, and so multiply them by combining in varieties, that the gift of counsel and the virtue of prudence, as well as the cool audacity of an apostle, are needed for the exercise of this love of souls. It is also a very laborious grace, wearing the spirit, fatiguing the mind, disappointing the heart. This is the reason why in so many persons it is a short-lived grace. It is a part of almost everybody's fervor, while it is part of the perseverance of very few. It is a grace which never grows old, never has the feelings of age, or the repose of age, or the slowness of age. Hence many men cast it aside as a thing which belongs to youth, as if it were a process to be gone through and then there were an end of it. The soul of an apostle is always youthful. It was mature in its young prudence; and it is impetuous in its gray-haired zeal.

But, if it is a grace hard to persevere in, it is one which gives marvellous unity and consistency to a man's life, and ultimately crowns it with inevitable and enviable success. If there is nothing in which work is harder, there is nothing in which success is more certain, than the love of souls. It is a perfect combination of spiritual nobilities. Of all single expressions of the Sacred Heart it is the broadest. It unites, as nothing else does, charity to God and man. On the one hand it seems intuitively to understand God, and on the other hand to have a supernatural attractiveness about it, which crowns it a king of men. It is a grace which makes a man surprisingly genial and inveterately happy. It delivers the heart from jealousy, rivalry, and all littleness; and by this especially do we know it from its counterfeits. Moreover, it works little miracles of its own; for it increases a man's intellectual power, at least in its own direction. This is a beautiful sight, and one of those palpable things of grace, which seem to supersede faith by sight—the beholding of the grand things accomplished, and the broad regions covered, by mediocrity of talent when raised above itself by zeal for souls. It lives equally in action and contemplation, and thereby supplies for a number of omissions in the spiritual life. It imparts a delightful simplicity to the character, sobering all gayety, and enlivening all seriousness. It is an emanation of apostolic grandeur, a touch of the vocation of the Apostles whose calling was above all others in the world, as their sanctity was special among other sanctities. It impregnates the soul with a strong personal love of Jesus, and is a participation in the adorable communicativeness of God. What a grace is this to possess! It is the grace which perhaps of all others is the most direct, natural, and inevitable grace of the Devotion to the Precious Blood.

In close connection with this grace we should name, as another fruit of the spirit of this devotion, a great devotion to the Sacraments. But this has been sufficiently dwelt upon in the course of the Treatise. A zeal for souls is naturally given to magnify the Sacraments. An apostolic man knows of them by experience. He has seen the magic of their operations. He has seen how they can lie in the bosom of corruption, like God's amulets, and charm away the vicinity, the relics, the associations, the roots, the attractions, of sin. He has handled their divine realities, and worships rather what he sees than what he knows of by the hearing of faith. But a great devotion to the Sacraments is not only an inseparable accompaniment of zeal for souls: it is also an antidote against all that is worldly, material, and anti-supernatural in the tendencies of the present day. It will increase in us, in proportion as we grow in devotion to the Precious Blood.

The effect of this devotion upon our devotion to our Blessed Lady may well be named as one of its graces, one of the revelations of its spirit. It makes our devotion to her an integral part of our devotion to Jesus. It makes the two devotions one. It draws her into the scheme of redemption so intimately, and at the same time with such splendors of separate exaltation, that the very highest language of the saints about her becomes easy to us, and is the only natural expression of our inward love. To be enthusiastic, our love of Mary only needs to be theological. The devotion to the Precious Blood clothes her with a new glory. It makes Mary magnify Jesus, and Jesus magnify Mary. It causes her individual mysteries to shine forth like stars, the Precious Blood forming the clearness of the purple night in which their peculiar brightness is more visible and more distinctive. He that can find another point of view, from which our dear Lady seems greater than before, has got a new means of sanctification; for he has acquired a new power of loving God: and the devotion to the Precious Blood is full of such points of view.

The devotion to the Precious Blood must also obviously im-

part to us a special love of the Sacred Humanity. It admits us into
the most secret recesses of our Lord's Human Life. Like its own
reiterated pulsations, each one of its mysteries urges upon our
faith and love the dreadest realities of his Created Nature, while
at the same time it seems to lay open before us the Hypostatic
Union, and to illustrate its strength. Our Lord is God; and we
all worship him as such. But there is a peculiar adoration of his
Divinity, which comes from a special love of his Humanity. We
would fain love God as he loves us. But there is a tenderness in
his love of us, which we dare not return because of his infinite
majesty. Yet somehow there is something in the particular adoration of our Lord's Godhead arising from special devotion to his
Humanity, which insinuates this element of tenderness into our
adoration without diminishing the sacred terror of our self-abasement. This element is one of the peculiar gifts of the devotion to
the Precious Blood.

One thing more. Where Jesus is, all honors and all glories
and all loves gather round the Father. Who can doubt, then, but
that the devotion to the Precious Blood is also a devotion to the
Eternal Father? Think of the immensity of the Father's love for
that redeeming Blood. Out of all possible creations he chose it
alone for the price of our redemption. Only its value could en-
rich the glory of the Creator, which the creature's sin had striven
to impoverish. Only from its victory would he condescend to receive back the dominion of which he had been despoiled. Only
its fulness could satisfy the claims of all his outraged perfections.
Only its sweetness could make universal peace in heaven and on
earth. It was to the Person of the Father, by appropriation, that
this dear price of our souls was paid. Nay, our devotion to the
Blood of his Son is only an imitation of the Father's complacency
therein. It is his joy, and his devotion. To join him in this devotion to the Blood of his Son is in truth to practice a distinct devotion to himself. Devotion to the Eternal Father! this is the sweet
grace to covet. Show us the Father, said Philip to his Lord, and it
is enough for us.

Now, reader, our task is done, and yet we would fain linger

over the subject. It so fascinates us that any conclusion we can make seems to be abrupt. The more we say, the more appears to remain unsaid. New glories of the Precious Blood are constantly coming into view, and new abysses opening to our contemplation. So it is with all divine things. They clothe themselves in the changefulness of divine love. They shine with a divine light upon them, and therefore their brightness is always new. They borrow the beauty of God, and so they satisfy our love by making it still more insatiable. We feel that all that has been said has been unworthy of the Precious Blood. Indeed, it has been unworthy even of our own conceptions of it. But what love has taught to one soul may waken the chords of love in others. What has been a light to one mind, and a joy to one heart, may carry light to other minds and joy to other hearts. May it be so, and Jesus more loved and God more glorified!

Let us recapitulate. We began with reflecting on the mystery of the Precious Blood, because all devotion starts best with doctrine. The incredibilities of divine love become more credible when we have learned them first as dogmas. It was also the more necessary to begin with doctrine in the case of a devotion which claims to be an adoration also. We then turned from God to man, and strove to form a right estimate of the Precious Blood by studying from various points of view our extreme need of it, and our immeasurable wretchedness without it. We then traversed its empire, learned its character by studying the method of its government, and judged of its magnificence by the splendor of its dominion. Our next step was to unfold its chronicles. We found there a whole revelation of God, and much of the secret history of his eternity. We discovered there our own place in creation by discovering our place in the procession of the Precious Blood. From its history we passed to its biography, to that notable characteristic of it which especially reveals its spirit—its prodigality. We saw then how God's prodigalities are not excesses, but most orderly magnificences; and also how our poverty is so extreme that we can only live on from day to day by being economical of God's most exuberant liberalities. As we had begun with doctrine and adoration, we have had to end with practice and devotion. The history, the characteristics, and the spirit of the devotion to the Precious Blood have been the concluding subjects of our reflections. We have thus considered the Precious Blood as a Doctrine, a Necessity, an Empire, a History, a Divine Prodigality, and a Devotion. In all these six aspects of it we have found it continually disclosing certain affinities, running into certain subjects, illuminating certain depths, and connecting itself with certain mysteries, and all this with so much repetition and so much constancy that we cannot believe its sympathy with them to be accidental. It bespeaks rather a divine law, and is a disclosure of the Divine Mind. These cognate subjects with the Precious Blood are three in number. They are first the Magnificence of God's Dominion, secondly the Church, and thirdly the Sacraments. As we grow in devotion to the Precious Blood, the sovereignty of God will become more dear to us, and clearer as it grows more dear. Our loyalty to the Church will become more and more a part of our spiritual life, and more and more a sanctifying exercise of the special virtue of religion. Our faith and joy in the Sacraments will be continually increasing, and our devotion to them will be at once our shelter and our shield from the dangers which at this day threaten both the minds and hearts of the faithful, while our more reverent frequentation of them will augment our union with God and make us saints. Such is devotion to the Precious Blood. It is a glory and an ornament to the Church. It is the life of the living, and the thirst of the Holy Dead. It is the song of angels. It was the light of all Mary's darkness, and the jubilee of all her woes. It was the device of the Holy Ghost, and the devotion of his love. It was the devotion and singular possession of Jesus himself. It was the devotion, the choice, and the complacency of the Eternal Father.

What more can we say? Sweet worship of the Blood of God! a worship with so many of man's peculiar rights in it, embracing all theology in itself, and then turning all its vast theology into tenderly triumphant song! Dear Fountain, that rises in the heart of God's human Mother, and flows down over the glorified souls of men into the Bosom of the Eternal Father, while those count-less souls, like the pebbles of the stream, make everlasting music as it flows! It is earth's beatitude to feel that the Precious Blood is bearing us onward into that adorable Abyss of Love. It is heaven's jubilee to be sinking evermore through that same Blood in the unfathomable depths of the Uncreated Bosom of the Father. All glory and all worship be to that mysterious River of the City of God, whose Spirit-fashioned streams are carrying us this hour with such breathless swiftness to our home—our home with the Mortal Mother and the Unbeginning Father of the Eternal Son!

If you have enjoyed this book, consider making your next selection from among the following . . .

Prices subject to change.

Prices subject to change.

Prices subject to change.

At your Bookdealer or direct from the Publisher.
Toll-Free 1-800-437-5876　　　　　　　　　　**Fax 815-226-7770**

Prices subject to change.

NOTES

NOTES

NOTES

NOTES